SOM journal

5

HATJE CANTZ

Contents

Introduction
Juhani Pallasmaa

After two decades of architectural euphoria brought about by unparalleled resources, new technologies and materials, novel possibilities opened up by the computer, and unforeseen media attention, we are unexpectedly in a situation where architecture seems to face the most dramatic shift of its paradigm since the breakthrough of modernism nearly a century ago. The urgency of the ecological perspective in architecture was not quite apparent even two years ago when the previous issue of the *SOM Journal* was published. In the current issue, Susannah Hagan calls the situation a "revolution"; now it is nature that is in revolt against human culture. The foreboding sense that our insensitive and unrestricted acts threaten the dynamic and subtle equilibrium of global natural systems has turned into an undeniable fact. Only during the past couple of years has global warming and its consequences come to our full knowledge. It is also becoming evident that the emerging situation, threatening the future of current technological culture altogether, is significantly caused by phenomena and processes related with construction. Now even architects cannot flee their responsibility. The unavoidable re-evaluation and re-orientation of architecture do not only concern the economy and technology of construction. The reassessment of the objectives, impacts, and responsibilities of architecture unavoidably imply new architectural ethics and aesthetics. Also the temporal perspective of design is bound to shift from nowness and newness to the evaluation of long-term impacts.

For roughly a hundred years, the functionalist ethos has served as the ideological and ethical backbone of architecture behind varying stylistic manifestations. However, functional and technical performance has been a metaphoric aesthetic motif, or architectural theme, rather than a question of actual and verified performance and efficiency. The era that we are entering now clearly calls for precise performance and an accountable efficiency, as well as an understanding of the causalities of all the environmental, material, energy, and social cycles related with buildings and their long-term use. Instead of being judged primarily as aesthetic objects, architectural projects will inevitably be assessed more as processes and cycles.

During the past two decades the most widely publicized phenomena in architecture around the world have been obsessively driven by the visual image and aesthetic seduction, most often at the cost of reason as well as functional, structural, technological, and economic logic, not to speak of ecological consequences. Even in terms of purely human values, architecture has too often turned away from building the material and institutional foundations for a democratic, emancipated, and egalitarian culture. Instead of creating a shared material culture aspiring for equality and human dignity, as the pioneering generation of modernism envisioned, architecture has frequently become directly tied with individual profit making and mental manipulation for commercial purposes. The current globalized and placeless architecture is a consequence of unlimited ideological and physical mobility, placelessly fluid and immaterial capital, as well as the universalizing impact of uncritically applied technology.

The computer has brought forceful and dramatic changes to the architectural practice. Acknowledging the undeniable benefits of the digital reality, computerized design also poses serious problems in relation to human imagination and sense of compassion. Alongside the current digital enthusiasm we need a serious assessment of creative design processes and, in particular, the significance of the senses and embodiment in the conception and experience of architecture.

In the architectural development of the past two decades or so, form has been forcefully detached from its essential architectural dependencies and given an exorbitant position. However, architecture is fundamentally an art of mediation. It mediates between different contexts, periods of history, cultural institutions, tradition and invention, society and individuals, material and spiritual.

Yet, today's formalistic buildings frequently appear autistic, devoid of wider cultural meaning, and incapable of establishing an existential foothold. In my opinion, an architectural "reformation" is inevitable, and the critical contributions in this *SOM Journal 5* confirm this view.

The breakthrough of modernity was largely guided by the invention and application of new building technologies and the metaphor of the functional machine. However, it is the violence, inadequacy, and insensitivity of our technology that is seen as the cause of our escalating environmental threat. Yet, it is a false conclusion, in my view, to demand that architecture should turn back to more primitive technologies in response to the current environmental imperative. This in fact has been the image frequently given to "green architecture" by many of the early proponents of this tendency. On the contrary, we need to develop a more refined, subtle, and responsive technological thinking. We need to conceive optimized systems that automatically monitor, regulate, and report on their performance. As architecture needs to become more "scientific" in terms of its true environmental impact, design has to be solidly grounded in research and follow-up studies. These requirements project a heightened responsibility, but at the same time, a special advantage to large scale multi-disciplinary firms with specific research sections. Instead of repeatedly conceiving and constructing buildings as unique prototypes as in today's standard practice, architectural projects can form a continuous process of accumulating knowledge and consequent improvement of performance. The resources, volume and varied range of projects, the large number and professional versatility of the staff, as well as the potential continuity of design principles through several designer generations, provides an opportunity for a large corporate firm like SOM to replace personal signature style by thoroughly research-based and professionally cumulative practice. During the four years since the meeting of the *SOM Journal 4* Jury in 2004, the firm has launched approximately 1100 projects, and it is evident that such a volume of work presents an enormous professional capital of knowledge.

It is also most likely that models and principles for the new and complex environmental and architectural systems will be sought within the endless richness of the biological world, and its unerring comprehensiveness and absolute performance. The new reformation could significantly be inspired and guided by the study of biological examples and systems instead of the ideal of the mechanistic machine of the modernists. The biologist Edward O. Wilson, who has introduced the notion of *biophilia*[1] and analyzed "human nature,"[2] argues, for instance, that the "superorganism" of a leafcutter ant colony is more complex in its performance than any human invention. The expanding interest in biological models is evident in new design concepts, such as *bionics, biomimicry,* and *biomimetics*. The complexities and marvels of natural systems can also teach us all a welcome sense of humility. The new interest in biological examples, however, needs to penetrate mere visual and formal parallels and enter an analysis and understanding of the very systems and strategies of the biological world. Currently emerging new fields of urbanism further expand ideas of responsive design, adapted to the dynamic principles and cycles of natural systems, to the scale of planning. Hagan writes appropriately about "artificial ecologies."

At the same time, the study of our own biological nature and bio-cultural historicity can provide new ground for a deeper understanding of architectural traditions, aesthetics and pleasure. Neurosciences as well as bio-psychology have already provided stimulating introductions to these perspectives. Yet, human construction cannot be reduced to mere systems, performance, or technology. Our buildings also need to settle our minds, memories, and desires. The cultural, mental, metaphorical, and aesthetic dimensions of architecture should not be underestimated or neglected, but they also need to be understood beyond the obsessions of momentary fashion.

•

In the previous *SOM Journals* the Jury's critical conversations were transcribed and published as a background to the presentation of the selected projects. The Editorial Board of *SOM Journal 5* found a transcribed conversation too anecdotal, fragmented, and sometimes too casual, or polemically critical. The often extremely complex architectural projects, that may well have taken years of collective research, design, and advancement through its own specific internal logic and set of constraints, can too easily be dismissed in a spontaneous conversation. As a result of this view, each member of the Jury (appointed by the external Editorial Board without any influence from the SOM staff) was asked to express his or her personal view of the important issues raised by the evaluation process, of either the awarded projects, or projects presented to the Jury, but not awarded.

In order to emphasize the independence of the Jury and the editorial process, the editor of the Journal did not function as a member of the Jury.

·

Considering the dominance of large-scale projects in the SOM practice, the fact that the Jury awarded mostly rather small-scale projects evokes questions. This choice certainly reflects the personal preferences of the individual Jury members, but it also suggests that small projects tend to permit or invite more experimental, articulate, and humane responses than huge projects that easily end up in more conservative and professionally safe solutions due to the heavy responsibilities involved. The author's individual hand may also be more visible in small projects in comparison with projects produced by a large team through division of tasks and responsibilities. Besides, in today's large-scale projects, the clients seem to know precisely what kind of performance and standards they expect, and these pre-specifications naturally limit the scope of architectural choices. Altogether, the role of the client in a design project is not much discussed today, but it is frequently decisive regarding the final quality of the project. The enlightened individual client of former times has often turned into a faceless organization or committee that fundamentally changes the fragile psychology of the design process. "Great poetry is possible only if there are great readers," Walt Whitman argued.[3] We can similarly argue that great architecture is possible only as long as there are great clients. Ludwig Wittgenstein, the philosopher, pointed out another even deeper interdependence between architecture and the cultural situation: "Architecture immortalizes and glorifies something. Hence, there can be no architecture where there is nothing to glorify."[4] Architectural projects have often lost their symbolic glory in our time as they have turned into mere instrumental structures of utility or investment opportunities instead of reflecting deeper cultural ambitions.

·

In his essay, Charles Waldheim, Chairman of the Jury, chose to discuss SOM's problems of planning, particu-

larly the frequent lack of vision in the scale of landscape, or urban planning and design. He focuses especially on the "mat building typology," a model of urban form that emerged in European architectural and planning projects after the mid-twentieth century. He points out that the mat building approach, that is the planning strategy of the project for the Kuwait Military Academy, was deployed in the campus designs by SOM simultaneously with the pioneering European examples.

In his personal report, Sean Godsell compares and contrasts the reality of architectural practices in the domestic scale of a small architectural studio like his own, and a global corporate practice like that of SOM. He particularly focuses on the issues of division of labor and methods of quality control at the two opposite ends of the scale. "Quality is a vexed issue in contemporary architecture where craftsmanship, traditions of building, and local skills are often found wanting." Godsell also provides a personal evaluation of the eight selected projects.

Marc Mimram chose to deliberate on the differences between two opposite modes of creative work; that of the solitary individual designer, and of a team within a large corporate firm. He points out apparent psychological differences as well as the extraordinary possibilities of a larger firm to create a continuum beyond individual designers, singular commissions, and momentary styles as an accumulation of research-based experience and knowledge.

Mary Miss, the artist member of the Jury, also points out the severity of current environmental problems, but places confidence in the power of artistic imagination: "Architectural firms can take the lead in bringing the imagination to bear upon the use of our diminishing resources; they can take the lead in raising these issues through the way their buildings are constructed." She suggests the possibility of architectural expressions that arise from the physical forces that impact the building, such as wind velocities at different altitudes, energy and water consumption, or carbon emissions. She also wishes to extend imagination from mere aesthetic concerns to "issues of social and environmental sustainability." In short, she proposes an aesthetics grounded in the facts of the world and life instead of being mere visual whims.

·

The Editorial Board commissioned two essays on subjects that are seminal in the development of architecture today, and two further essays that survey essential aspects of the history of SOM following the line already adopted in the previous issues of the Journal.

Professor Susannah Hagan's essay "Sustaining Architecture During a Revolution" is a forcefully argued declaration of the new ecological paradigm for architecture. "Historical inevitability is this time found in unavoidable ecological limits… Social and economic turmoil will follow climatic turmoil as the biosphere struggles with its gathering disequilibrium, and we are tossed around." She argues for a new econo-ethical understanding: "Our attitudes to profit and nature must shift if we are not to be bankrupted by the efforts of global warming." She points out that the real challenge is not in designing new structures to meet the requirements of sustainability, but the task to retrofit the billions of existing buildings around the globe. She rejects the idea of returning "to some pre-industrial arcadia," and calls for a "radically reconfigured architecture." In her view, the ecological performance of new architecture is a new challenge to scientific rationality and technologically oriented architecture. Finally, Professor Hagan cites examples of current visions in urban systems, the "artificial ecologies," that seek to function in accordance with the circular dynamics of natural systems.

One of the structural engineers to have recently significantly expanded the boundaries of structural thinking is Dr. Mutsuro Sasaki of Japan. Francesco Dal Co introduces Sasaki's basic approach and a few of his projects carried out in collaboration with leading Japanese architects, such as Toyo Ito, Arata Isozaki, and Kazuo Sejima and Ryue Nishizawa / SANAA. His characteristic undulating structures are partly based on analyses of Antoni Gaudí's organic forms originally defined by means of physical structural models.

In her essay entitled "Art, Soul of the Corporation," professor Joan Ockman surveys the emergence and interactions of corporate art and architecture. Corporate interest in art originated in the ambitious collections of art (by mostly European masters) by powerful financiers and industrial magnates during the first decades of the twentieth century. Also the 1935 congressional ruling that allowed businesses tax deductions for charitable gifts channeled funds for ambitious corporate art projects.

The ultramodern Terrace Plaza Hotel, designed by SOM and opened in Cincinnati in 1948, is an early showcase of corporate art. The Romanian-born artist Saul Steinberg (an architect by training) executed a huge mural in the hotel's Skyline Room depicting Cincinnati landmarks. In the Gourmet Room, twelve floors above, Joan Miró painted another modernist mural. Two further site-specific works were executed for the Terrace Plaza: "Twenty Leaves and an Apple," a mobile by Alexander Calder, and a kinetic group of light sculptures by James Davis.

After the war years, the ideal of New Monumentality called for a grand-scale synthesis of arts. This "civic" ideal of monumentality was radically translated after the war by SOM and its capitalist clients in the skyscrapers and corporate headquarters of the postwar urban landscape.

It has been customary in previous Journals to include essays on the important individual creative talents behind the corporate image of SOM. In *SOM Journal 5*, Nicholas Adams, the author of *Skidmore, Owings & Merrill: The Experiment since 1936,* presents the career and contributions of Myron Goldsmith (1918–1996), the author of numerous important SOM building projects. The writer summarizes Goldsmith's philosophy of architecture based on structural clarity and expression (the title of the essay, "Structural Architect," conveys concisely the essence of Goldsmith's art), and analyzes one of the architect's lesser-known buildings, Arthur C. Keating Hall, the gymnasium of the Illinois Institute of Technology. The campus was planned by his mentor Mies van der Rohe, in whose office Goldsmith worked from 1944 to 1959. The building "provides an imaginative structural and aesthetic solution for a gymnasium in an educational institution turning the transparent box into a translucent container." In its reductive expression the project precedes today's Minimalist aspirations and diversified uses of light.

•

In order to underscore the Jury's independence from the SOM offices in New York, it has become customary to hold the Jury meetings outside the United States. The Jury for *SOM Journal 5* first planned to meet in the mythical Maison de Verre by Pierre Chareau and Bernard Bijvoet (1928–31) in Paris. As this proved to be impossible due to the current renovation of the house, the Jury met in the Maison Carré, designed by Alvar Aalto between 1956 and 1959, outside of Paris (see pages 209–15).

1   Edward O. Wilson, *Biophilia: The Human Bond With Other Species* (Cambridge, MA, 1984).

2   Edward O. Wilson, *On Human Nature* (Cambridge, MA, 1978).

3   As quoted in Joseph Brodsky, *Less Than One* (New York, 1997), p. 179.

4   Ludwig Wittgenstein, *Culture and Value* (Oxford, 1998), p. 74.

Sean Godsell, Juhani Pallasmaa, Mary Miss, Marc Mimram, and Charles Waldheim during the Jury review at the Maison Louis Carré

SOM Journal 5 Jury Report

Charles Waldheim

The *SOM Journal 5* Jury (2007) included Sean Godsell (Melbourne); Marc Mimram (Paris); Mary Miss (New York); and Charles Waldheim (Toronto), Chairman. Juhani Pallasmaa (Helsinki), editor of the *Journal*, served as a jury advisor and member ex-officio; Amy Gill (SOM, New York) provided administrative and logistical support. The Jury met for two days in October, 2007 at the Alvar Aalto–designed Maison Carré (1956–69), outside Paris, France.

Over the course of its work, the Jury reviewed seventy-four projects executed by various offices of Skidmore, Owings & Merrill (SOM) over the past three years. Based on that review process, the Jury can report the following findings:

The Jury applauds SOM for inviting critical peer review of its projects and for convening this process. The Jury was impressed by the quality and range of work presented, particularly the diversity of high-quality design work executed by the firm. At the same time, the Jury was underwhelmed by the seeming lack of engagement or evidence of high-quality projects over a range of issues, including but not limited to contemporary urban design; landscape architecture and design; and serious commitment to environmental sustainability.

Collectively the Jury examined eight projects executed by SOM over the past three years. These projects are published.

The Jury found each of the eight projects worthy of critical attention and exemplary in a variety of ways, including the following observations (the projects are listed in the order they were presented to the Jury):

North Mosque Bahrain Bay

The project resonates with contemporary architectural interests in indeterminate geometric patterns and traditional Islamic prohibitions on figural representation. The project embodies two-dimensional patterns of the lived experience on the site over the time of day and the seasons of the year.

Bridging the Rift

The project is exemplary of a regional environmental response embedded in building typology, and passive environmental strategies indexing local landscape conditions. The scheme is a compelling political statement of inhabiting border space.

BioPods

The project is an innovative sculptural response to chronic institutional needs for flexibility, privacy, and presence embodied through design. The project offers a playful approach to social grouping, workplace identity, and security. The proposal presents a strong critique of uncritical interior design conventions and the inevitable cubicles of conventional office compartition.

Kinetic Curtainwall Prototype

The proposed façade system is an excellent example of indexing environmental phenomena through building technology. The idea transcends simple technical response, connecting the building's identity to weather, and human emotive response to subtle ongoing transformations of light, air, and wind.

Balance Bridge

The bridge proposal is a wonderful example of infrastructure as catalyst for urban connectivity. It is also a successful integration of sustainability into an otherwise efficiently engineered object. The scheme is a convincing resolution of aesthetic, technical, and environmental aspects in the context of an explicitly urban agenda.

The Mill Center for the Arts

The project is a coherent and cohesive essay on a modest institutional program reflecting a specific culture, context, and climate. The project successfully articulates regional identity, institutional aspirations, and material presence through a modesty of means.

Kuwait Military Academy

While the Jury found aspects of this commission controversial and acknowledges the politically charged nature
of the program, it applauds the architectural organization
of a large scale institution in the vast horizontal context of
the desert. The project connects profitably to the tradition
of SOM projects for military and educational institutions
while offering a reinterpretation of the historical mat-
building type. It offers a coherent relation of individual
details to the overall site strategy through layering of
horizontal and vertical surfaces, each modulating harsh
environmental conditions.

Elizabeth Academic High School

While this is a building of modest means with clear limitations of design intent and resolution, it is a noteworthy
example of SOM's engagement with public programs
and challenging social contexts. Through this work, architecture is brought to a site and a situation in which it
typically fails to present itself. The Jury encourages SOM
to continue this form of engagement with modest building projects for challenging social conditions. Through
this work, architecture is brought to bear on the social,
environmental, and cultural challenges of the contemporary city and its citizens.

In addition to the collective appraisal of these eight projects, each member of the Jury has been invited to author
their own critical reflections on both the specific projects
presented and larger thematic issues available through
the body of work.

The eastern end and façade of Maison Louis Carré, with kitchen and servants' bedrooms above, and the bedroom terraces on the south side

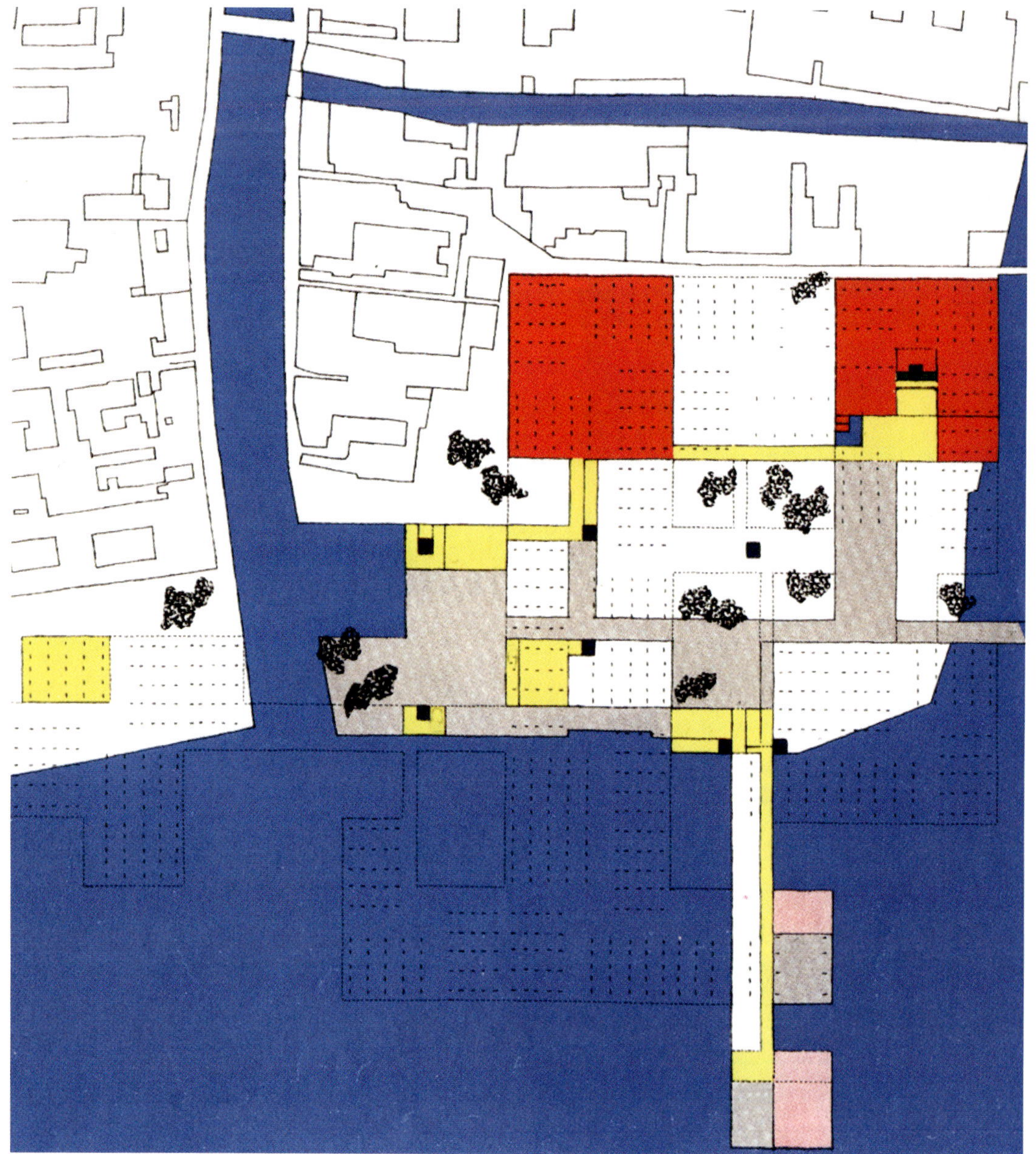

Le Corbusier, Venice Hospital, (1964); first floor plan

SOM on the Mat
Charles Waldheim

Charles Waldheim is Associate Dean and Director of the Landscape Architecture Program in the Faculty of Architecture, Landscape, and Design at the University of Toronto. Waldheim's work examines the relationships between landscape and contemporary urbanism. He coined the term "landscape urbanism" to describe the recent emergence of landscape as a medium of urban order for the contemporary city.

Waldheim has received numerous awards and honors for his work, including the Rome Prize Fellowship from the American Academy in Rome; the Visiting Scholar Research Fellowship at the Study Centre of the Canadian Centre for Architecture; the National Citation for Outstanding Professional Achievement from the Canadian Society of Landscape Architects; the Citation for Excellence from the Association of Collegiate Schools of Architecture; and the Sanders Fellowship from the University of Michigan. He was elected Fellow of the Institute for Urban Design, and named Honorary Member of the Ontario Association of Landscape Architects. He has taught as a visiting faculty member at Harvard University, the University of Pennsylvania, the University of Michigan, the Swiss Federal Technical Institute (ETH), Zurich, the AHO School of Architecture, Oslo, and the Technical University, Vienna.

North American architectural culture has enjoyed a renewed interest in the topic of contemporary urbanism over the past many years. These developments have included a vibrant discourse over the history and future of urban design and planning, as both disciplines enjoy renewed critical scrutiny and increased relevance. Among the subjects of this ongoing discussion has been the increased role of landscape as an element of the urban field. Equally, this discussion has been informed by the historical reconsideration of modernist urban planning. Not unrelated to this has been the historical rereading of urban design's founding half a century ago as a medium for the "urban minded" architect. In many ways these developments have brought focused attention to the role of design in the complex urban environments that increasingly characterize global culture. Often this attention has the effect of reconsidering the perceived failures of modern architecture in shaping the city.

Surveying the design projects produced by Skidmore, Owings & Merrill over the past few years, one is struck by the relative absence of these commitments and questions in much of their recent work. Of course this is both a generalization and overstatement. However, given the enormous scope of SOM's production globally and the range of sites and situations that its projects propose, one is surprised to find a relative absence of critically engaged and productively provocative approaches to contemporary urbanism. This holds true generally whether the work in question is an architectural commission that simply implies an urban attitude or an explicitly commissioned project of urban design or planning.

This general critique is particularly evident given the abundance of high quality design projects produced over the past decade by a range of international designers that frame urban issues to inform their architectural propositions. Based on that survey it is true that several of SOM's recent architectural commissions successfully refer to their urban contexts and many imply charged urban and environmental conditions. Yet, few of the firm's urban design and planning projects successfully articulate a contemporary model of urban form. This is particularly regrettable given SOM's body of work on the subject and its historic contributions to discussions of urban design in the modern era. The mandate of this journal and its associated peer review of SOM's work is to articulate these findings.

The relative absence of a strong portfolio of urban design and planning projects cannot be credibly excused due to a lack of opportunities to engage in urban commissions. SOM enjoys a privileged access to premier commissions in urban design and planning internationally. As such, it could be expected to occupy a position of leadership in those disciplines. Many of the firm's recent projects afford it singular opportunities to illustrate a renewed commitment to innovation in urban planning and design. The relatively small number of SOM projects that do successfully attempt to animate architectural production with a critical position on contemporary urbanism might be categorized in two ways. First, SOM's work has included a range of educational and institutional campus designs. Of these, many imply a latent urbanism and are most successful when they are situated in a highly charged historic context. Second, SOM's production has recently included a number of significant architectural projects that despite the absence of an explicit urban figure infer an urbanistic concept as a method of shaping future decisions in rapidly urbanizing contexts. Both of these lines of work have been relatively more successful than their direct commissions for urban design precincts or planning projects globally.

More often than not, and in the overwhelming majority of these projects irrespective of continent or culture, SOM's approach to contemporary urbanism devolves all too quickly into nostalgia for a lost nineteenth-century street fabric, and an all too often generic approach to the gridding of sites to be rapidly consumed in urbanization. Most often this approach is paired with nostalgia for pastoral images of highly constructed landscape. This combination it should be noted is not specifically associated with SOM alone, but could equally characterize the overwhelming majority of urban design work produced by North American firms for sites across North America, Europe, and Asia.

Among SOM's recent projects a small number of more carefully crafted and critical urban proposals can be found that avoid this general trend. Among those, one project especially reveals a renewed commitment to questions of urban form and holds great promise for contemporary discourse on these topics. The Kuwait Military Academy project designed in the New York office of SOM (in 2006) offers a brilliant counter argument. This project simultaneously sheds light on discussions of contemporary urbanism and reconnects with an historic typology of urban design. In so doing, it reconfirms SOM's leadership in contemporary discourse on urban design and planning, while advancing practices of progressive urbanism.

The Kuwait Military Academy is a vast institutional campus designed for an enormous empty site in the Kuwaiti desert. As such it is situated in an unlikely context for discussions of contemporary urbanism, yet it promises a much needed built example for those interested in new models of urban form. It does so by recalling a model of urban form that is over a half century old, the mat building typology. The project as conceived by SOM is a large mat building complex in which a vast array of horizontal buildings, courtyards, and larger territorial landscapes are held together with an armature of connective tissue. The project successfully reinterprets the mat typology as an essentially horizontal field of low-rise, high-density urbanization.

The mat, or carpet, typology was first proposed in discussions of twentieth-century urbanism as a solution to accommodating vast institutional programs as a form of city in their own right. While those first mat types were conceived for European cities, the discourse and typological strategy quickly came to inform North American discourse on urbanism in the middle of the twentieth century. Not coincidentally, SOM's successful reanimation of the mat typology coincides precisely with a broader revival of interest in the mat as a topic of contemporary concern. This so-called mat revival has been described in a number of recent publications, most notably in *Case: Le Corbusier's Venice Hospital* (2002). This volume focuses on Corb's unbuilt proposal of 1964 for Venice Hospital and situates that project in the longer genealogy of mat building or carpet strategies. This history includes Candilis, Josic, and Wood's project for the Berlin Free University (1963), as well as the popularization of the type by prominent members of Team 10, including Alison and Peter Smithson, among others.

In part, the perceived appeal of the mat building in the early 1960s was the type's seeming ability to reconcile rapidly growing institutional programs within existing urban fabrics. Equally significant was the mat's potential for flexibility with respect to changing institutional programming over time. Not unrelated to this were claims that the mat building type afforded multiple relationships between interior and exterior while implicating larger landscapes associated with the metropolitan condition. Not surprisingly, SOM's Kuwait Military Academy successfully reanimates the firm's historical contributions to the development of the mat building type. That lineage is

Myron Goldsmith, partner, Skidmore, Owings & Merrill, United Airlines World Headquarters, Elk Grove Village, Illinois, 1962. Photo: Hedrich Blessing, courtesy United Airlines

Gordon Bunshaft, partner, Skidmore, Owings & Merrill, Connecticut General Life Insurance Co. Headquarters, Bloomfield, Connecticut. Photo: Ezra Stoller, courtesy ESTO

Gordon Bunshaft and Walter Netsch, partners, Skidmore, Owings & Merrill, U.S. Air Force Academy, Colorado Springs, Colorado, 1959

Gordon Bunshaft and Walter Netsch, partners, Skidmore, Owings & Merrill, U.S. Air Force Academy, Colorado Springs, Colorado, 1959. Photo: Hedrich Blessing, courtesy Chicago Historical Society

Skidmore, Owings & Merrill, University of Illinois at Chicago Circle Campus, aerial view, 1974. Photo: Hedrich Blessing, courtesy Chicago Historical Society

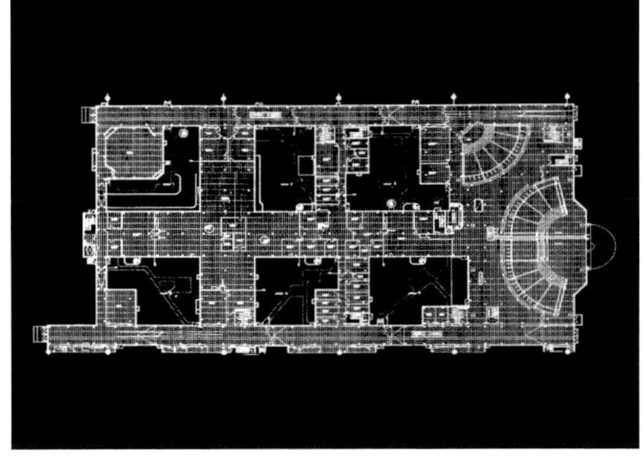

Candilis, Josic, Woods; plan approach at Berlin Free University, 1963

itself deserving of serious scholarship and remains to be completed. Among SOM's modernist projects contributing to the genealogy of mat building, Gordon Bunshaft's Connecticut General Life Insurance Headquarters (1957) might be considered an early American antecedent to the mature European examples of the early 1960s. Equally, Myron Goldsmith's United Airlines Headquarters (1962) can be read as relevant to that lineage. Both projects propose a campus constructed out of repeating low-rise elements organized around internal courtyards and connected to a larger campus beyond.

Equally relevant to the history of the mat building are two SOM campus designs: Gordon Bunshaft and Walter Netsch's Air Force Academy (1956–62) and Netsch's University of Illinois at Chicago (1961–65). Both extend an interest in the mat as a horizontal organization of vast institutional programs. Both projects realize the promise of the low-rise, high-density array of multiple buildings around a series of courtyard and landscape spaces. As such, these projects reveal interesting precedents for current reconsideration of the mat as realized in the design of the Kuwait Military Academy.

As the earlier institutional SOM projects, the Kuwait Military Academy utilizes the mat as an organizational strategy to array a vast and ever changing set of institutional requirements into a coherent urban field. The project successfully deploys a horizontal connective tissue and extensive roofscape as its primary ordering device. That roof, while ordering and subsuming the enumerable individual buildings within it, equally modulates the intense desert sun. It does so through an innovative use of complex three-dimensional apertures in the roof. These openings are precisely shaped so as to allow sunlight to enter at specific points in the field at precise times of day, literally illuminating the day to day movement of bodies through a landscaped urban field. These apertures are replicated in the vertical surfaces and screens separating individual building spaces from one another and the courtyard spaces that afford the collective institutional realm.

At the larger scale of the site, the Kuwait Military Academy effectively deploys a territorial landscape strategy to situate the carpet or mat building within the regional ecology. The landscape proposes native plant material in a vivid pattern of planting effectively buffering the project while situating it within its otherwise enormous and vacuous site. This innovative landscape strategy mitigates windblown sand and arid heat, and insulates the institution from the most severe of its environmental conditions. As such, the landscape strategy of the project reanimates the potential of the mat building as campus, and effectively resonates with current interests in the topic. SOM's Kuwait Military Academy project aspires to rival SOM's Air Force Academy as a truly significant architectural achievement. In so doing, it reanimates discourse on contemporary urban form and renders SOM's work more relevant to contemporary design culture.

Glenburn House working sketch by Sean Godsell Architects

Glenburn House by Sean Godsell Architects

Architecture and the Tyranny of Scale

Sean Godsell

Sean Godsell graduated with first class honors from the University of Melbourne in 1984, and in 1999 obtained a Masters of Architecture from RMIT University, entitled "The Appropriateness of the Contemporary Australian Dwelling." His work has been published in the world's leading architectural journals. In July 2002 the influential English design magazine wallpaper *listed him as one of ten people destined to "change the way we live."* Time *magazine named him as one of seven designers in "Who's who—the new contemporaries," in their 2005 design special. He has lectured widely in Australia and overseas.*

He has received numerous local and international awards, and in July 2003 he received a Citation from the AIA (American Institute of Architects) for his work for the homeless. He lives and works in Melbourne, and is currently working on projects in the USA, China, and Australia.

In his brief acceptance speech when receiving the 1961 AIA Gold Medal, Le Corbusier famously stated "It is Le Corbusier who cleans the toilets at 35 Rue de Sevres —that's why he's still the boss." It was an observation made late in the history of the office when, having swelled to overflowing in the heady days of Chandigarh, La Tourette, Ronchamp, and others, it was back down in size: "Once upon a time we were forty here; it was crazy and everyone had the right to say what he thought; it was civil war. Now we are four, it works better—Do you want to work for me?" While I hesitate to draw any comparisons between my office (currently four people) and Corb's, I do actually empty the bins in my office and pay the bills, lick the stamps, do the working drawings, answer the phone, and administer the contracts, as does my long time assistant Hayley Franklin. The hierarchy and office politics are fairly simple, and the day to day pressures usually center around money (or the lack thereof) and therefore, survival without resorting to architectural prostitution, something that so far we have managed to avoid.

Recently our office received its first big commission (The Big One), a new post graduate school for design research for RMIT University in Melbourne—a fifty million dollar project. The office grew instantly by 100%, from two to four, and suddenly we found ourselves dealing for the first time in my practice's history with issues of scale. Everything got bigger—the meetings, the fees, the "issues," the stakeholders, the problems, the processes. It has been a salient reminder of the fragility of the art of architecture and at the same time an exhilarating ride into the world of larger buildings.

The majority of the seventy-four projects executed by SOM's various offices over the past three years and exhibited for the *SOM Journal 5* Jury are this scale or larger. The luxury of small practices is that they are uncommercial. Design is everything. In a good year we break even. The problem of small practices is that they are uncommercial. Large practice is burdened by the commercial realities of scale. The management of project costs is far more critical, as are the cost repercussions should a project the scale of say, the Kuwait Military Academy, go off the rails. SOM faces this reality every day and as a jury we witnessed evidence of how various design teams had been able to cope with the exposure of the creative process to issues of scale. The three larger scale projects that were permeated—North Mosque Bahrain Bay, Bridging the Rift, and Kuwait Military Academy, each demonstrated a conceptual clarity that is reinforced in the architectonic resolution of each scheme.

The Kuwait building draws on a regional archetype— the massive walled courtyard building—to support other ideas of climate control, in particular extreme heat and dust, and then expands these ideas into a poetic light-dappling, time-tracking eave detail. The simple, place-making, circular, landscaping *partis* doubles as a wind barrier and dust filter. The ambitions of this scheme are controlled and measured. Its ultimate success is largely dependent on how rigorously the coffered façades are pursued.

"Bridging the Rift" uses the same archetype—massive walled courtyards—and uses the kind of air over water exhaust / cooling system that Corb exploited in India, for example, as a passive cooling device. The building's program—a scientific research facility—has been extended to one of place making, in this case a neutral zone on the Israel / Jordan border. In doing this the authors demonstrate their understanding of how simply this can be achieved using urban design principles—the street, the square, and so on—as organizing devices. While I am not convinced that the laws of the still life composition necessarily apply to architecture, as the author attests, the relatively simple, almost Barragan-like forms provide the basis for further development.

Similarly, the North Mosque combines a simple plan and form with a thorough understanding of the cultural and religious requirements that come with the building typology. The rigor in analysis of the program and cultural and geographical context is exemplary. A number of projects, including the Mosque, explore the potential for complex outer skins to filter light and help shade buildings while at the same time producing intricate light patterns during the day.

The Mill Center for the Arts uses irregularly spaced and deliberately crude timber battens to achieve a similar effect. Like the other schemes its success lies in no small part to the simple organization of functional spaces, in this case around a central common, or "performance green" as described on the drawings. The simple *partis* of these schemes is what underpins their relative success. All good architecture can claim this, regardless of scale. However in the context of a large practice it is more likely that a relatively simple idea clearly articulated and well researched will stand the torrent of extraneous forces placed upon it during the design process. Thus the Mill Center should continue to evolve into a well resolved and successful project. There is parsimony about this project which is appealing, particularly when viewed in the context of seventy-four projects, many of which must have had enormous budgets.

This can too be said for the Elizabeth Academic High School, which was explained to the jury as a highly ambitious (and noble) project in the context of the American public school system, where architecture rarely plays a role. It should be noted that very few large practices would have the courage to take on such a project and SOM must be commended and encouraged to do more commissions where the challenge is to make architecture out of very little. The scheme was selected as much for what architecture can do for people who could never afford to commission a building. Everybody benefits from good design and this project is an example of where scale, in this case the sheer critical mass of SOM, can enable a well-designed project to proceed, properly serviced by the firm and therefore potentially make a meaningful difference, to young students in this example.

Research is a critical part of any serious design. Planning and constructing buildings is in many ways a banal pursuit and can be done without the involvement of architects altogether. Solutions can be repeated, techniques mimicked, and buildings rushed out the door as quickly as possible. This is notoriously a big practice trait around the world. SOM has a deeply entrenched position in the history of modernism in the US, underpinned by serious research into, for example, typology (the tower), technology (the curtain wall), and practice (the evolution of the contemporary office). It is therefore encouraging to see projects such as BioPods—a highly creative and thoroughly considered response to the need for flexibility within a scientific research facility; Balance Bridge—a poetic and imaginative solution to the need to raise and lower a bridge by using solar powered, water filled ballast tanks; and a kinetic curtain wall prototype—a sun tracking operable outer skin that both gathers solar power and deflects radiant heat—are given serious consideration within the firm.

Inherent in these works is an optimism for the possibility that prototypical design solutions will evolve into built responses that themselves may become repeated again and again—in research facilities, in the case of the BioPods, or as mainstream construction systems, in the case of the Kinetic Curtainwall. This is practice within practice, and while not evident in all the projects submitted, it clearly exists within the culture of SOM. Somewhat ironically then it is these smaller, research-based works that are in many ways the most enticing. In *An American Architecture,* Wright famously says, "It doesn't matter whether you're doing a chicken shed or a cathedral— it's quality that counts." Quality is a vexed issue in contemporary architecture, where craftsmanship, traditions

of building, local skills, and so on are often found wanting. In a small practice like mine, quality control is pretty
easy—nothing goes out the door without my initial on it.
I spend a lot of time on site, honing, refining, and changing details. The distance between the author of a building
and the building itself in a large office is far greater however, and the involvement of the author on site is often
non-existent (that's another department).

Rigor in the design process is also a hallmark of quality,
and in that sense the role of the architect is put under
duress on a daily basis. The sheer number and scale
of projects produced over three years by SOM around
the globe is remarkable. Buildings both good and bad
become permanent reminders of the architect's stamina
and determination (or lack of) as much as their design
skill or the ability to detail. There is evidence of all this
in the works presented to the Jury. With the selected
projects there was, however, common ground—clarity,
simplicity, and, most of all, a sense that the commission
was treated with the utmost importance—regardless of
scale.

I have a beautiful excerpt from a lecture given by
Louis Sullivan to graduating students in Chicago, in
1900, pinned above my drawing board. It serves as a
daily reminder of the privilege that comes inextricably
with any architectural commission:

"A great occasion is yours, the occasion confronts you,
the future is in your hands—will you accept the responsibility or will you evade it? That is the only vital question
I have to put to you. Do you intend or do you not intend,
do you wish or do you not wish to become architects
to whose care an unfolding democracy may entrust the
interpretation of its material wants, its psychic aspirations."

Beng Bu bridge, Tianjin, China by Marc Mimram

Individual Versus Collective:
Generic Versus Specific

Marc Mimram

Born in Paris in 1955, Marc Mimram holds a Master's Degree in Mathematics and graduated as an engineer from the École Nationale des Ponts et Chaussées. He is a DPLG architect and holds a Master's in Civil Engineering from the University of California, Berkeley in addition to a post-graduate degree in Philosophy. He founded his own consultancy and architecture-engineering firm in 1981, and has completed a good many civil engineering structures and architectural projects in France and abroad.

Marc Mimram has taught at the École Nationale des Ponts et Chaussées, at the École Polytechnique Fédérale de Lausanne, and at Princeton University. He was appointed Professeur des Écoles d'Architecture (Professor of Architectural Schools) at the École d'Architecture de Marne-la-Vallée.

He has given numerous lectures in France, as well as Brasilia, London, Tokyo, Berlin, Stuttgart, Venice, Geneva, Montevideo, New York, Los Angeles, and Boston.

It is common in French literature to contrast the lonely individualism of Sartrean existentialism with the more collective and social personality of Levi-Strauss' structuralism. Antoine Roquentin, the protagonist of the novel *Nausea* by Jean-Paul Sartre, could be compared to the architect working alone or on a small team (and usually also working on small-scale projects), whereas the working process of a large firm in corporate architecture would represent a collective and more anonymous production.

As a large company, SOM has produced great buildings that have become references for smaller architectural offices. Some of the projects are even regarded as signature works of individual artistic designers, although the works primarily represent the firm as a whole. In this way, we could here refer to Claude Levi-Strauss' statement, "Every artist wanting to be lonesome is bound to develop an illusion, as we are never alone on the path of creation."[1]

The Jury reviewed seventy-four projects by SOM conceived during the past three years. Somewhat surprisingly, the majority of projects did not really appear as the production of a single corporate team, nor did they appear as a reflection deriving from the accumulated experience of one firm. On the contrary, the projects often appeared as if they were the very first project of the authors.

Given the submitted skyscraper projects which reflect SOM's acclaimed tradition for high quality, most of the schemes appeared as exceptional projects in a challenging and artistic way. Curiously, those projects seem like the work of a small-scale company rather than of a knowledge-based firm such as SOM. At a moment when so many huge towers are being planned (in China, UAE, Russia, etc.), it looks as if the projects produced by SOM attempt to become iconic and exceptional, instead of forming a part in the shared culture of the company as a team or as a work in progress based on its long and fantastic history. Instead of being based on the accumulated knowledge of the firm, these projects aspire for astonishing effects, arising from formalist principles. It appears as if innovation were opposite to tradition, technological innovation against invention, and that new curtain wall concepts had nothing to do with precedent. If that is the case, knowledge would be considered a weakness, and a team would be considered a handicap in comparison to the supposedly more innovative lonely artist. Antoine Roquentin's phantasm would be considered a privilege.

I originally believed that SOM's production would be largely based on the firm's unique accumulated experience, on the strength of the shared knowledge arising from varied professional backgrounds, and that the company culture would inform architectural, urban, and technological issues alike.

Most of the selected finalist's projects were based on a clear development of identifiable principles, and in consideration of a shared architectural research orientation.

As such:

In the Kinetic Curtainwall Prototype project, the traditional relationship between façade and structure, interior
habitability, and exterior appearance are fused through
a technological innovation. These ideas present the
preoccupation with sustainability into clear architectural
concepts.

In the North Mosque Bahrain Bay scheme, the geometric
elaboration is based on new mathematical tools used in
relationship with local traditions, as well as clear associa-
tions between support and surface, façade and gravity,
light and materiality.

The Balance Bridge infrastructure is linked to an ani-
mated structure in relation to the equilibrium of the water
tank (based on a photovoltaic device). The movement
legitimates the structural shape. The balance of forces
organize the form of the counterweight and the bridge's
appearance at a larger scale.

The Pin-fuse Frame and Studies in Structural Topology
are concerned with the development of technological and
conceptual tools for the later generation of design projects. It is obvious that SOM's culture has always been
based on theoretical structural principles. Basic research
can provide a real development of knowledge that can
later turn into tools for actual design projects, not only in
terms of form but also conceptually.

Working on architectural principles such as geometry,
structure, habitability, technology, and contextual considerations, provides the basis for a continuing development of a real and deep design philosophy. This culture
can be shared by the team, and eventually, the entire
company. It doesn't imply that the project designer would
lose his personal identity in the group, nor does it mean
that the project will turn generic, or less linked with urban
and local circumstances. On the contrary, the strength
of simple principles like the reality of construction, the
pleasure of materiality, the relationship with the geogra-
phy and the landscape, will permit the development of
specific projects based on a real design culture giving a
new meaning to the term corporate architecture.

1 Claude Levi-Strauss "Tout artiste en se voulant solitaire se berce d'illusion car on n'est jamais seul sur le sentier de la création"; in Claude Levi-Strauss, *La Voie des Masques* (Geneva, 1975), p. 124.

The Sixth International Alvar Aalto Symposium, "Architecture of the Essential," held in Jyvaskyla, Finland, addressed the issues of building within the context of diminishing resources, installation by Mary Miss

The Power of Imagination
Mary Miss

Mary Miss, an artist known for her environmentally based artwork, lives in New York. For more than four decades Mary Miss's work has examined the intersection of sculpture, architecture, environmental engineering, and installation art in projects and proposals ranging from riverfront walkways to infrastructure sites. Grounded in the context of place, Miss creates installations that allow the visitor to become aware of the site's history, its ecology, and its surrounding environment.

Permanent installations include Framing Union Square *at the Union Square subway station in New York City, and a wetlands preservation project in Des Moines, Iowa. Recently she was a lead designer of the collaborative team that won the competition to design the 1300 acre Orange County Great Park, currently being built in Irvine, California.*

Entering the twenty-first century only one thing seems clear: we must redefine how we use our resources, build our communities, and lead our lives. Our imagination and ability to envision alternatives are our greatest resources. How can the insights of architects, designers, and artists, i.e. those who are "visual thinkers," be brought to bear upon these issues? Environmental engineers, ecologists, and hydrologists are researching and developing new systems to support sustainable ways of building, providing energy, and tracking our resources. However two questions arise: how can innovative means of implementing these practices and research be developed, and how can urban design, new buildings, or new infrastructure sites communicate these practices experientially and viscerally to the communities in which they appear? It seems apparent that individuals who make up these communities are key to developing a new paradigm for creating a sustainable future. Making them aware of the innovative practices that are being implemented within their communities is a strategic part of this complex puzzle of sustainability.

In reviewing the seventy-four submissions from five different SOM offices, the strengths of the firm's tradition were apparent. There is a wide range of territory covered from master planning to skyscrapers, infrastructure to restoration, smaller scale educational and cultural projects to industrial design and engineering. The firm has also mastered the programming of large complex projects, and how to manage their implementation for governmental and institutional clients around the globe. The budgets, scale, and range of projects are impressive. An issue to be considered, however, is how this firm can re-invent and renew itself to adapt to the rapid changes that inform our lives as we move forward. The mastery the firm has achieved in other areas could also be utilized in answering the current demanding questions.

The issues are daunting. We are dealing with intense global urbanization while climate change is forcing us to reconsider and reverse our relationship to the natural environment. We are faced with diminishing resources and ever greater demands upon them. While previously it seemed a luxury to consider these issues (only the enlightened client would ask for a "green" building), it is apparent that they are becoming unavoidable. A sea change is occurring as political will builds globally and begins to cross party lines. The corporate client is starting to embrace issues of conservation for a variety of reasons, not all of which may be solely altruistic. This is an opportunity for the designer to use the skills of this field to become an operative in dealing with the issues with which we are all confronted. Architectural firms can take the lead in using their imagination to concentrate on the use of our diminishing resources; they can take the lead in raising these issues through how buildings are constructed. These buildings can help us understand our relationship to our environment through what they communicate and how they are perceived.

In the Energy Positive Building project, Quai du Moulin de Cage, in Paris, the goal of building a sustainable project is commendable. However, this seems to have been achieved by going down a list of accepted green building methods and checking off one of each. In the process, any possibilities for how the building could work urbanistically seem to have been put aside. The field of green building and design has barely begun to develop. It seems that a firm like SOM, where design is so highly valued, would do well to make a major investment in researching new means of creating green buildings while ensuring that innovative design is not left out of the equation. This is an area dealing with our current needs that should be investigated and developed in every office.

Many of the submitted schemes were highly visible projects, a large percentage of them skyscrapers. If we assign architects and designers the expanded role of "operatives" in both inventing and communicating new ideas through the design of buildings, the question arises: how can an interface be created with the environment both functionally and visually? Can such buildings reveal natural phenomena that might otherwise go unseen, can they index natural forces? The Kinetic Curtainwall Prototype project begins to do this with shutters that move in relation to the course of the sun. Having this visual expression apparent on the façade announces the building's connection to the environment.

The proposal for the Transbay Joint Powers Authority in San Francisco seems less successful in this regard. This transit oriented development aims at mitigating car congestion and the resulting pollution within the city. It would be assumed that making this new facility a clear expression of sustainable practices is a priority. There are many sustainable aspects to the project, but even if the building qualified for a LEED Platinum Certification, how would anyone know? The only thing that is immediately apparent is that a new structure towering over the city appears on the skyline. Is there a new way to think about what such a building communicates beyond the traditional role of identity and power? Can the temporal, visual, audio, or tactile qualities of form and space be used to this end? Could new content be embedded in these structures? We could imagine a tall building that reveals changing wind currents at different heights of the structure, or one that indicates what percentage of its energy consumption is being supplied by alternative sources, or what its carbon emissions are, or one that tracks water consumption in the immediate area.

The imagination has been identified as a primary territory of the architect, designer, and artist; it should allow issues of social and environmental sustainability to be made visible and tangible, and inserted into the public realm. It is imperative that as builders and thinkers we begin to assume a leadership role in addressing these issues. It may be through small-scale interventions that are imbedded in larger projects, or through something as large and imposing as a skyscraper or infrastructure project. SOM is in a position to investigate and invest in these new fields. This expanding area of expertise can only be a great resource in the coming years.

Journal 5
Submissions

1 Park Place,
London, UK

101 Warren Street,
New York, NY, USA

Ninth Avenue Development,
New York, NY, USA

Adirondack Museum, Lake Placid Branch,
Lake Placid, NY, USA

Al-Hamra Firdous Tower,
Kuwait City, Kuwait

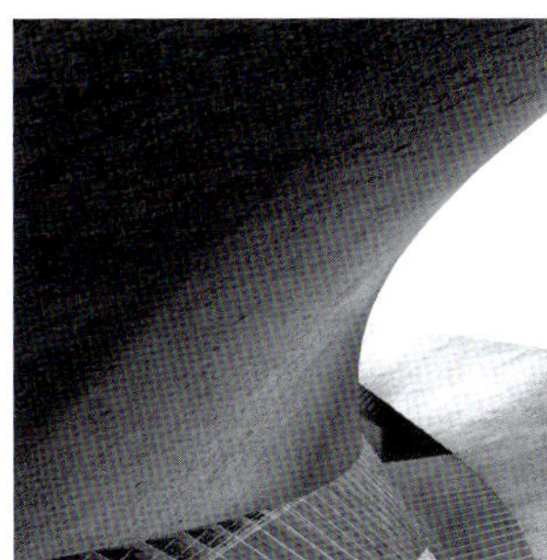

Al-Rajhi Bank Headquarters,
Riyadh, Saudi Arabia

Al-Rayyan Masterplan,
Doha, Qatar

Al Sharq Tower,
Dubai, UAE

Allied Irish Banks Capital Markets HQ,
Dublin, Ireland

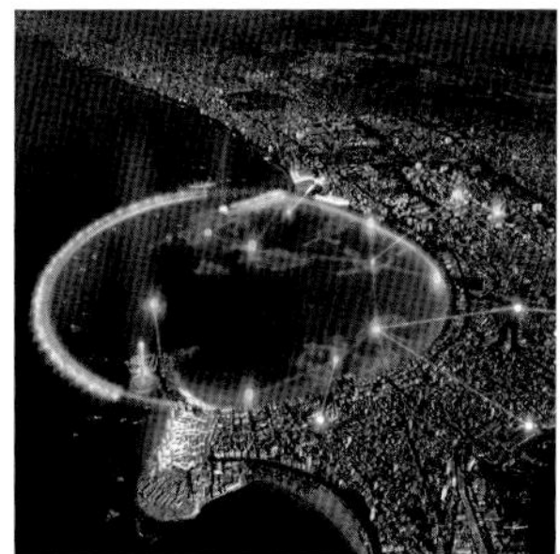

The Arc of the Sun,
Alexandria, Egypt

Balance Bridge,
Bergen, Norway

Beach Road Crescent Gardens,
Singapore, Singapore

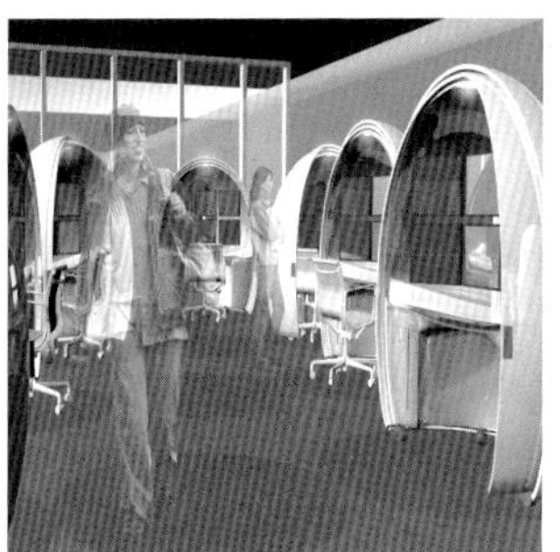

BioPods,
Chapel Hill, NC, USA

Bridging the Rift,
Border of Israel (Central Arava) & Jordan
(Wadi Araba)

Brunswick Upper School Renovation,
Greenwich, CT, USA

Castlelands Headquarters,
Bishopstown, Cork, Ireland

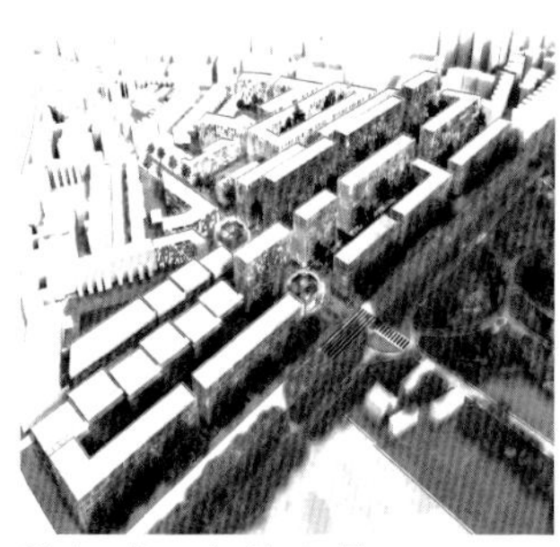

Chelsea Barracks Master Plan,
London, UK

Chicago 2016 Olympic Games,
Chicago, IL, USA

City Front Center,
Chicago, IL, USA

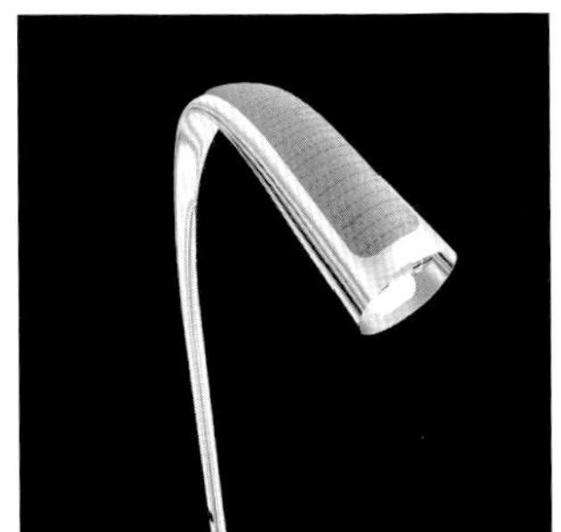

City Lights Design Group

City Santa Fe,
Mexico City, Mexico

Conde-Nast Cafeteria,
New York, NY USA

Crossharbour II,
London, UK

Cyrus Capital,
New York, NY, USA

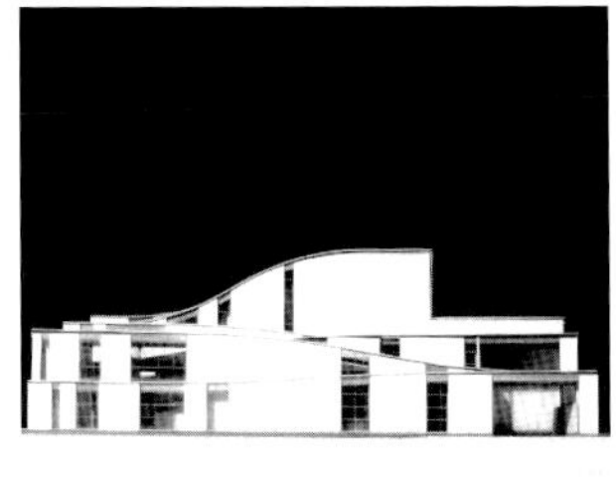

The Dallas City Performance Hall,
Dallas, TX, USA

DePaul Center for the Arts,
Chicago, IL, USA

Dia Art Foundation,
New York, NY, USA

Elephant and Castle Master Plan,
London, UK

Elizabeth Academic High School,
Elizabeth, NJ, USA

Energy Positive Building,
Paris, France

The Exchange Tower,
Shenzhen, China

Four Seasons Hotel and Office,
Manama, Kingdom of Bahrain

Harvard University Northwest Laboratory,
Cambridge, MA, USA

High School of Art and Design and P.S. 59,
New York, NY, USA

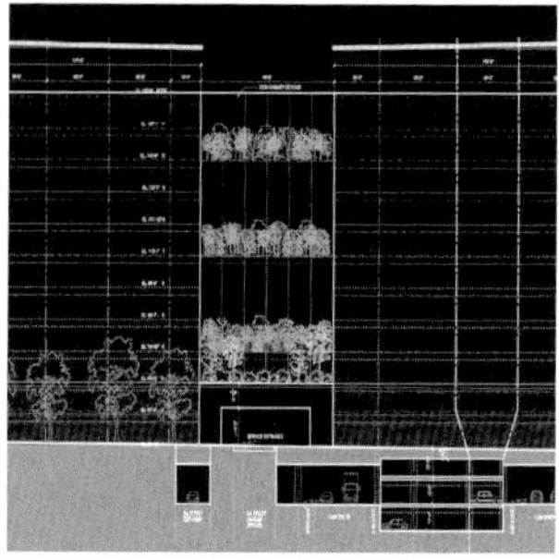

I-395 air rights development,
Washington, DC, USA

Infinity Tower,
Dubai, UAE

Kinetic Curtainwall prototype

Kuwait Military Academy,
Al Jahra, Kuwait

Leamouth Peninsula,
London, UK

Lotte Super Tower,
Seoul, South Korea

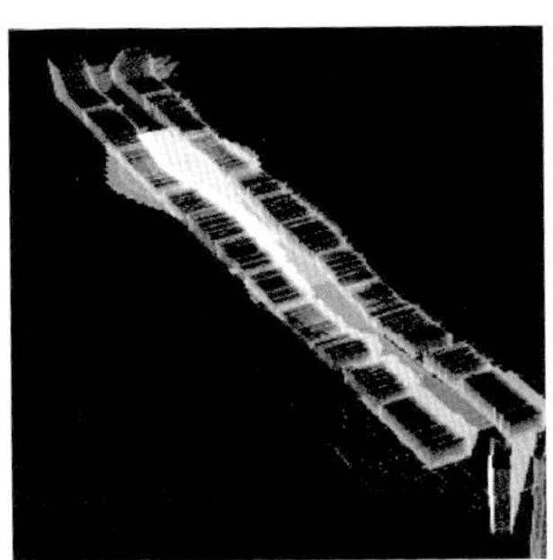

Lusail Masterplan,
Lusail City, Qatar

Mill Center for the Arts,
Hendersonville, NC, USA

Moscow Media Center,
Moscow, Russia

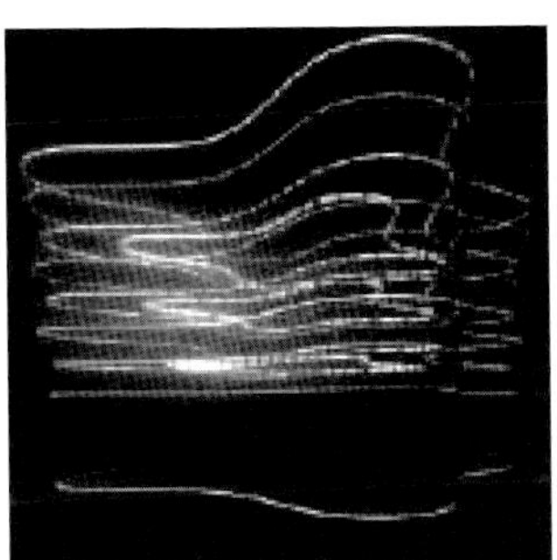

North Bund White Magnolia Plaza,
Shanghai, China

The New Beijing Poly Plaza,
Beijing, China

The New Pulkovo Airport,
St. Petersburg, Russia

The world's largest cable net wall,
Beijing, China

North Mosque Bahrain Bay,
Manama, Kingdom of Bahrain

New York Jets Training Center
and Corporate Headquarters,
Florham Park, NJ, USA

The Park Hotel,
Hyderabad, India

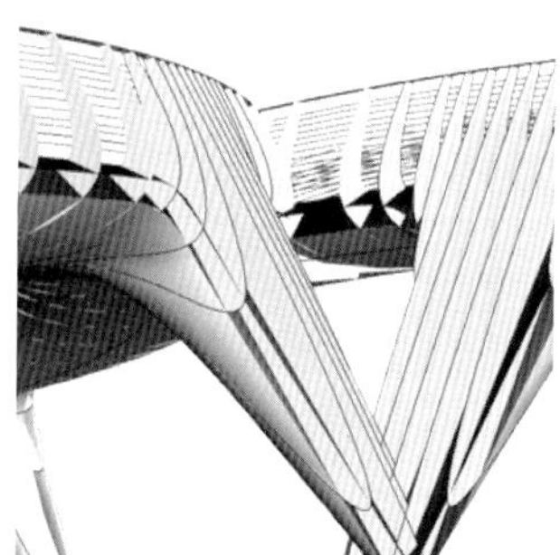

Pedestrian bridges,
University of North Carolina,
Chapel Hill, NC, USA

Pin-Fuse Frame and Link-Fuse Joint,
US Patents Pending

Poly International Plaza,
Guangzhou, China

Regenstein Library Addition,
Chicago, IL, USA

Rolex Tower,
Dubai, UAE

Seven Tower Bridge,
Conshohocken, PA, USA

Shanghai Center,
Shanghai, China

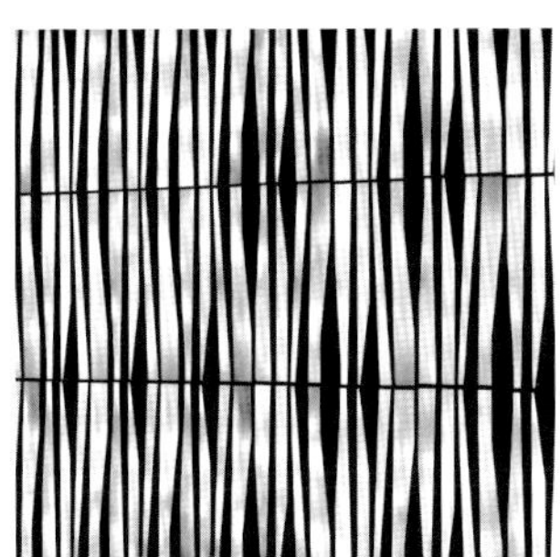

Silvus

St. Albans School, Centennial Hall,
Washington, DC, USA

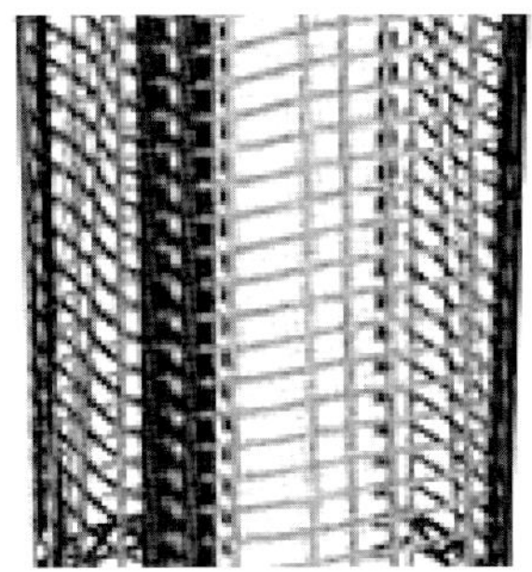

Studies in structural typology

Teda Mixed Use Towers,
Tianjin, China

Tokyo Midtown,
Tokyo, Japan

Tour M,
Paris, France

Transbay Terminal,
San Francisco, CA, USA

The Transbay Tower,
San Francisco, CA, USA

Tyrol Tower,
Wörgl, Austria

University of North Carolina Genomic
Science Laboratory Building,
Chapel Hill, NC, USA

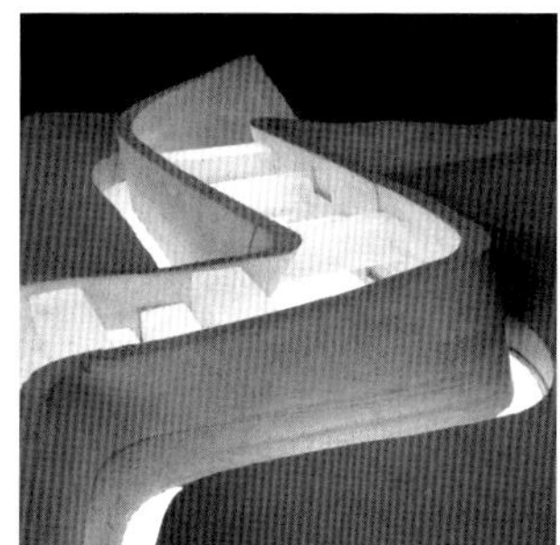

The Wadi,
Doha, Qatar

Washington Headquarters Services,
Fairfax County, VA, USA

World Trade Center Marketing Suite,
New York, NY, USA

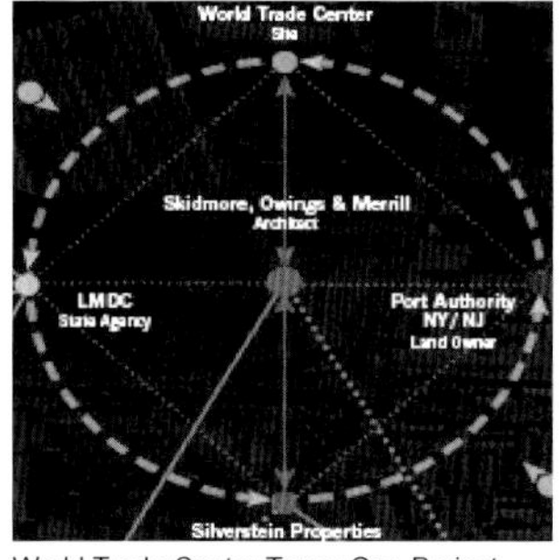

World Trade Center Tower One Project
Management,
New York, NY USA

Wuxi Times Square,
Wuxi, China

Yale University School of Management
Competition,
New Haven, CT, USA

Yokohama Kitanaka – Dori North District
Design Competition,
Yokohama, Japan

The North Mosque

Manama, Kingdom of Bahrain
Designed 2006

The Bahrain Bay Master Plan is the flagship map for the future growth of Bahrain and its capital city of Manama. It is part of a larger response to economic development in the Arabian Gulf, and will be the catalyst and model for growth and development in the greater North Manama Master Plan. Its close proximity to the airport, Bahrain Financial Harbor, World Trade Center, and the Diplomatic Area, make it a prestigious site bursting with potential.

The Bahrain Bay Master Plan consists of approximately 450,000 square meters of land constructed as fill in the Manama Bay. It is programmed as a residential and commercial island that joins a newly constructed Marina Bay just off the coast of Manama and the Arabian Sea to the north. Its strong radial organization is bisected by a commercial mixed-use boulevard that begins and ends in two grand, public open spaces which connect to a new waterfront and an active pedestrian promenade.

The North Mosque site is located at the intersection of the Bahrain Bay Water Promenade and the Canal Promenade. The Bahrain Bay Water Promenade, a curving waterfront spine, connects in its path the South and North Mosques along with other components of the master plan's civic program. The heart and main public space of the master plan, The Canal Promenade, is an axis formed by a canal that divides the island and opens up a straight connection and a clear view corridor to the inner harbor. Being the most prominent parcel within the development, the North Mosque site was intended to house a building that would serve a civic program. Because of the parcel's strategic location and its public nature, the architectural approach centered on designing an iconic piece that would emphasize and celebrate Bahrain's culture and religion.

The strategy was to condense the program towards the most open and unconstrained corner of the site; generating an object-like structure which maintains a significant distance from the surrounding buildings. The basic footprint is then rotated towards Mecca to achieve the correct orientation of the Qibla wall. That same footprint is extruded upward to create a perfect box. The pure form allows the exterior treatment to be enhanced by layers of ornamentation derived from historic Islamic patterns, which clothe the building, and provide its fundamental structure. The program is divided into two main volumes: a platform linking public and private areas, and a suspended cube which serves as the primary prayer space. To accentuate the condition of the suspended cube, the volume is shifted in two directions, cantilevering towards the two main intersecting axes. A unique screen wraps the outer cube, simultaneously ornamenting the volume and providing the thin screen with a three-dimensional structural sense of weight.

< 1 Bahrain Bay master plan aerial view
2, 3 Geometric precedents: a combination of
shapes from a small number of units
4 Screen design studies
5 Unfolded elevations of primary and
secondary structural members

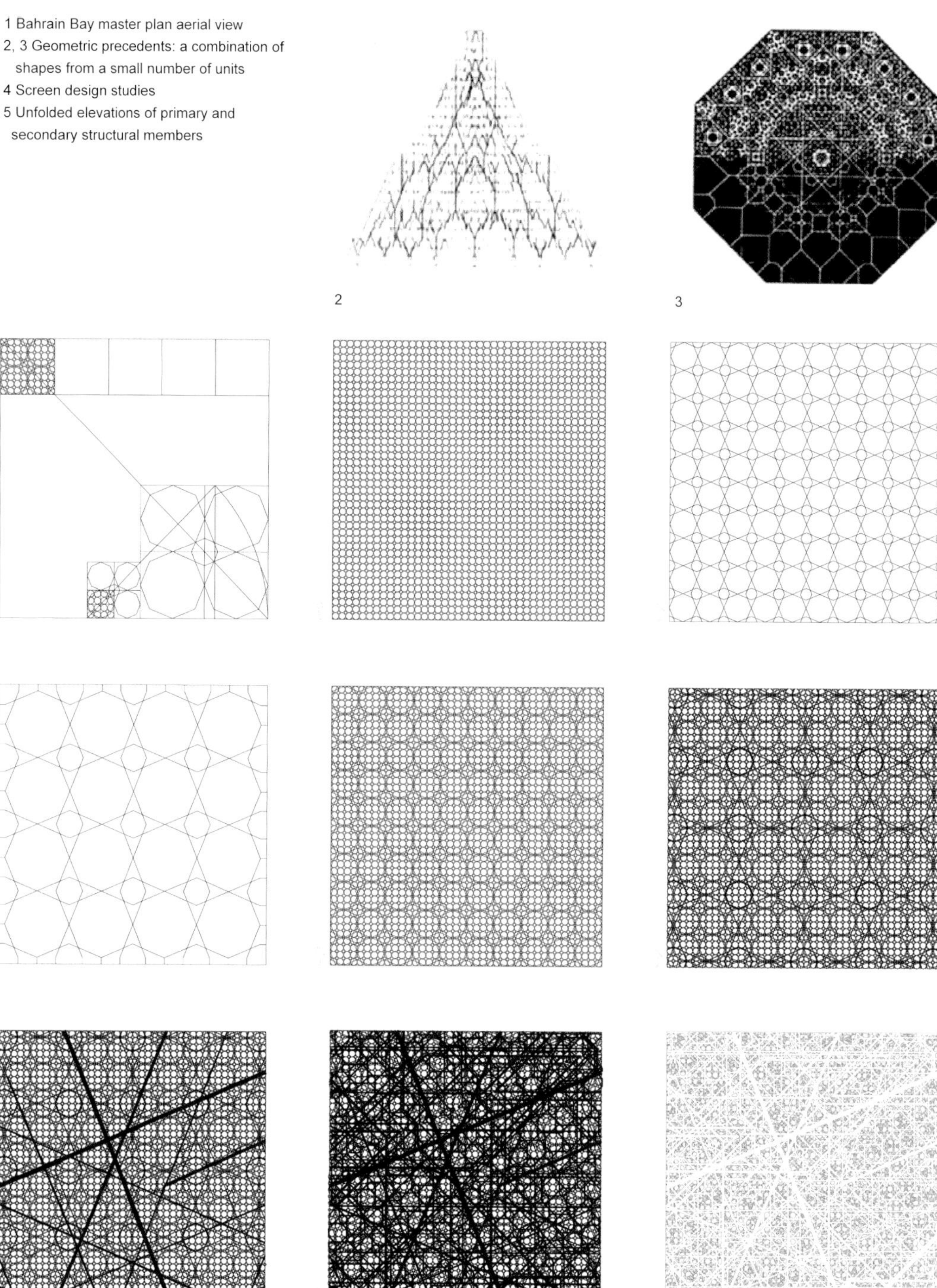

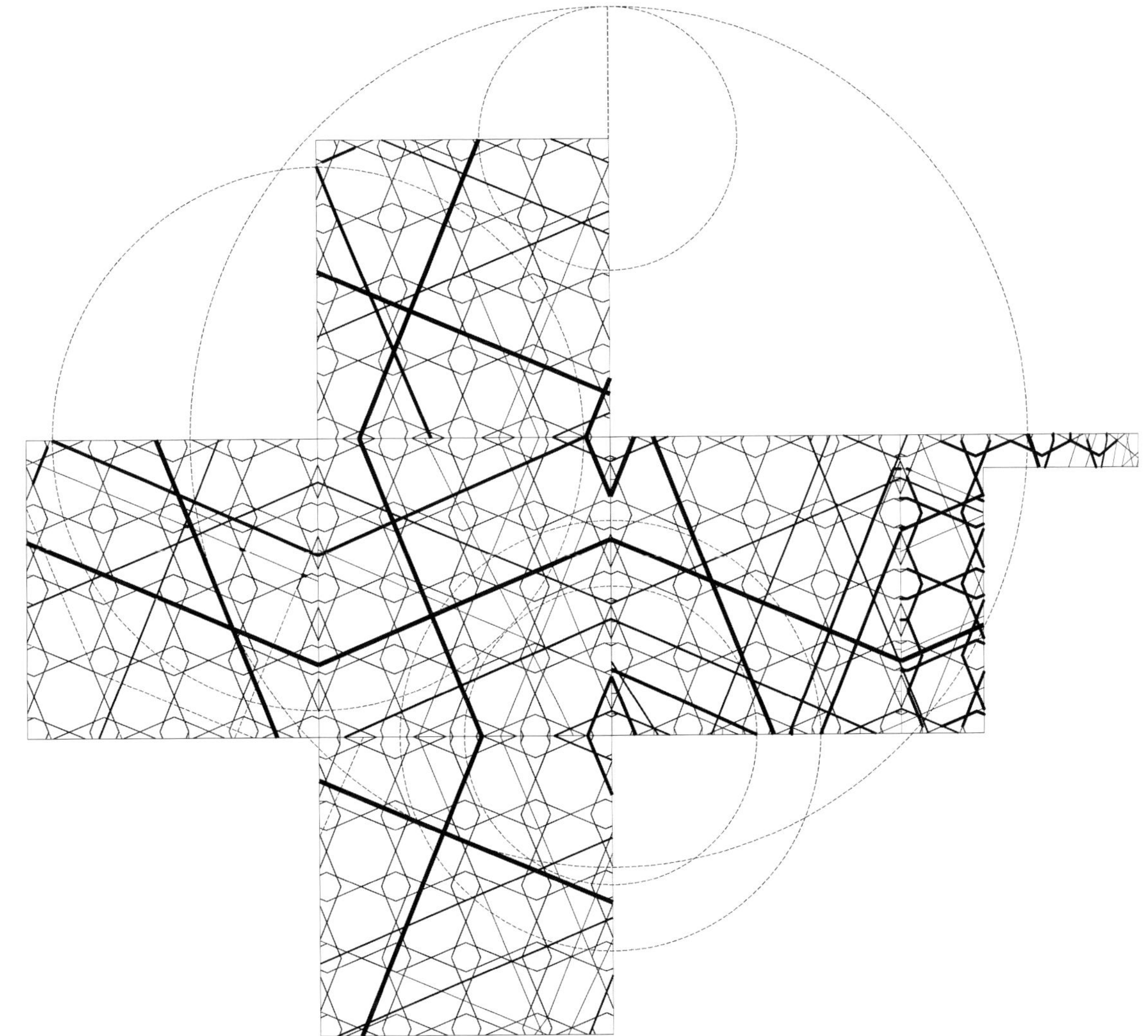

6 Self-supported steel composed of
  primary diagonal framing members and
  braced in-plane with an octagonal
  lattice of secondary framing members
7 Outer cube corner module isometric
8 North Mosque trademark screen
9 Steel lattice composed of IPE 600 and
  IPE 400 for primary diagonal framing
  and secondary members respectively >

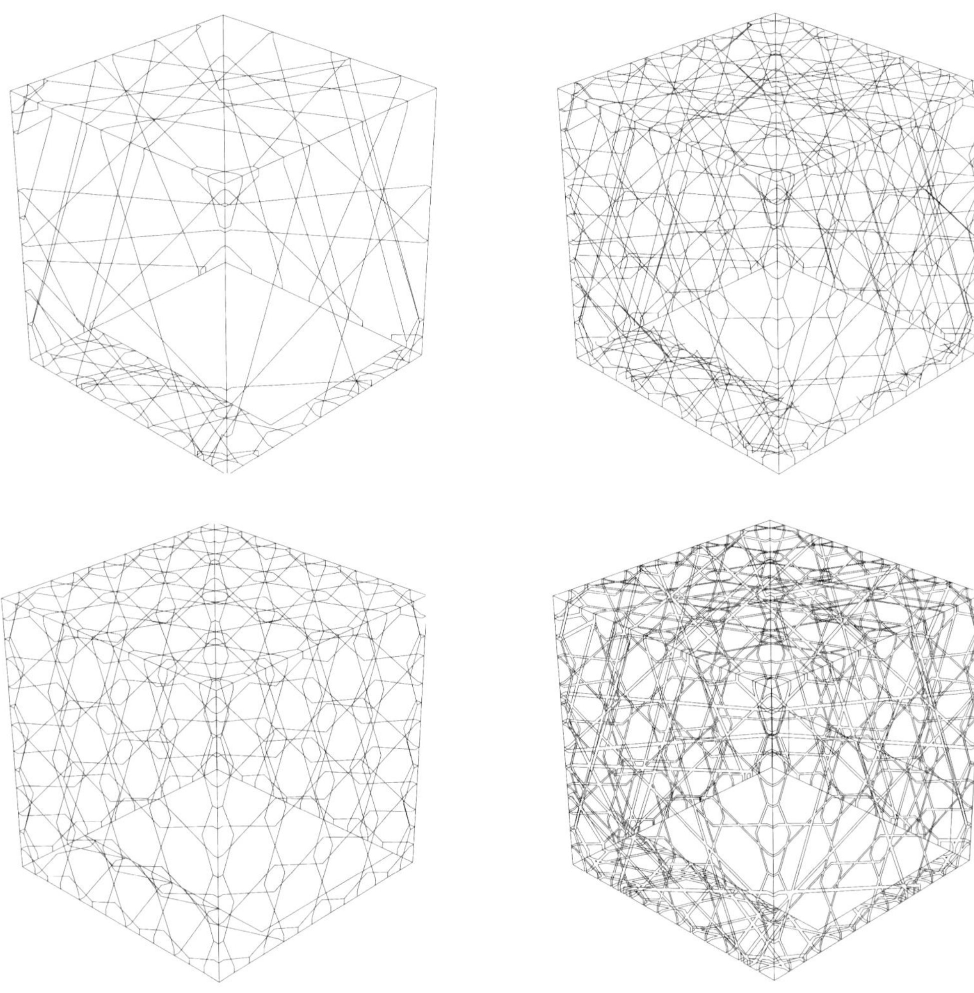

6

OUTER CUBE STRUCTURAL
STEEL PRIMARY MEMBERS
~3950
~3950
SHOP-FABRICATED, FULLY-
WELDED RIGID FRAME WITH
STIFFENERS AS NEEDED
WEST
SOUTH
~3950
RIGID CONNECTION (IN FIELD)
TO ADJACENT PRE-FABRI-
CATED STRUCTURAL MODULE,
TYPICAL AT ALL MODULES

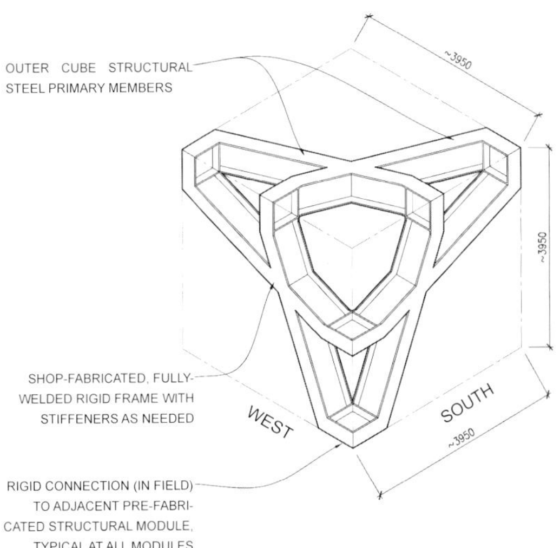

7

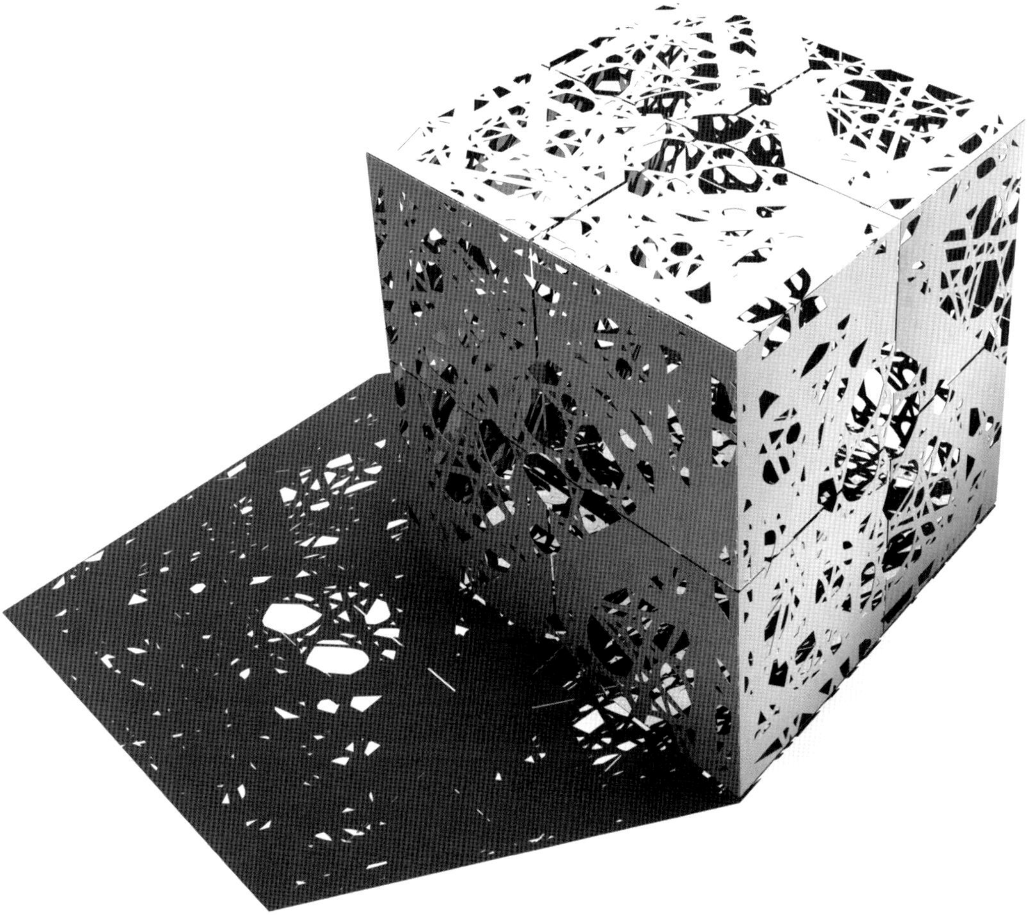

8

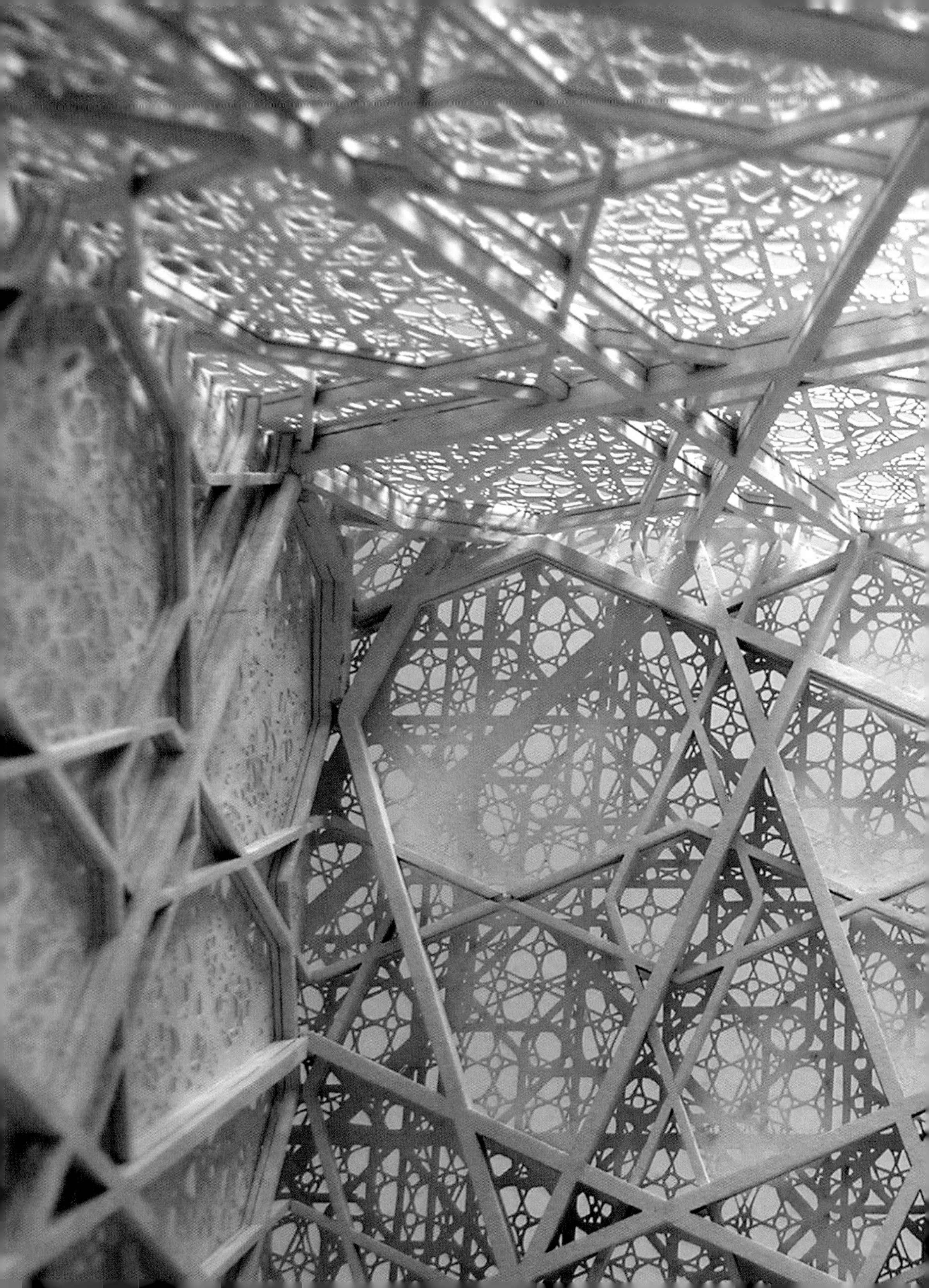

10 Men's Prayer Hall

11 West wall section

12 West elevation; the design organizes
   the program into two main elements:
   a monolithic black platform that links
   public and private areas, and a porous,
   suspended cube which serves as the
   main prayer hall

13 First floor plan EL. +12.00m >

14 North Mosque viewed from the Bahrain
   Bay Canal Promenade >

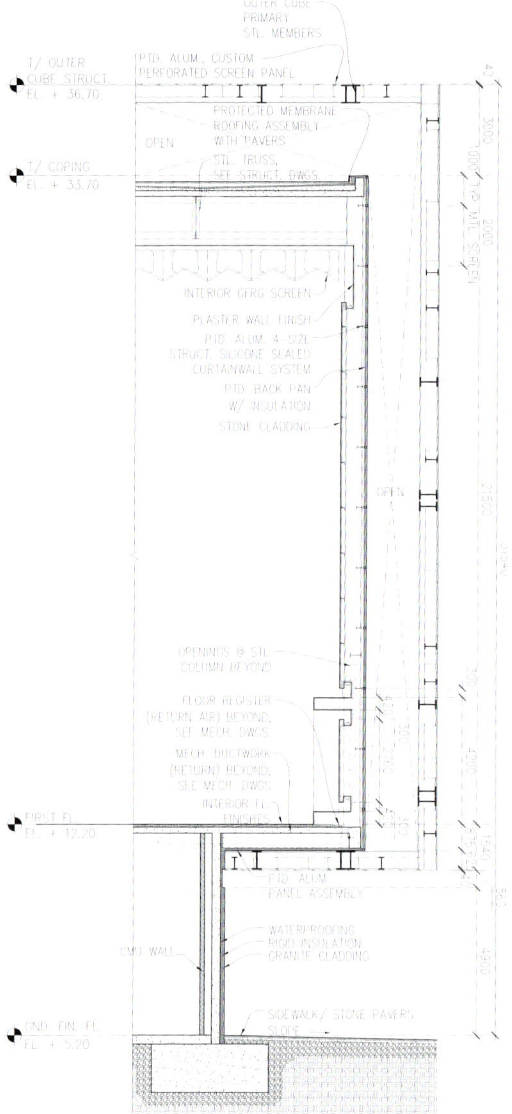

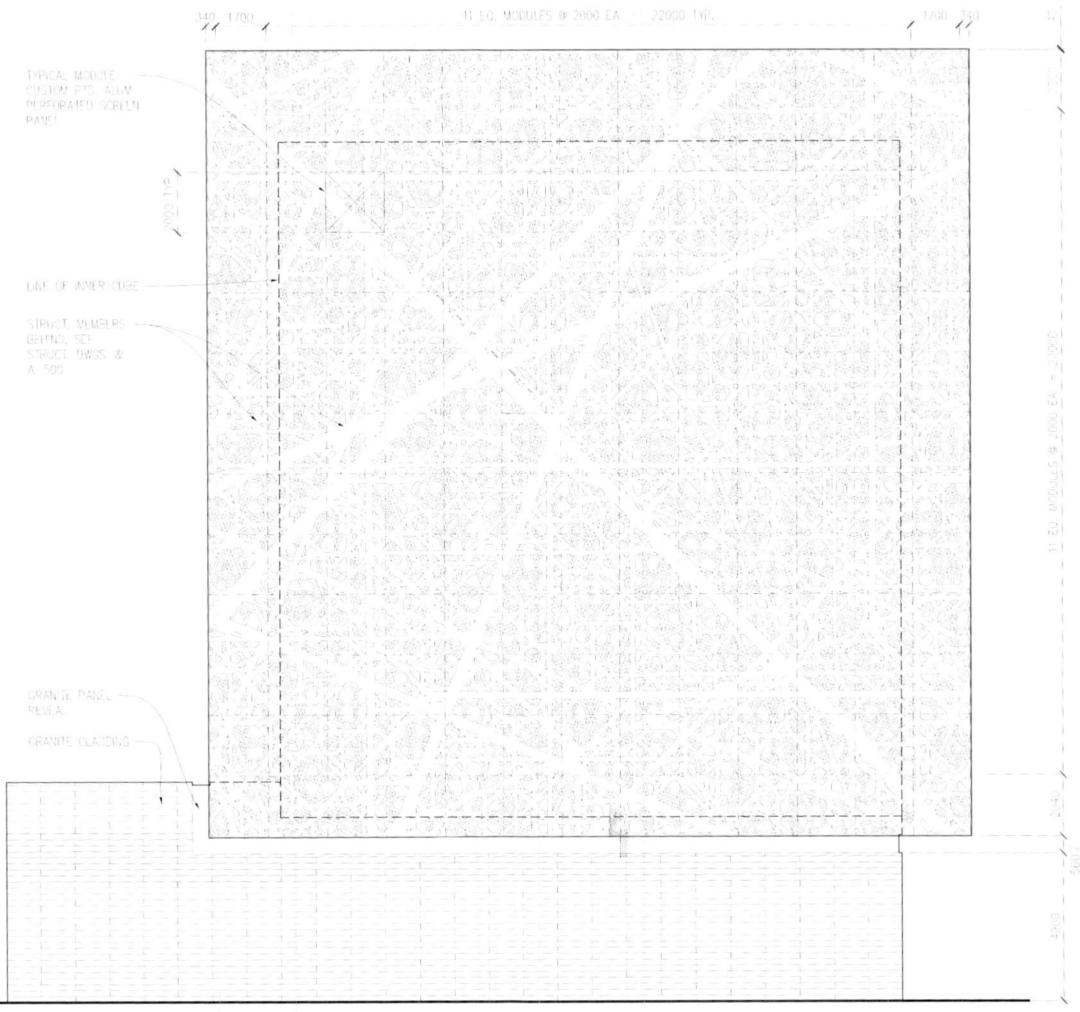
340 1700
11 EQ. MODULES @ 2000 EA. = 22000 TYP.
1700 340
TYPICAL MODULE CUSTOM PTD. ALUM PERFORATED SCREEN PANEL
2000 TYP
LINE OF INNER CUBE
STRUCT. MEMBERS BEHIND, SEE STRUCT DWGS & A 500
11 EQ. MODULES @ 2000 EA. = 22000
GRANITE PANEL REVEAL
GRANITE CLADDING
SCALE: 1:250

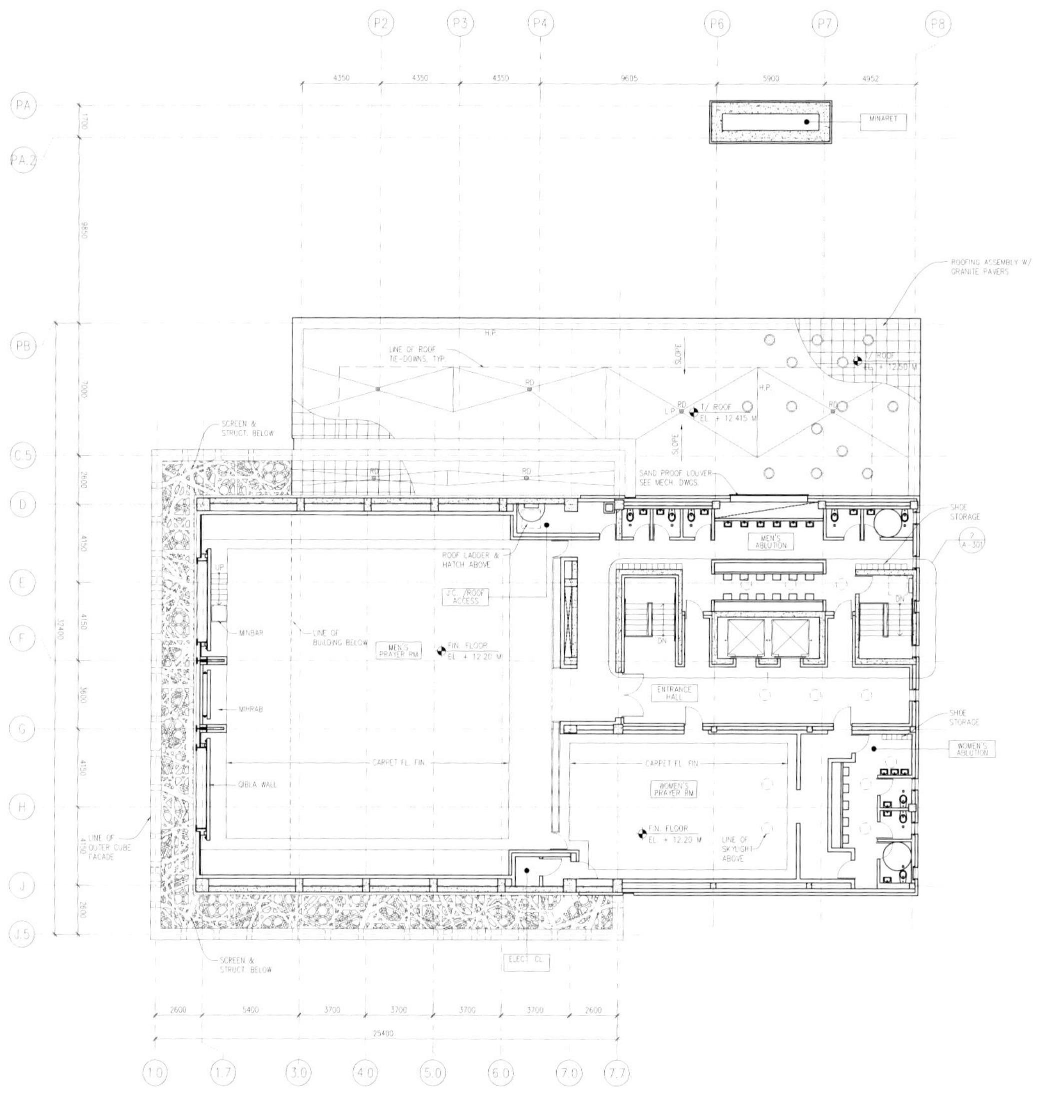

P2
P3
P4
P6
P7
P8
4350
4350
4350
9605
5900
4952
PA
PA.2
PB
C.5
D
E
F
G
H
J
J.5
MINARET
ROOFING ASSEMBLY W/
GRANITE PAVERS
LINE OF ROOF
TIE-DOWNS, TYP.
H.P.
SLOPE
ROOF
EL + 12.560 M
RD
RD
H.P.
L.P.
RD
T/ ROOF
EL + 12.415 M
RD
SLOPE
SCREEN &
STRUCT. BELOW
RD
RD
SAND PROOF LOUVER
SEE MECH. DWGS.
SHOE
STORAGE
MEN'S
ABLUTION
ROOF LADDER &
HATCH ABOVE
J.C. /ROOF
ACCESS
DN
2
A-301
UP
MINBAR
LINE OF
BUILDING BELOW
MEN'S
PRAYER RM
FIN. FLOOR
EL + 12.20 M
DN
DN
SHOE
STORAGE
MIHRAB
ENTRANCE
HALL
WOMEN'S
ABLUTION
CARPET FL. FIN.
CARPET FL. FIN.
QIBLA WALL
WOMEN'S
PRAYER RM
LINE OF
OUTER CUBE
FACADE
FIN. FLOOR
EL + 12.20 M
LINE OF
SKYLIGHT
ABOVE
SCREEN &
STRUCT. BELOW
ELECT. CL.
2600
5400
3700
3700
3700
3700
2600
25400
1.0
1.7
3.0
4.0
5.0
6.0
7.0
7.7
SCALE: 1:400

ISRAEL
SYRIA
JORDAN
WEST BANK
GOLAN HEIGHTS
NEGEV
GAZA STRIP
DESERT
DIMASHQ (DAMASCUS)
AMMAN (PHILADELPHIA)
Jerusalem
Tel Aviv-Yafo
Haifa/Hefa
Gaza
Ashdod
Ashqelon
Be'er Sheva (Beersheba)
Al Karak
Irbid (Arbela)
Ar Ramtha
As Suwayda
Al Mafraq
Az Zarqa'
Ar Rusayfah
Petra
Ma'an
Al 'Aqabah (Aqaba)
Al Tafilah
Ash Shawbak
Zefat
Teverya
Naharyya
Akko
Shefar'am
Nazerat (Nazareth)
Bet She'an
Janin
Nablus
Ramallah
Bayt Lahm (Bethlehem)
Hebron
Al Khalil
Jericho
Madaba
Dhiban (Dibon)
Mu'tah
Al Mazar
Ramat Gan
Bat Yam
Holon
Rishon LeZiyyon
Nes Ziyyona
Rehovot
Ramla
Qiryat Gat
Dimona
Yeroham
Mitzpe Ramon
Eilat
Rafah

Bridging the Rift

Border of Israel (Central Arava) and Jordan (Wadi Araba)
Designed 2005

The Bridging the Rift project is conceived as an extra-territorial neutral enclave where scientific discourse can be conducted in an environment unburdened by the political divisions existing in the Middle East. To achieve this goal, a precinct was created by land donated from Jordan and Israel where an envisioned campus would bring together academics and researchers whose focus is to understand the genetic heritage of desert plants and species. With the involvement of academic institutions such as Stanford, Cornell, and Harvard, a research community has evolved that focuses on the natural resources of the Great Rift Valley. This cooperation among scientists, absent of political overtones, will lead to agricultural strategies that would equally benefit the inhabitants of the region. To turn this vision into reality, a large master plan was developed that would ultimately house a community of 1000 people. In the meantime, knowing that the implementation of the master plan would take many years, a pilot project was designed that would jump-start the activities on the site and act as an experimental prototype in building forms that specifically responds to the harsh desert climate.

The first building, a small structure in the context of the overall plan, is conceived as a marker in the desert that straddles the Israel / Jordan border. Inspired by traditional forts and caravansaries, the compound is envisioned as a pure rectangular form with clean geometric lines that establish a strong presence in the undifferentiated desert plain. Rising from the desert, the protective walls around the compound at once blend with the environment by their materiality and yet are juxtaposed by its saturated color.

A path defined by the borderline that connects the arrival court through the building and ends in a landscaped courtyard that is slightly depressed in the desert floor is used for contemplation and casual interaction. Within this "excavation," building forms and landscape elements are carefully sculpted to create a still-life-like composition within the desert.

Beginning with the construction of a massive stone wall surrounding three sides of the complex, a thermal mass is created to absorb the direct heat of the harsh sun to the eastern, southern, and western exposures. Within this protective mass, the building "floats" above the desert floor forming a cavity between the research facility floor and the earth below. An air chimney located at the center of the complex pulls air passively from under the building where air cooled by the low nighttime desert temperatures is stored. A pool of water located within an inner court adds to the cooling process and introduces humidity to the air before it enters the building.

For symbolic reasons, the building sits literally on the former border between the two nations and physically brings the thirty scientists gathered there together. Three research laboratories are organized in clusters that are dispersed around larger programmatic spaces, including a lecture hall, dining hall, and library. Each of the laboratory clusters relate to the outdoors through intimate courtyards that allow for researchers to expand their indoor environments when the climactic conditions are tolerable. The larger programmatic elements containing shared functions such as libraries, cafeterias, and lecture halls are housed in tall volumes that protrude upward onto a roof-level terrace. This raised and partially shaded terrace can accommodate larger gatherings and serves as a viewing platform to the future campus of Bridging the Rift.

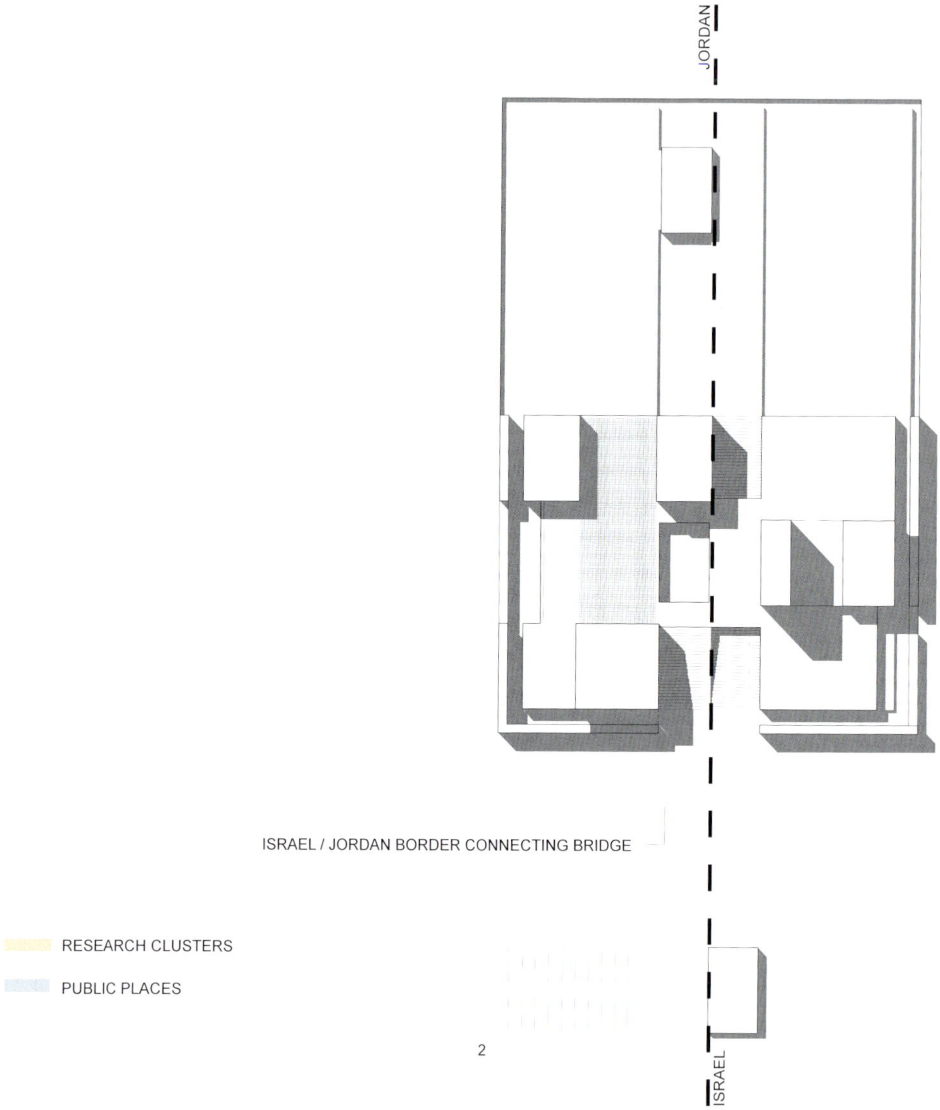

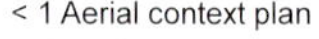

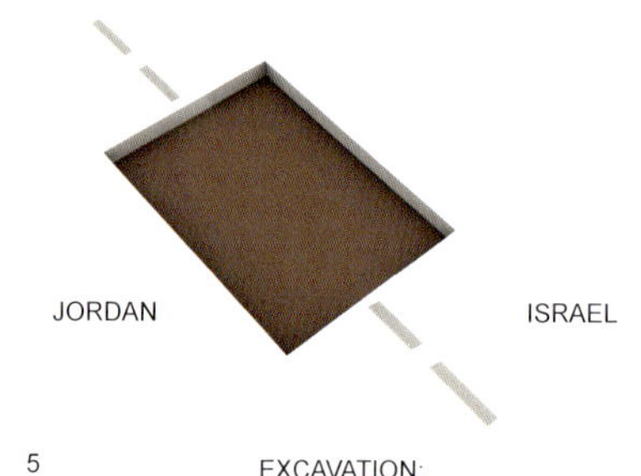

< 1 Aerial context plan
2 Roof plan
3 First floor plan
4 Second floor plan
5 Parti diagrams
6 View of new science and research center
on Israel / Jordan border >

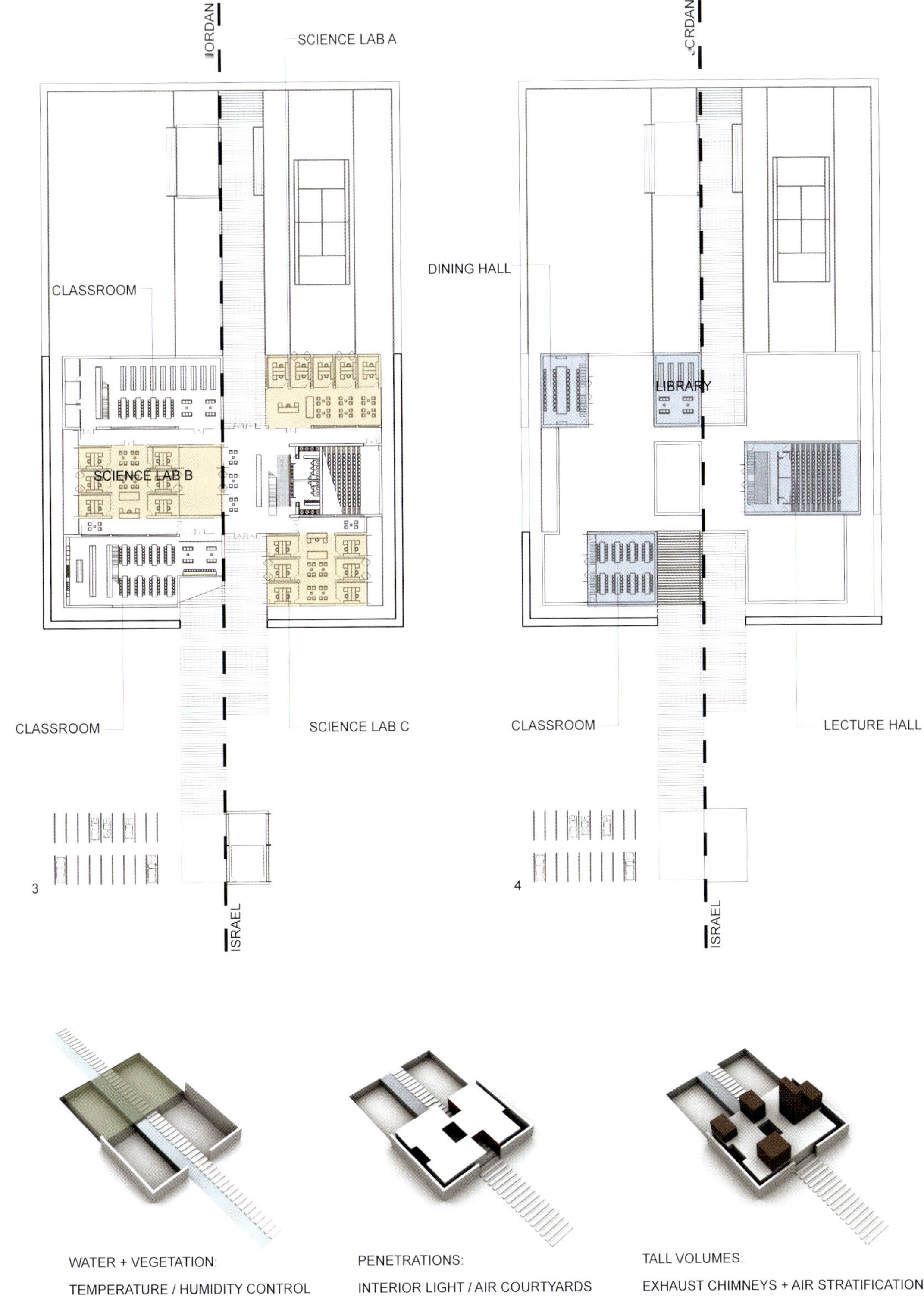
JORDAN
SCIENCE LAB A
CLASSROOM
SCIENCE LAB B
CLASSROOM
SCIENCE LAB C
3
ISRAEL
JORDAN
DINING HALL
LIBRARY
CLASSROOM
LECTURE HALL
4
ISRAEL
WATER + VEGETATION:
TEMPERATURE / HUMIDITY CONTROL
PENETRATIONS:
INTERIOR LIGHT / AIR COURTYARDS
TALL VOLUMES:
EXHAUST CHIMNEYS + AIR STRATIFICATION

7 Sustainable design concepts

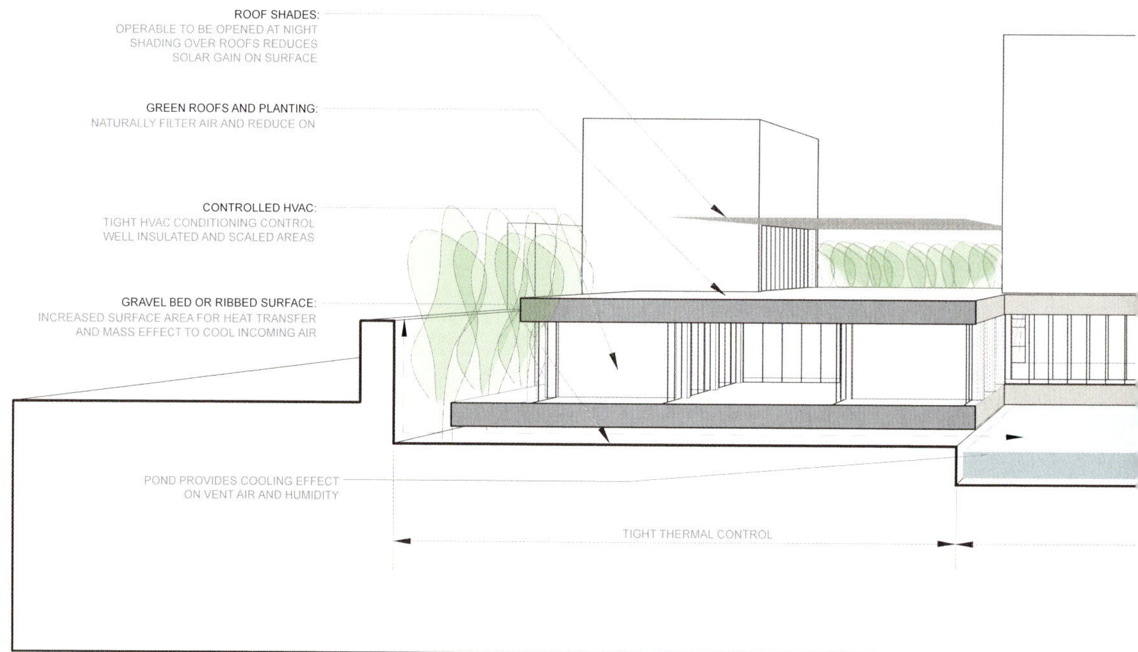

7

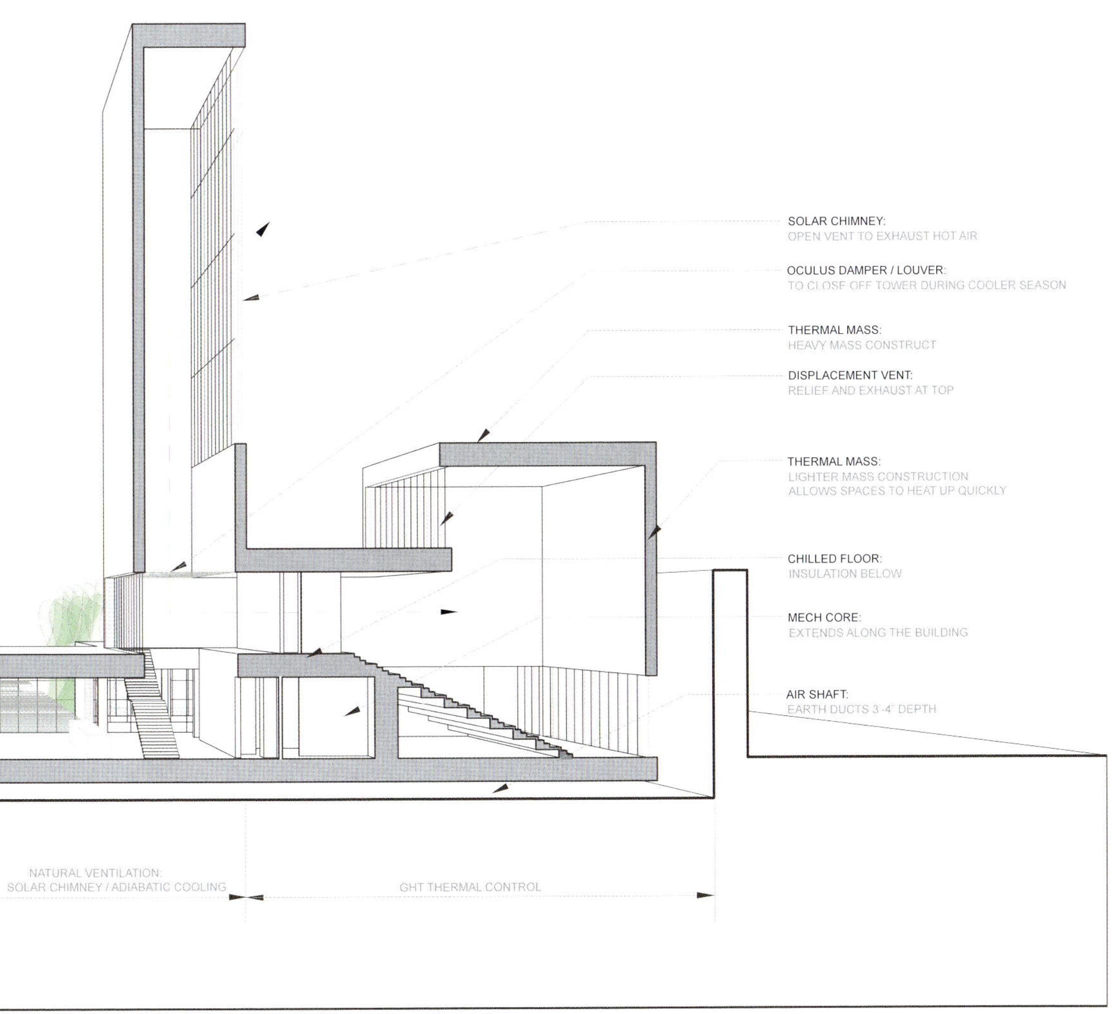

SOLAR CHIMNEY:
OPEN VENT TO EXHAUST HOT AIR

OCULUS DAMPER / LOUVER:
TO CLOSE OFF TOWER DURING COOLER SEASON

THERMAL MASS:
HEAVY MASS CONSTRUCT

DISPLACEMENT VENT:
RELIEF AND EXHAUST AT TOP

THERMAL MASS:
LIGHTER MASS CONSTRUCTION
ALLOWS SPACES TO HEAT UP QUICKLY

CHILLED FLOOR:
INSULATION BELOW

MECH CORE:
EXTENDS ALONG THE BUILDING

AIR SHAFT:
EARTH DUCTS 3'-4' DEPTH

NATURAL VENTILATION:
SOLAR CHIMNEY / ADIABATIC COOLING

GHT THERMAL CONTROL

8 Aerial view showing building forms and
  landscape elements carefully sculpted
  to create a still-life-like composition within
  the desert
9 View of tall volumes that protrude upward
  onto a roof-level court
10 Shaded view towards main campus
11 Intertwined science and research
  program >
12 Solar chimney >

8

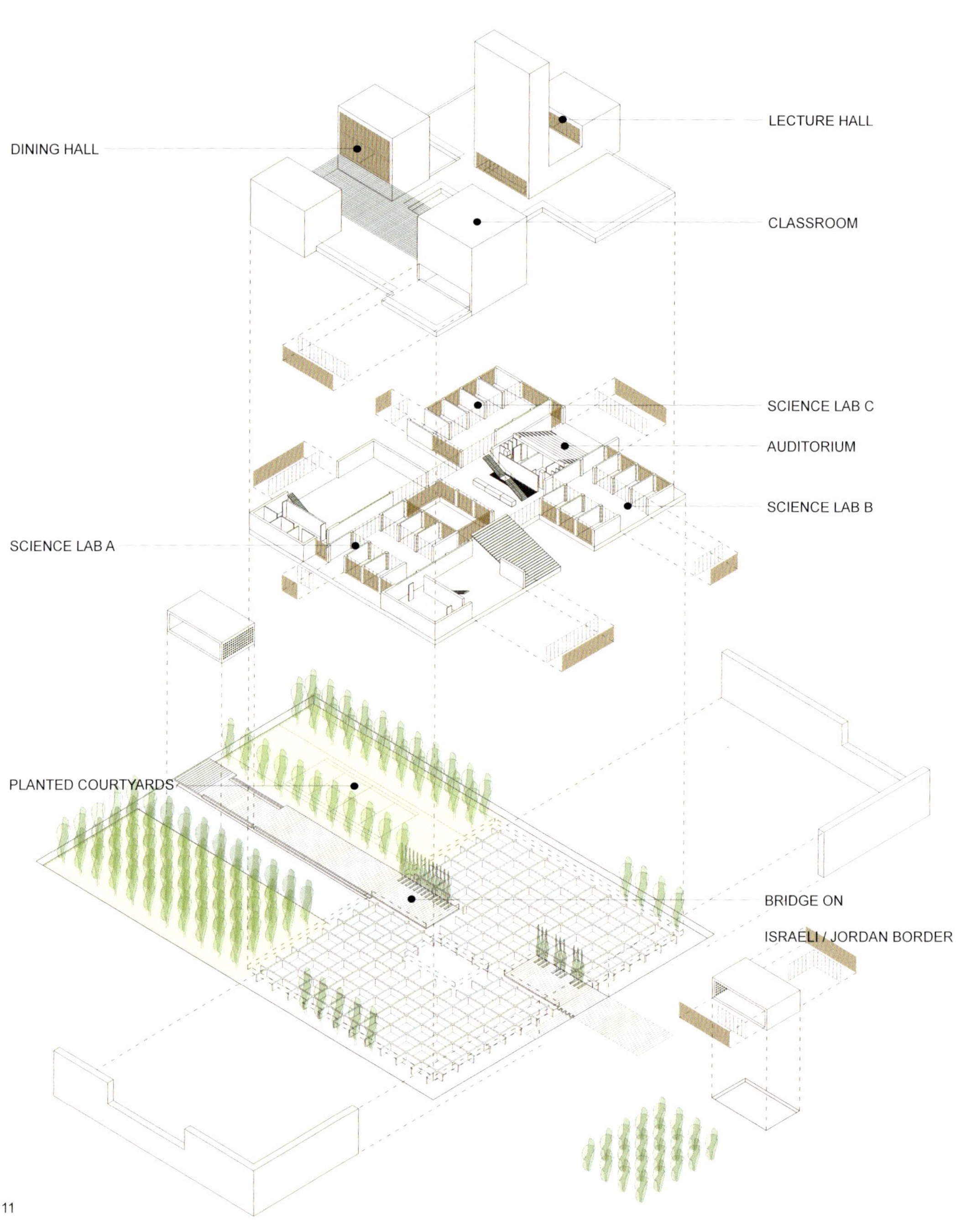

DINING HALL
LECTURE HALL
CLASSROOM
SCIENCE LAB C
AUDITORIUM
SCIENCE LAB B
SCIENCE LAB A
PLANTED COURTYARDS
BRIDGE ON
ISRAELI / JORDAN BORDER
11

12

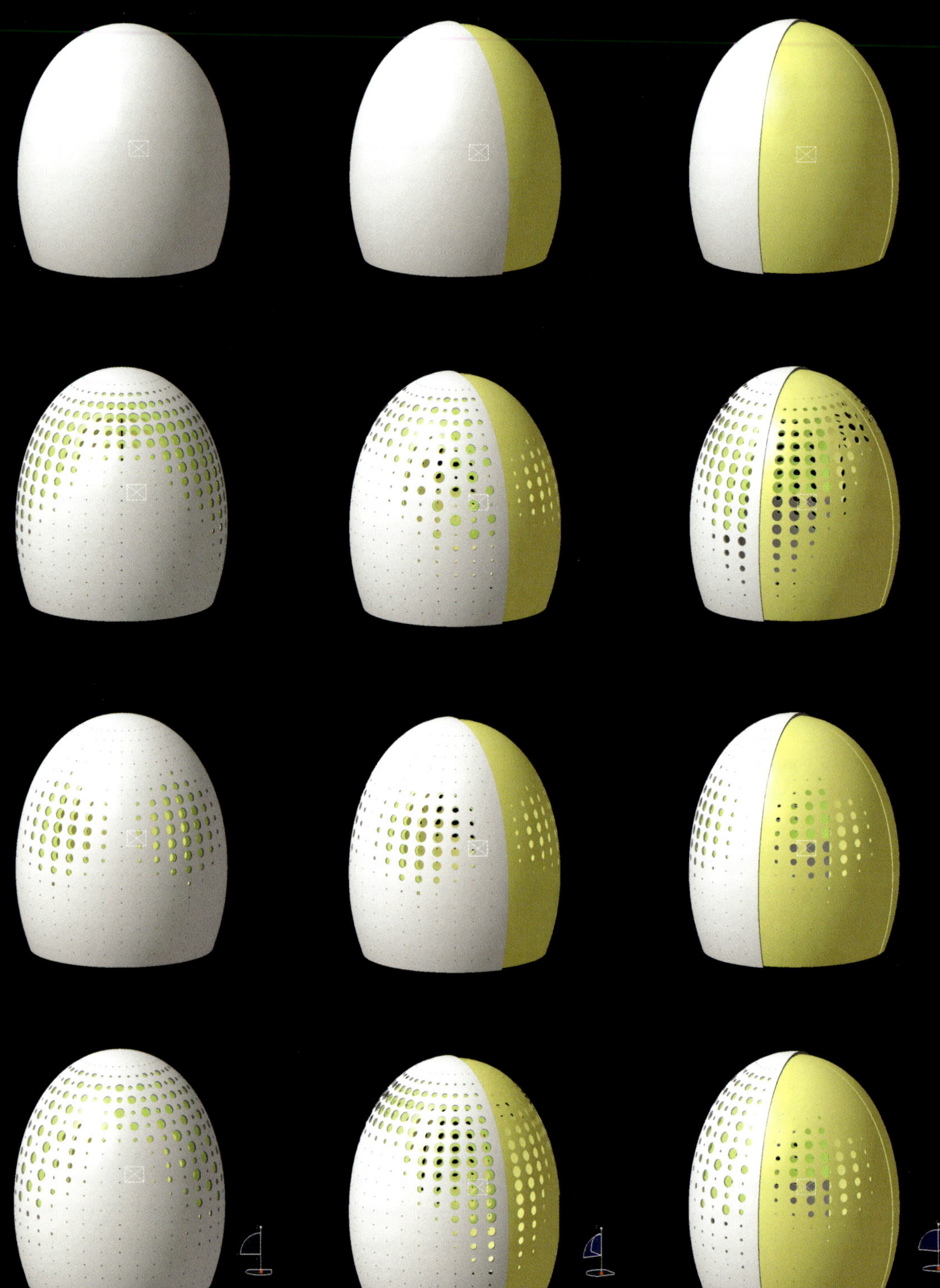

BioPods
Chapel Hill, North Carolina
Designed 2007

The Genomic Science Building (GSB) at the University of North Carolina is comprised of three identical lab modules that pinwheel around the public plaza below. The BioPod was created for the BioInformatics Lab, a specialized group at the university, as a place to collect and interpret research data generated by plant material grown in a secured greenhouse on the roof.

The BioPod is an unconventional workplace solution designed for an unconventional user. It was developed as a branding mechanism for the BioInformatics research team, an introverted group of scientists who desired a work environment that could be equally collaborative and private. In the new GSB, the BioInformatics team is front and center, highly visible from the public plaza below and to visitors circulating the building. The BioPod provides an opportunity to give them a new identity; to introduce them to the campus and to attract researchers in a notoriously competitive recruitment process.

The university and the design team desired an open, transparent work area for the group consistent with the interstitial space they were given. The SOM team began to analyze the conventional space plan and found that traditional furnishings were limiting. The resulting cellular shaped BioPod is a world unto its own that allows the user to entirely reinterpret traditional space planning. The multiple spatial envelopes create a more interactive environment where the forms can be reconfigured as easily as pieces in a game of chess.

The BioPod is a room within a room and accommodates the individualistic preferences within the BioInformatics group. While each pod has an inherently private nature, it is also malleable to the needs of collaboration. The design incorporates wheels that allow unlimited configurations depending on the needs and density of the department. Once each pod is moved to its desired location, it is then plugged into one of the many docking ports in the raised access floor. The BioInformatics group was also concerned with acoustical distractions and a need for securing their work area. To address these concerns, each molded fiberglass unit is a self-secured, self-illuminated, self-ventilated interior surface that acts as an acoustical barrier. Each unit can accommodate up to six pole-mounted flat screen monitors and two CPU units as specified by the user.

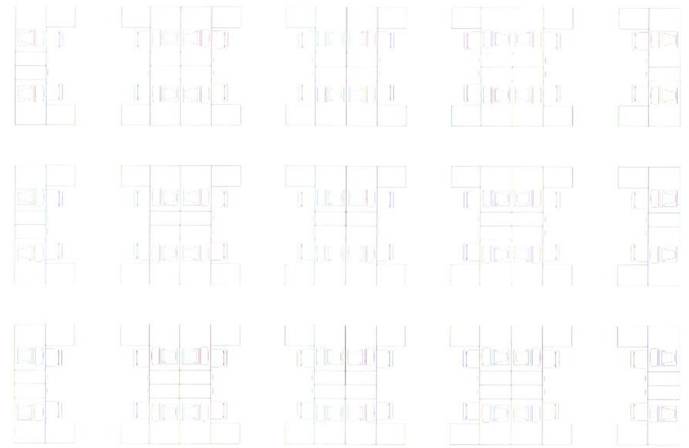

TOTAL NUMBER OF WORKSTATIONS: 48

TOTAL NUMBER OF WORKSTATIONS: 30
TOTAL NUMBER OF DOCKING STATIONS: 35

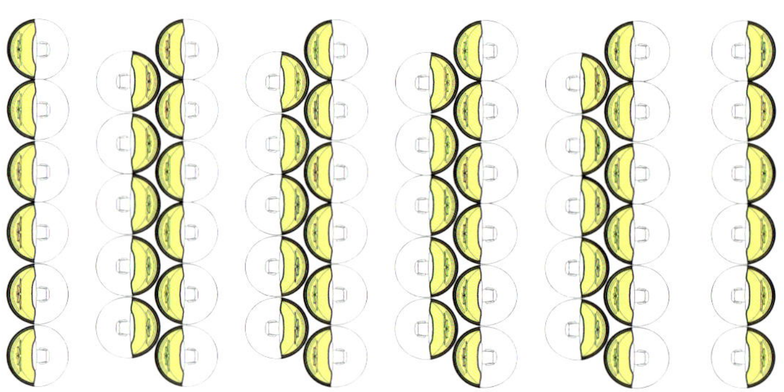

TOTAL NUMBER OF WORKSTATIONS: 56
TOTAL NUMBER OF DOCKING STATIONS: 56

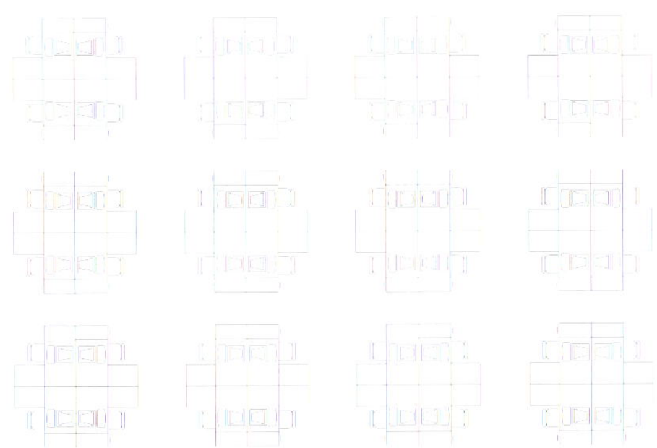

TOTAL NUMBER OF WORKSTATIONS: 48

TOTAL NUMBER OF WORKSTATIONS: 26
TOTAL NUMBER OF DOCKING STATIONS: 72

2

TOTAL NUMBER OF WORKSTATIONS: 23
TOTAL NUMBER OF DOCKING STATIONS: 45

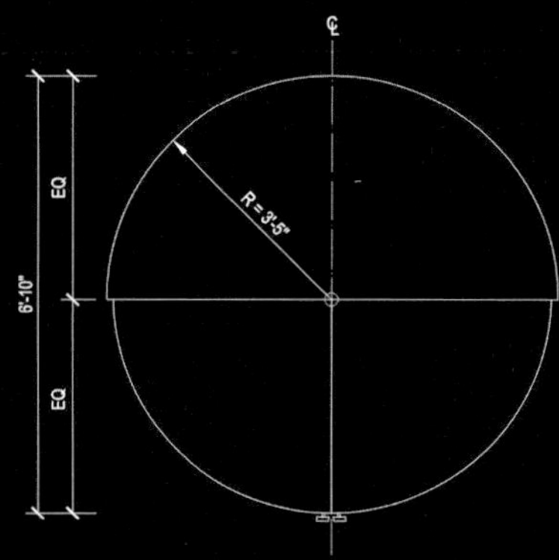

LOCATION PLAN

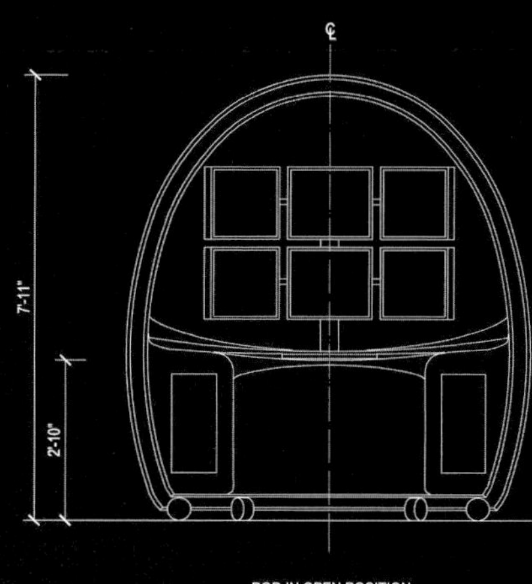

POD IN OPEN POSITION

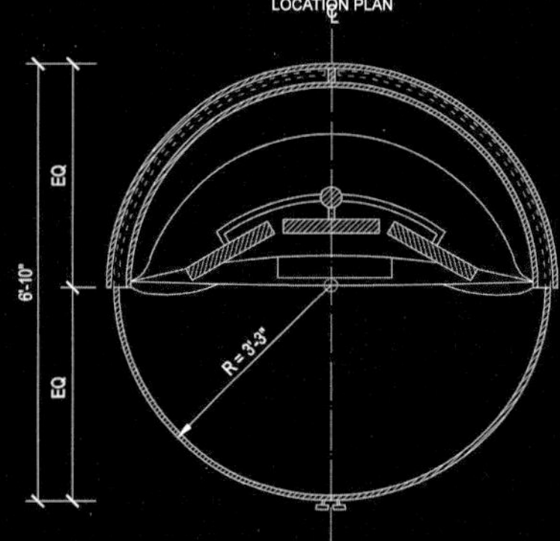

WORKSPACE PLAN

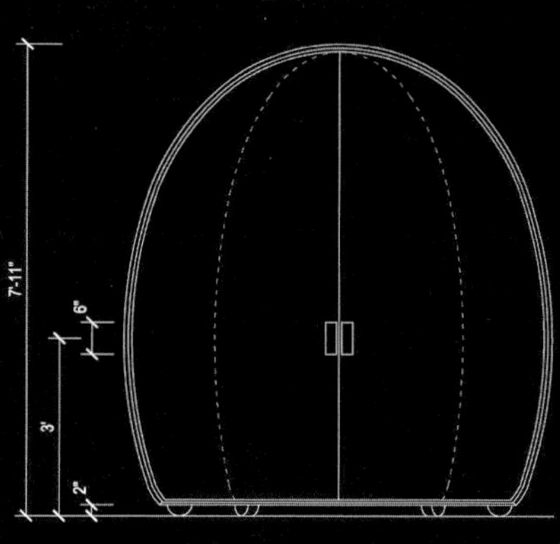

POD IN CLOSED POSITION

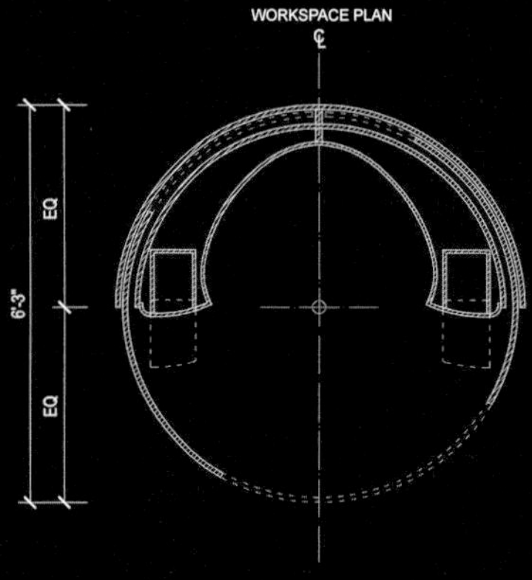

PLAN OF CPU STORAGE

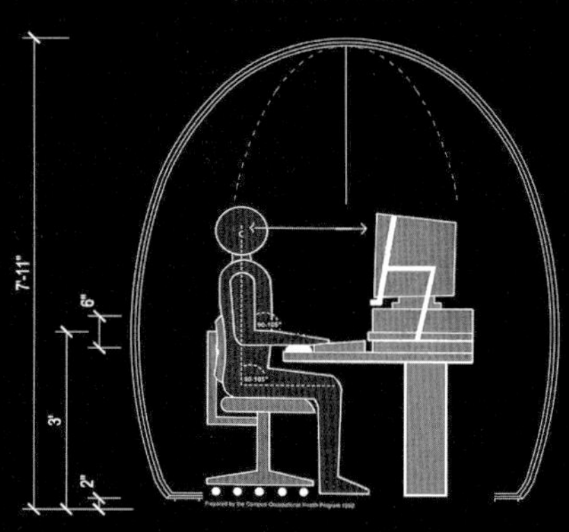

POD FOR ONE PERSON

6 Light study of typical shell perforation
  type
7 Single pod, closed

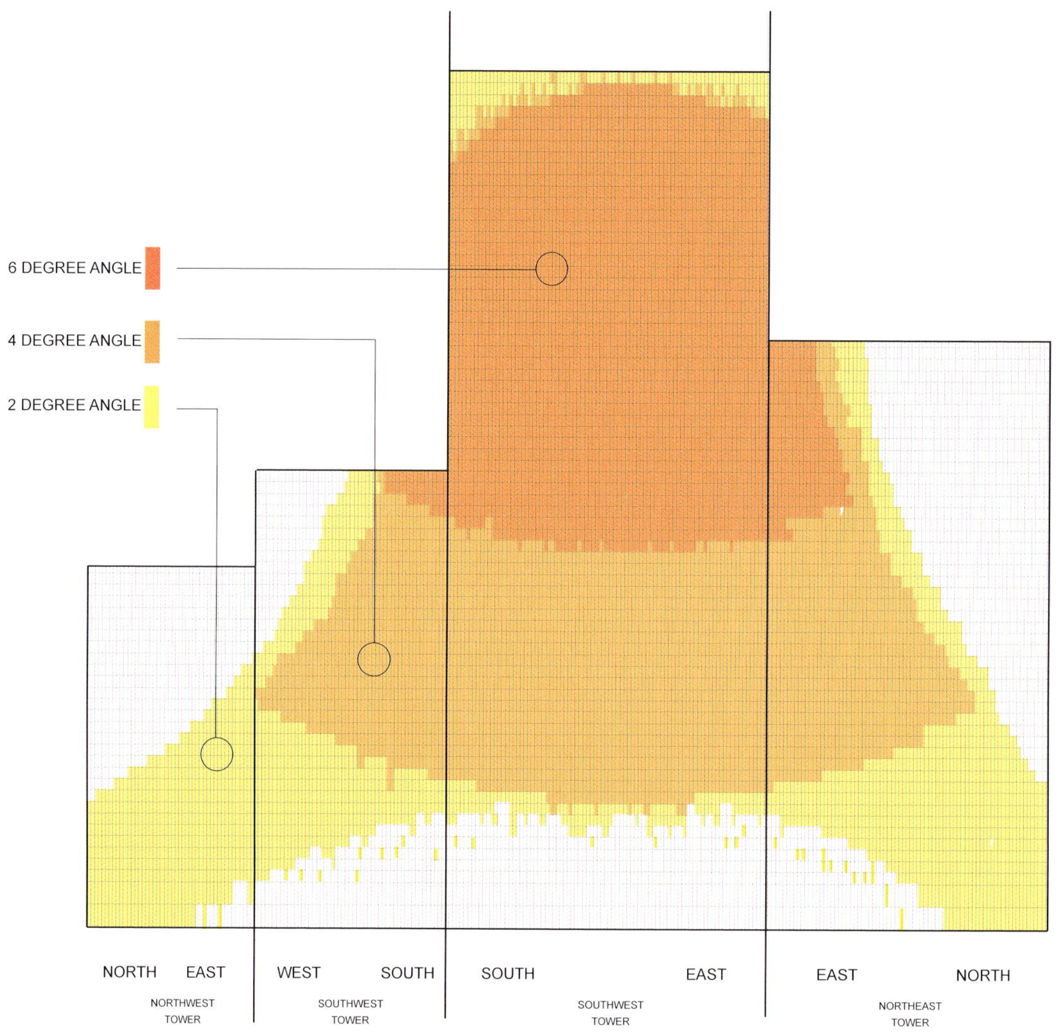

6 DEGREE ANGLE
4 DEGREE ANGLE
2 DEGREE ANGLE
NORTH   EAST
NORTHWEST
TOWER
WEST   SOUTH
SOUTHWEST
TOWER
SOUTH   EAST
SOUTHWEST
TOWER
EAST   NORTH
NORTHEAST
TOWER

Kinetic Curtainwall Prototype

New York, New York
Designed 2007—ongoing

The Kinetic Curtainwall Prototype was an independent research project that developed out of an interest in producing a curtainwall system that could generate a positive response to changing environmental conditions in real time.

With the understanding that solar conditions are constantly changing over the course of the day, and over the course of the year, we realized that a building could adjust to reflect or absorb more or less solar heat and light, which in turn could mean significant cost savings of the heating and cooling systems of the building, and an increased efficiency in applied photovoltaic systems. There is an opportunity to accomplish this if one allows for a building's curtainwall to adjust accordingly.

The Kinetic Curtainwall Prototype is designed as a double skin curtainwall system where the exterior glass pane and the face of the spandrel panel are hinged together and pinned to a track that allows the assembly to slide out or "bend" up to six degrees out of the perpendicular plane. Photovoltaic cells laminated into the face of the spandrel panel power a small motor connected to a thermal sensor and magnetic release switch. These motors control when and to what degree the assembly slides out. During the hottest part of the day, the glass plane will lean out six degrees, and the spandrel panel will lean in so that its face is at a nearly forty-five degree angle to the sun. This change in the surface angle helps to deflect a large portion of the sun's rays, reducing solar heat gains by twenty-five percent. Additionally, the angle of the photovoltaics in the spandrel panel is optimized to the sun's angle, providing enough energy to operate the building systems when energy demands are at their peak. During the summer months, employing this system on a medium-large building could produce 175 kilowatts a day, and offset from the electrical grid nearly fifty-two pounds of carbon dioxide. When there is little sun, or it is cold outside, the assembly remains in the zero position, and the air cavity created between the layers of glass provide an added layer of insulation for the building.

Where it was exposed during the day, photo-luminescent paint on the backside of the spandrel panel glows into the night, reminding viewers of the building of the twelve hours of light that preceded the night.

4 Section, Kinetic Curtainwall IGU
5 Section, photovoltaic (PV) panels in
  flat position
6 Section, photovoltaic (PV) panels in
  angled position

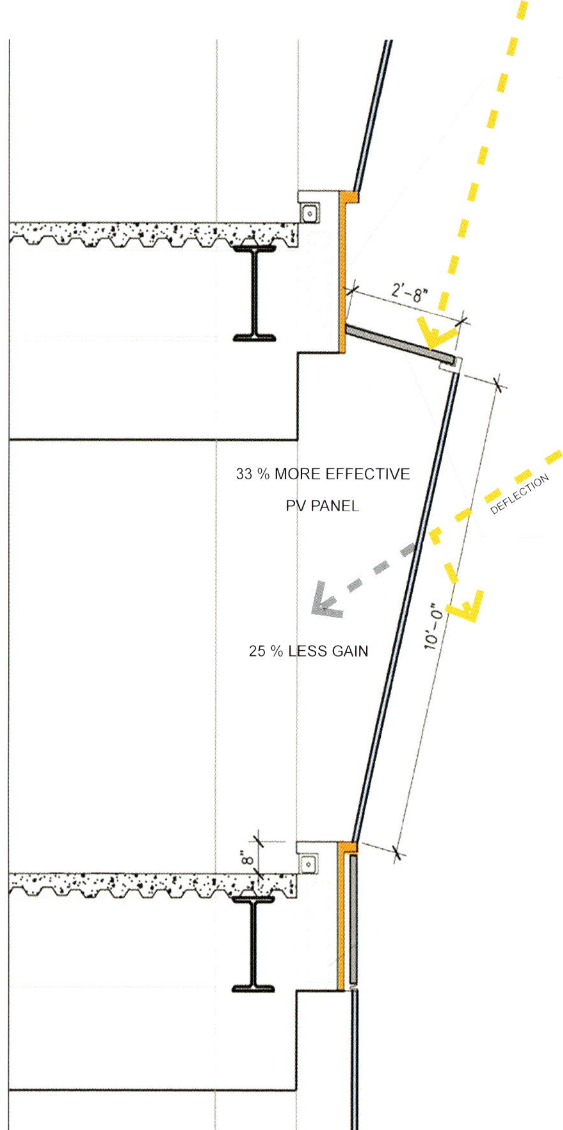

PHOTO LUMINESCENT SPANDREL PANEL RE-
VEALED (GIVES TOWERS A GLOWING PRESENCE
AT NIGHT)

BUILDING INTEGRATED PV PANEL LAMINATED
INTO ADJUSTABLE SPANDREL PANEL; ADJUSTS
ACCORDING TO SOLAR PATH OVER THE COURSE
OF THE DAY

INSULATED GLASS UNIT WITH SOLAR SHADING
5'-0" X 10'-0" TYPICAL (ANGLE REDUCES SOLAR
HEAT)

SPANDREL PANEL, SURFACE PAINTED WITH PHO-
TO-LUMINESCENT PAINT

4

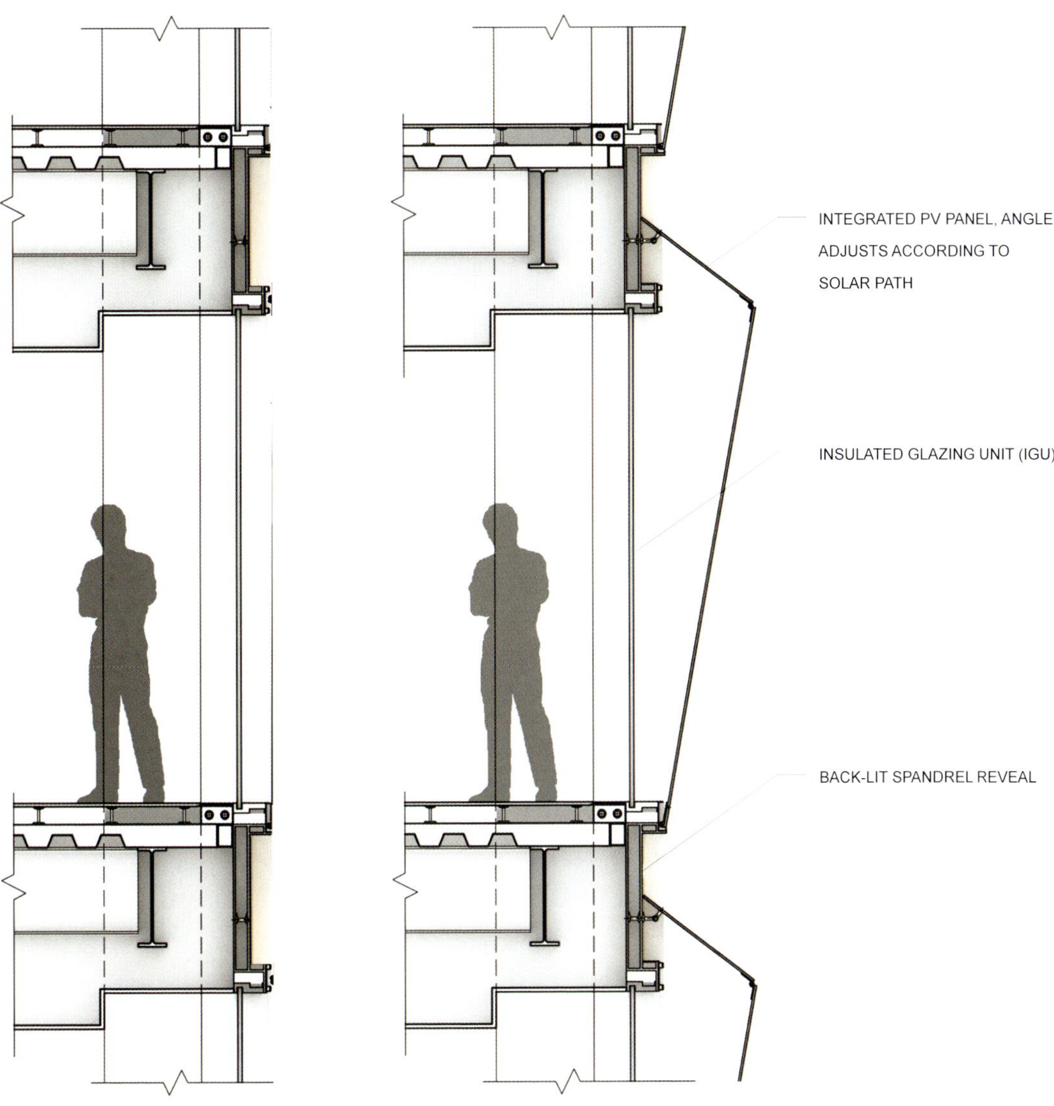

INTEGRATED PV PANEL, ANGLE ADJUSTS ACCORDING TO SOLAR PATH

INSULATED GLAZING UNIT (IGU)

BACK-LIT SPANDREL REVEAL

5

6

TILTED CURTAINWALL

OBJECT ID	OBJECT TYPE	SURFACE (FT^2)	EXPOSED AREA (FT^2)	UNDER GROUND (FT^2)	AZIMUTH ANGLE (DEG)	ORIENTATION (DEG)	TOTAL RADIATION (WH/M^2)	TOTAL DIRECT RADIATION (WH/M^2)
ZONE: NORTH GLASS	WINDOW	180	180	0	90	29	150615	45644
ZONE: SOUTH GLASS	WINDOW	180	180	0	-90	-151	301509	196265
ZONE: EAST GLASS	WINDOW	180	180	0	0	119	369681	264574
ZONE: WEST GLASS	WINDOW	180	180	0	180	-61	356356	151796

FLAT CURTAINWALL

OBJECT ID	OBJECT TYPE	SURFACE (FT^2)	EXPOSED AREA (FT^2)	UNDER GROUND (FT^2)	AZIMUTH ANGLE (DEG)	ORIENTATION (DEG)	TOTAL RADIATION (WH/M^2)	TOTAL DIRECT RADIATION (WH/M^2)
ZONE: NORTH GLASS	WINDOW	180	180	0	90	29	155414	60244
ZONE: SOUTH GLASS	WINDOW	180	180	0	-90	-151	358700	263530
ZONE: EAST GLASS	WINDOW	180	180	0	0	119	405566	310396
ZONE: WEST GLASS	WINDOW	180	180	0	180	-61	378628	283458

7

7 Flat and angled curtainwall radiation analysis
8 Deflection analysis study models
9 Tank philosophy—geometry to beat the heat

8

WWI GERMAN (AC7 TANK)

GULF WAR (M-1 ABRAMS TANK)

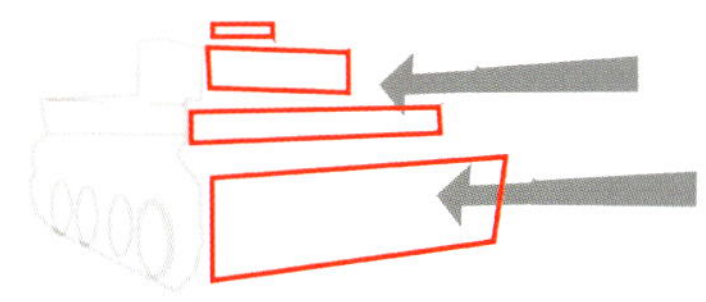

FULL IMPACT (PANELS PERPENDICULAR TO DIRECT HIT)

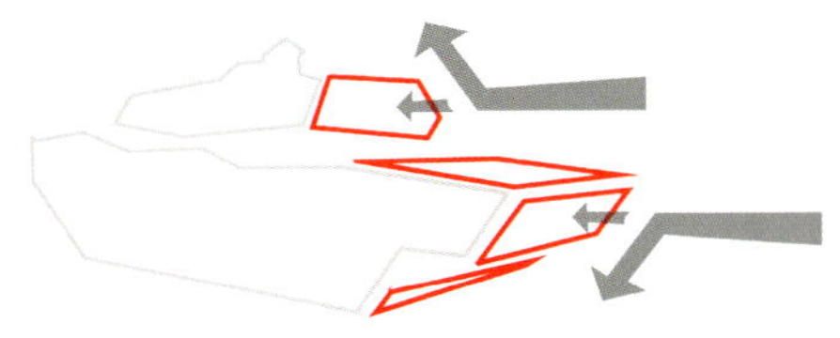

DEFLECTION (PANELS REDUCE EFFECTS OF DIRECT HIT)

9

MORE DEFLECTION

MOST DEFLECTION

10

11

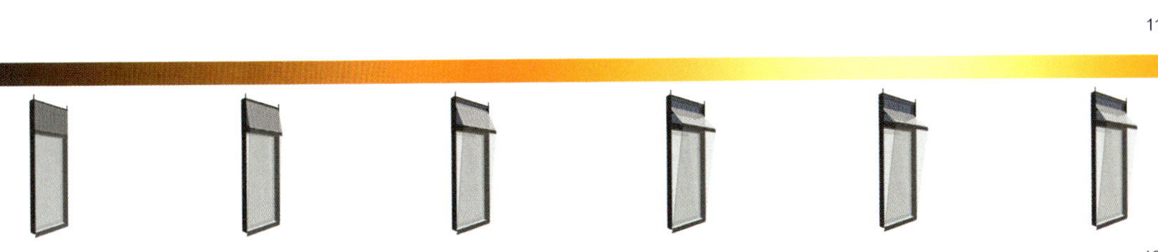

12

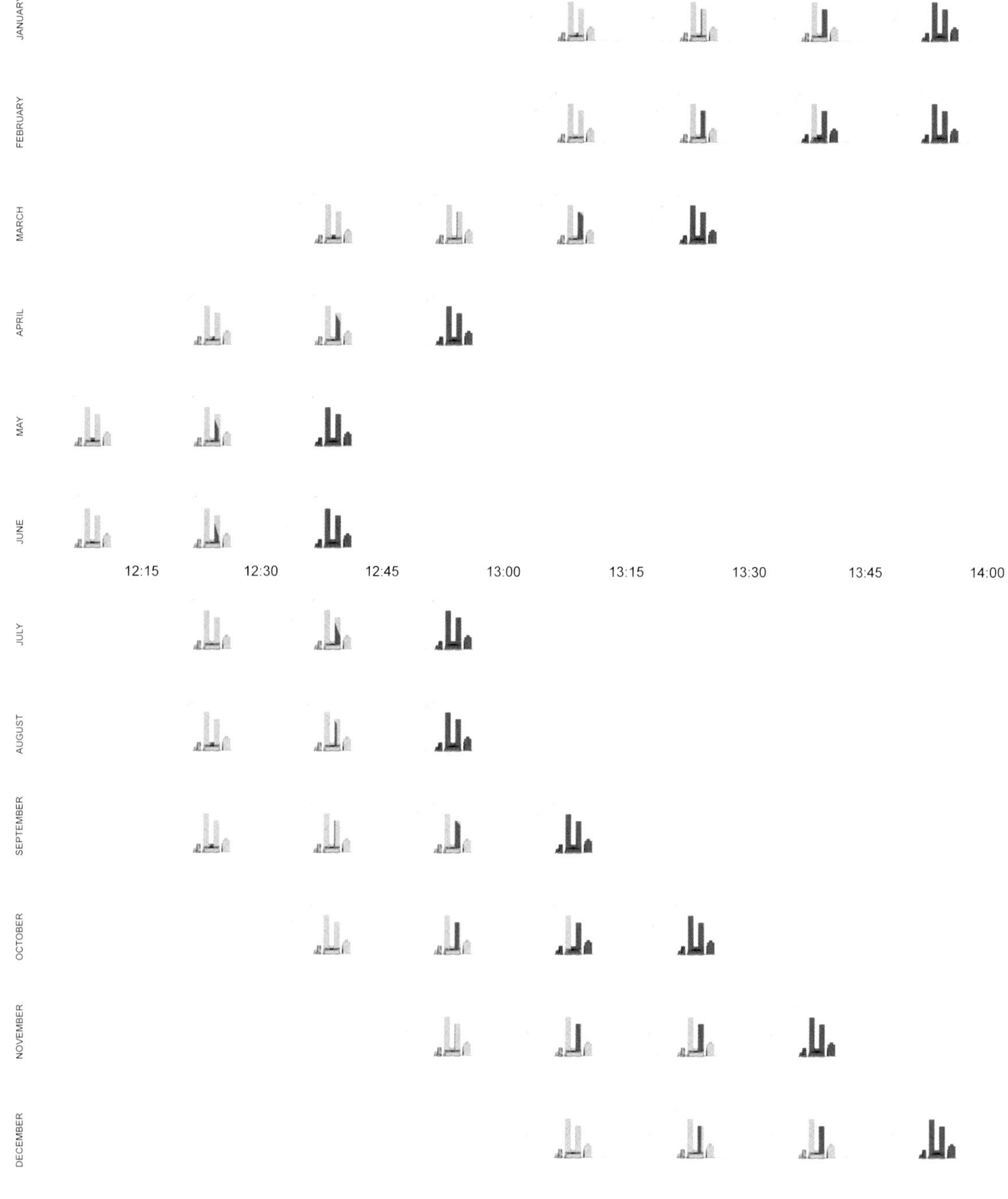

JANUARY
FEBRUARY
MARCH
APRIL
MAY
JUNE
12:15
12:30
12:45
13:00
13:15
13:30
13:45
14:00
JULY
AUGUST
SEPTEMBER
OCTOBER
NOVEMBER
DECEMBER
13

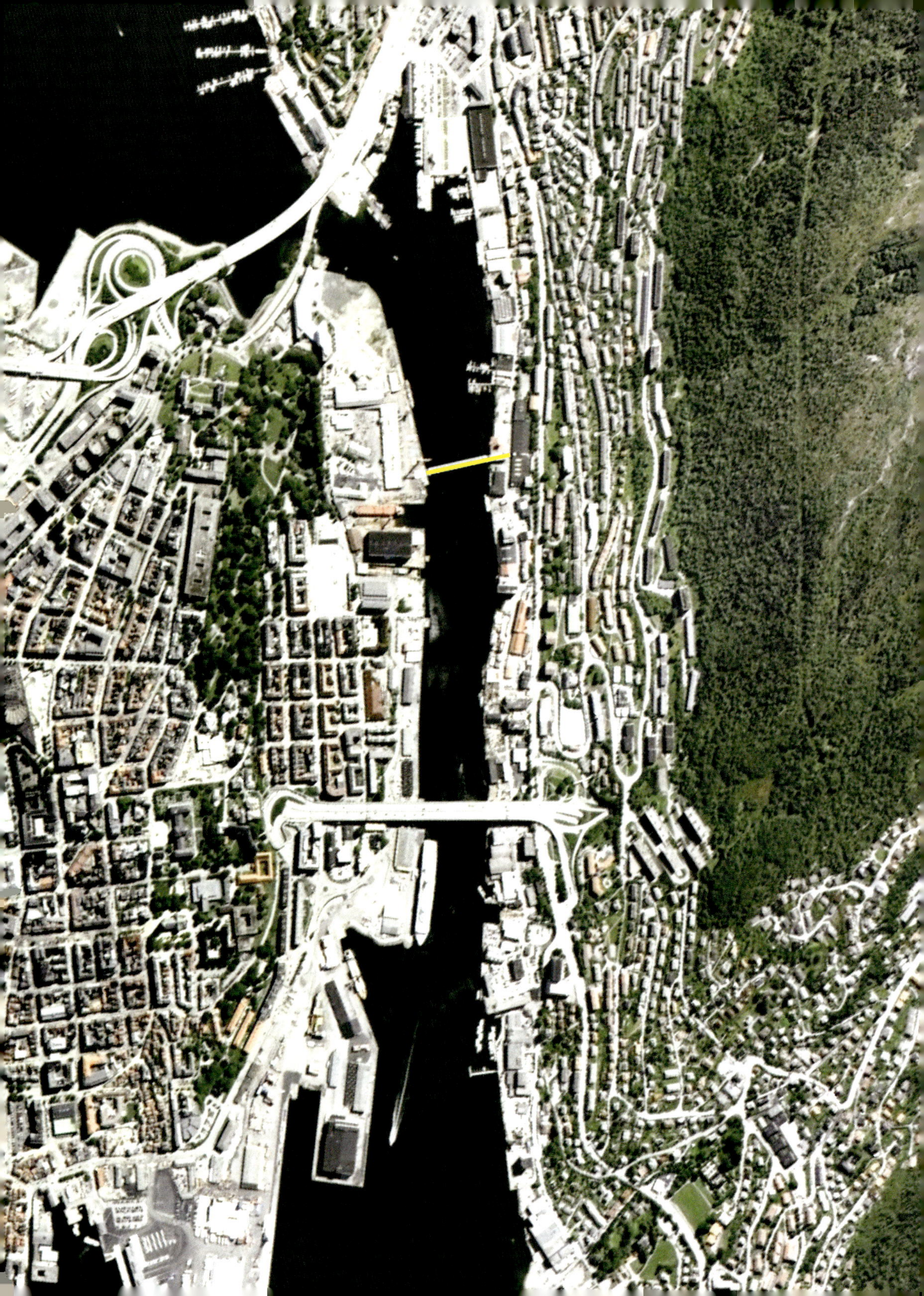

Balance Bridge

Bergen, Norway
Designed 2005

This footbridge has been conceived as a dramatic gateway to Bergen, a city on the west coast of Norway that dates back almost a thousand years. The aesthetic of the bridge is intended to be elegant and forward looking, yet in keeping with existing industrial structures found in the vicinity. While the bridge in operation will have a unique quality, it is based on well-tested principles.

The two cantilevered spans avoid the expense and environmental issues associated with structural supports within the river. A simple and cost effective mechanism has been devised to raise the bridge sections. Pumping water between internal chambers in the tank-back-span structure will alter the location of the water mass and allow gravity to open the bridges clear of the navigation channel without hydraulic actuators or mechanical drive mechanisms. This can be accomplished with the energy generated by an array of solar cells mounted on the top surface of the water chamber. The electric pump used to move the seawater is also mounted within the back span of the bridge, making the assembly self-contained, and ideally, self-sufficient.

The illumination of the bridge at night defines the walking surface and water tanks. A warm glow from the internally lit water tanks welcomes pedestrians to the crossing. This light shifts with the water as the bridge operates, highlighting its dynamic quality. The surface of the bridge is illuminated for the safety of the pedestrians and cyclists without marring views across the water.

The material palette is intended to be economical, durable, and easy to maintain. A painted galvanized steel structure, combined with galvanized high-strength steel cables is efficient and lightweight. The proposed walking surface is a stainless steel grating with porous ceramic infill to allow for drainage. The stainless grating is left exposed on the bicycle path to further facilitate drainage and to differentiate between uses. The reinforced acrylic water tanks are supported by a perforated steel structure, which allows the movement of water to be visible.

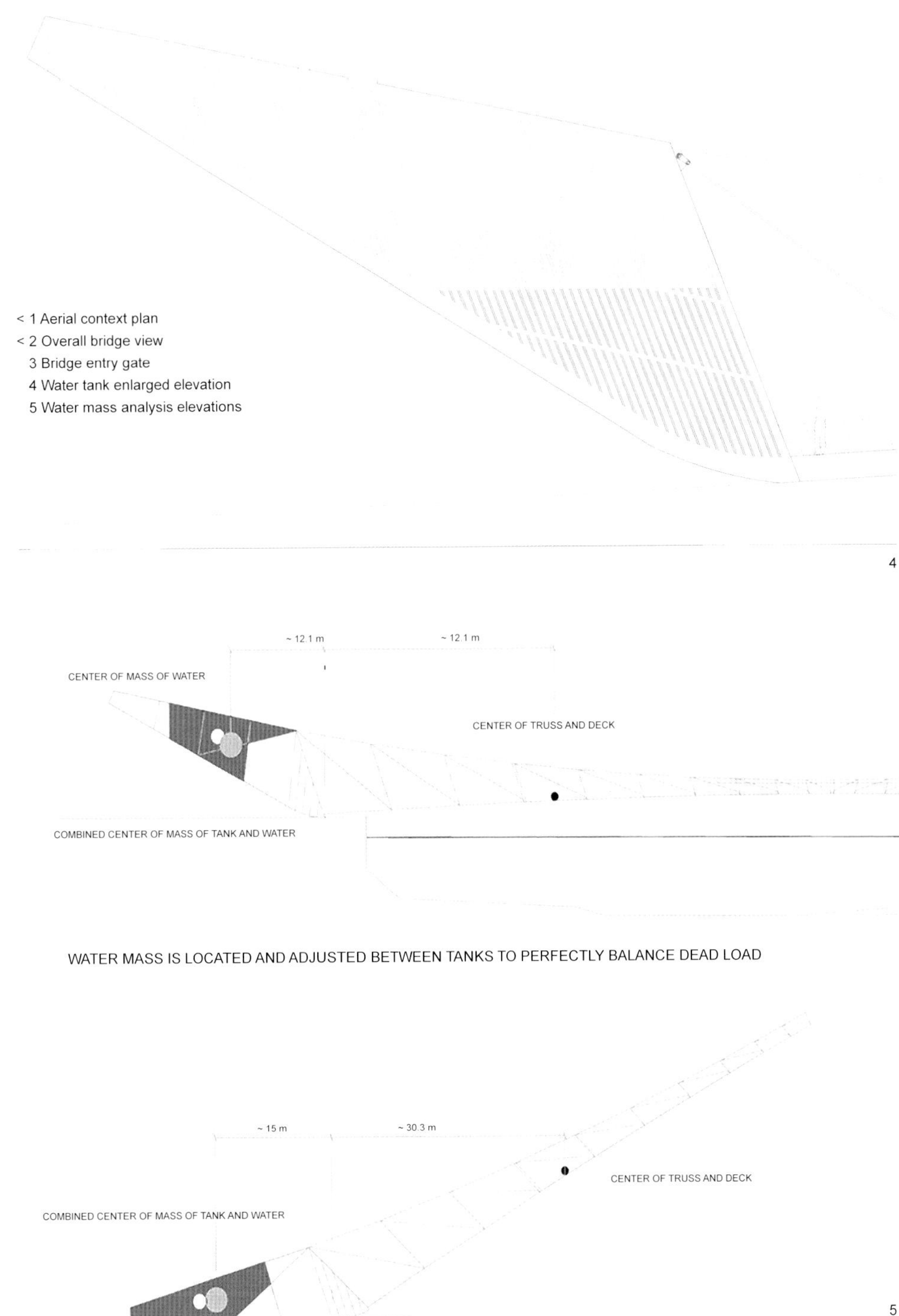

WATER MASS IS LOCATED AND ADJUSTED BETWEEN TANKS TO PERFECTLY BALANCE DEAD LOAD

WATER IS PUMPED TO CHAMBER TO LIFT BRIDGE

10 Typical section at bridge
11 Elevation
12 Typical section at decking

10

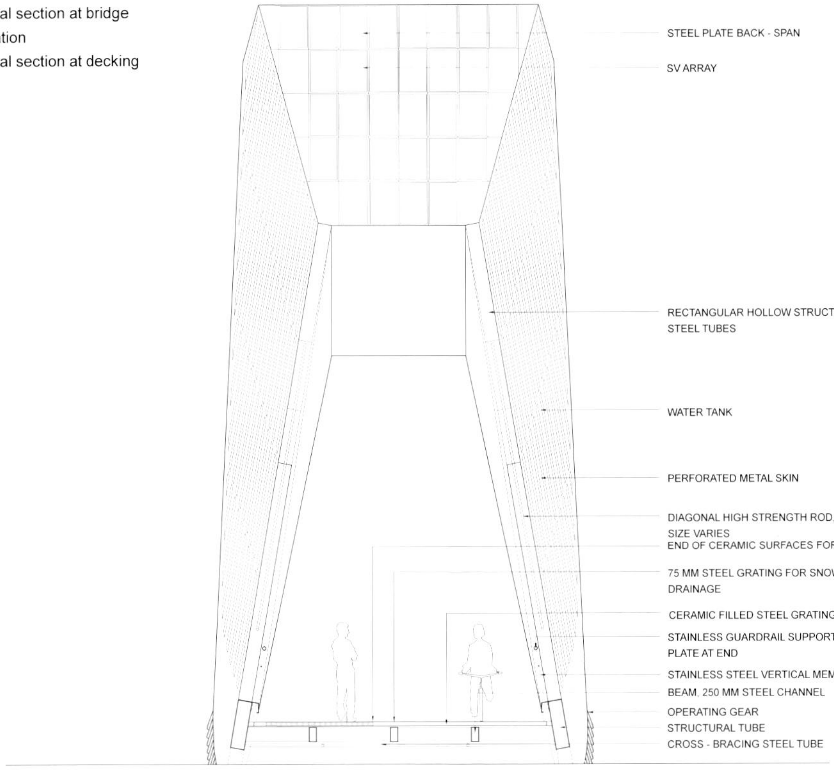

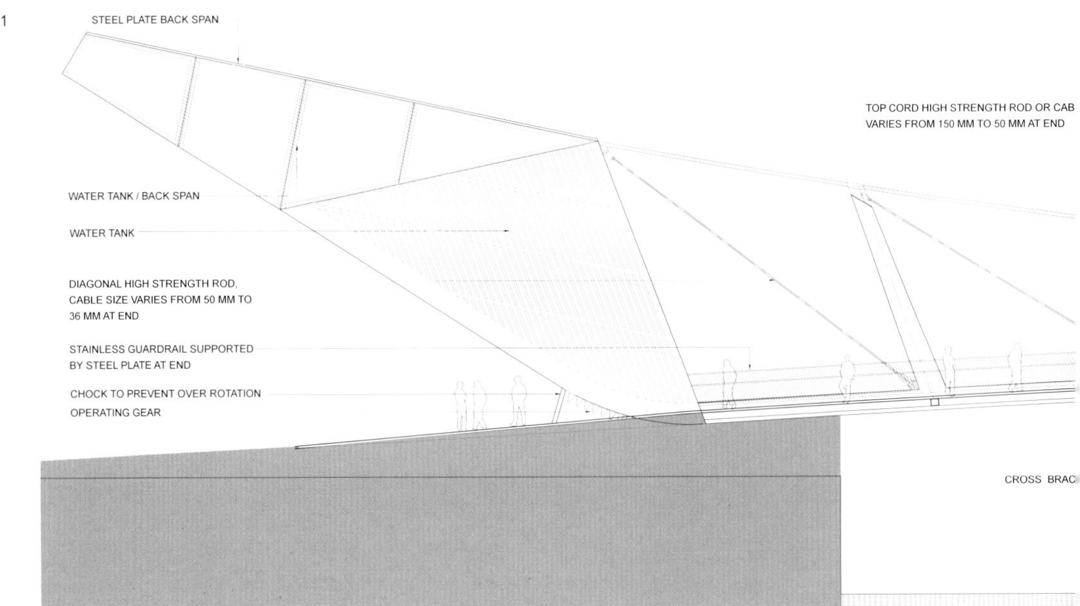

11

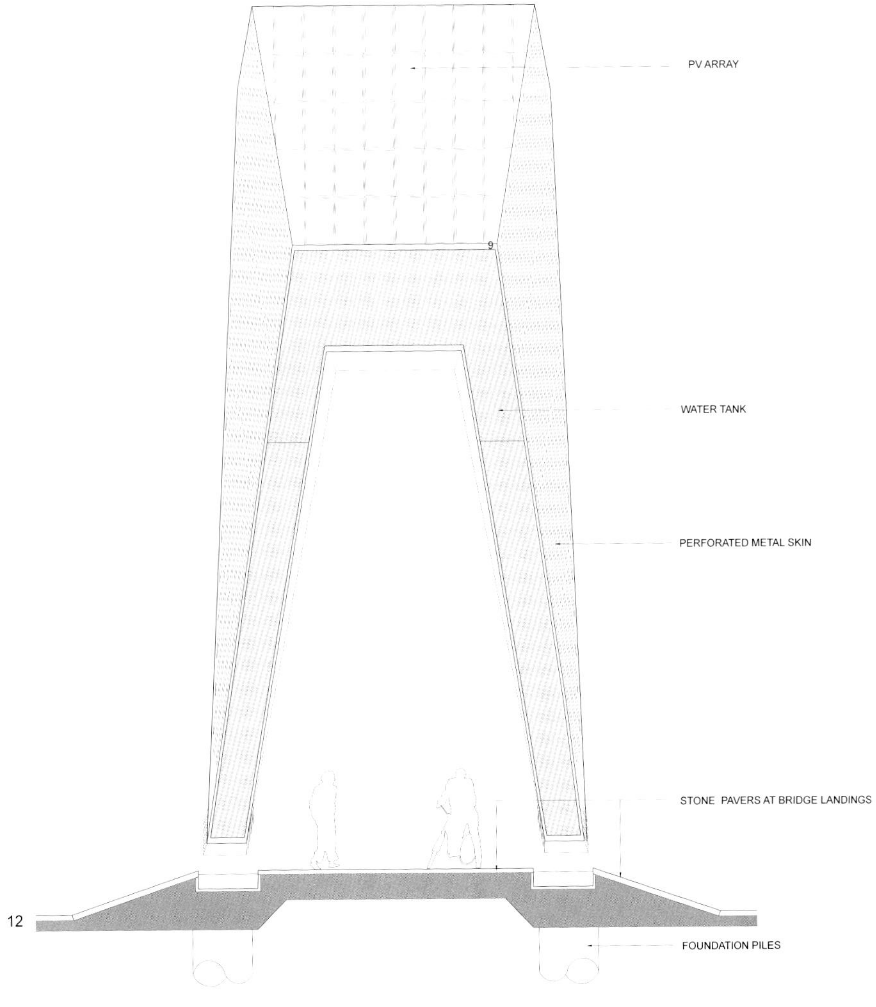

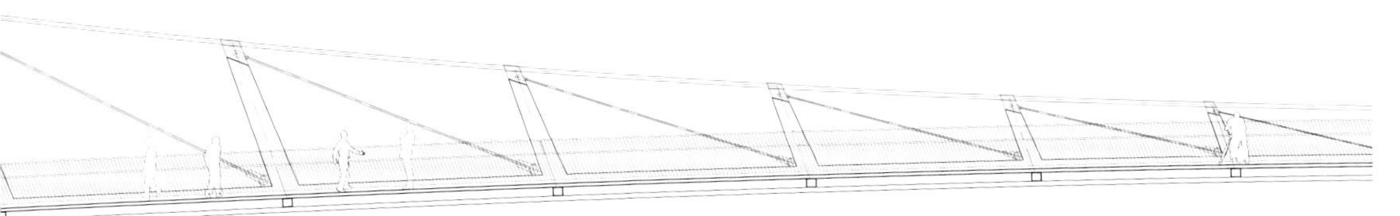

PV ARRAY
WATER TANK
PERFORATED METAL SKIN
STONE PAVERS AT BRIDGE LANDINGS
12
FOUNDATION PILES

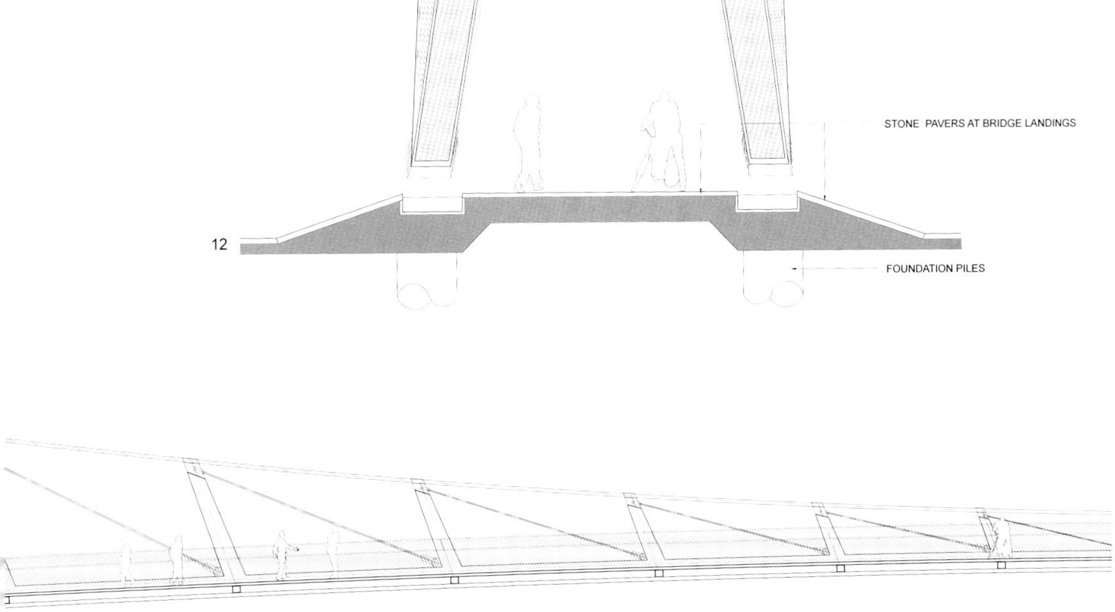

The Mill Center for the Arts

Hendersonville, North Carolina
Designed 2005

The Mill Center for the Arts is located in Hendersonville, North Carolina, a small town west of Charlotte. The mission of the Mill Center is to facilitate the creation and operation of a self-sustaining community complex that will fulfill the vision of providing a variety of arts, entertainment, and educational programs and events. Its program includes a 1,200-seat multi-purpose hall and a 300-seat black box theater for regional performing arts groups, in addition to a children's museum, events hall, art studios, classrooms, and gallery space for the community.

The center is designed to harmonize with the scale and materiality of the surrounding neighborhood. Four buildings, including a renovated historic textile mill, house the program with an efficiency that allows for a phased construction process. The exterior perimeter of the buildings are arranged to provide major entrances from each adjoining street, while the rear façades frame a lawn that can be used for outdoor events. Each structure is designed to open out to the lawn with large doors and porches. Overhead, a trellis of steel cables suspended between the buildings supports light and sound for events while also providing an armature for planting that shades the courtyard during warmer months.

In complement to the existing brick mill that houses art studios, gallery space, and classrooms, each new structure is built of a unique material. Loosely stacked field stones are used to build the walls of the children's museum, allowing light to filter through the voids. Rough hewn wood slats clad the main theater building, dappling and diffusing light throughout the interior. Corrugated metal panels wrap the black box and event hall, consolidating the spaces under one roof. The lawn at the center of the complex provides a simple backdrop for each building to be clearly legible.

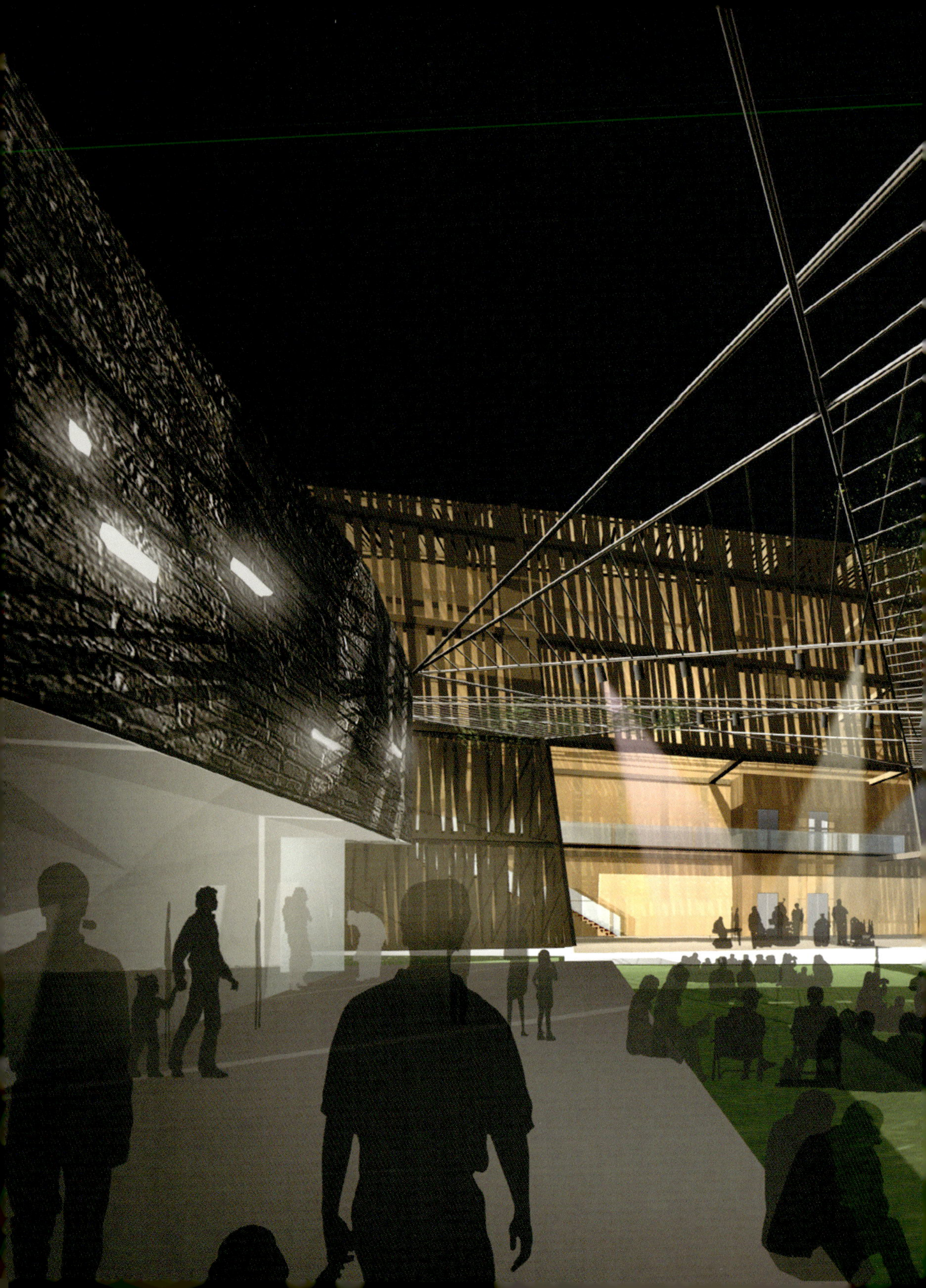

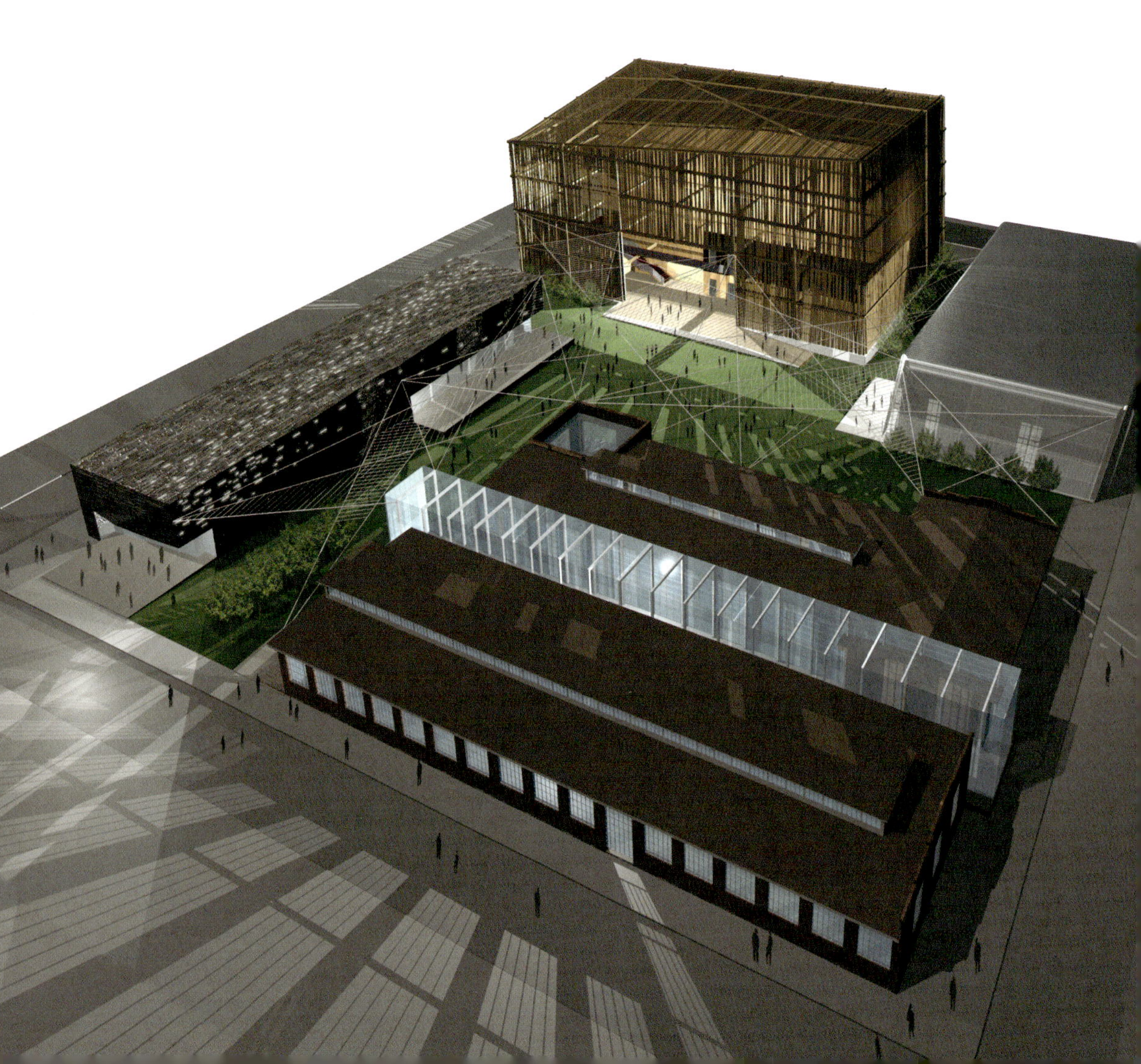

< 1 Aerial context plan
< 2 Public courtyard at night
3 Overall scheme
4 City block program distribution plan

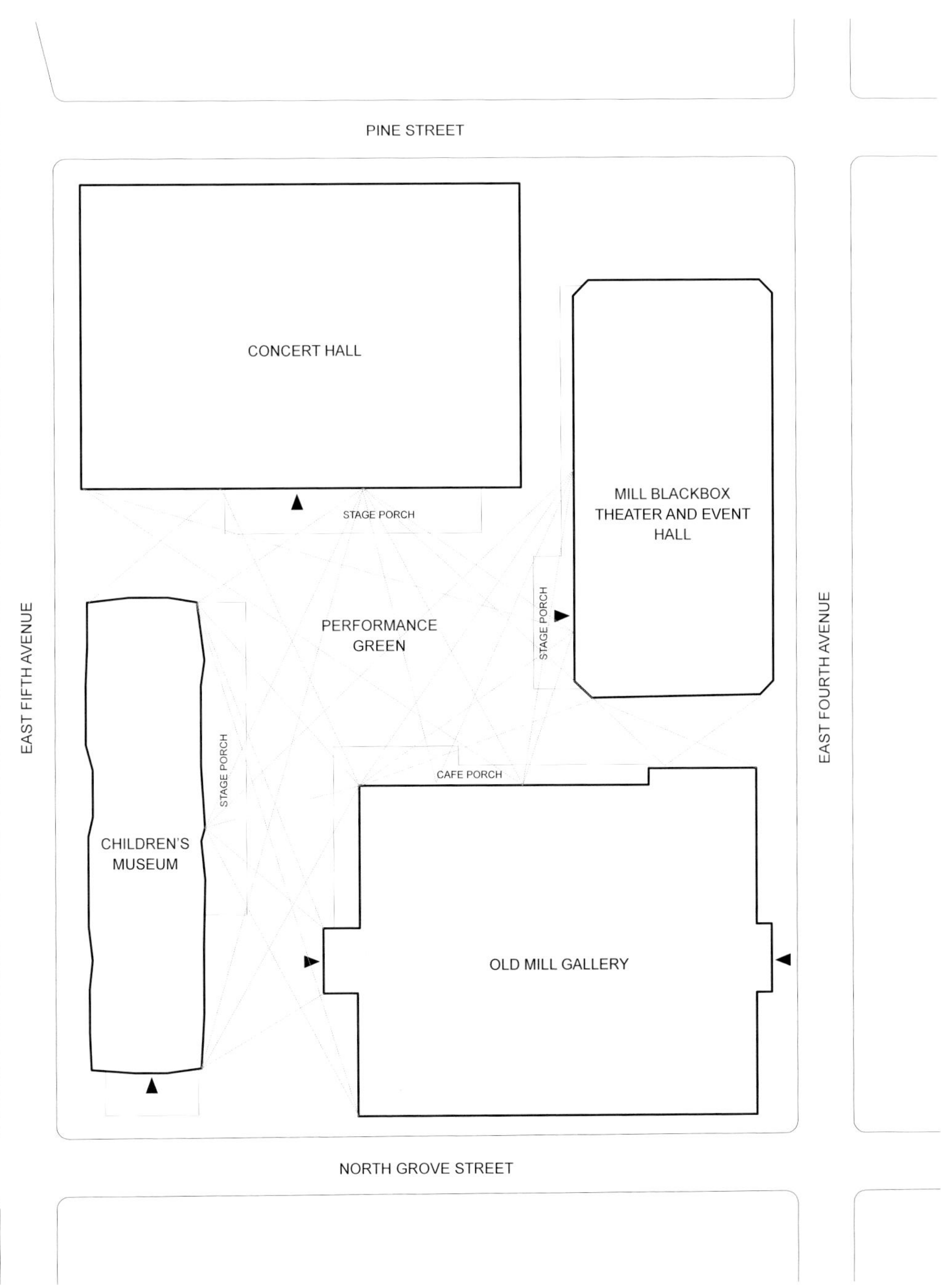

PINE STREET
EAST FIFTH AVENUE
EAST FOURTH AVENUE
NORTH GROVE STREET
CONCERT HALL
STAGE PORCH
MILL BLACKBOX THEATER AND EVENT HALL
STAGE PORCH
PERFORMANCE GREEN
STAGE PORCH
CAFE PORCH
CHILDREN'S MUSEUM
OLD MILL GALLERY

5

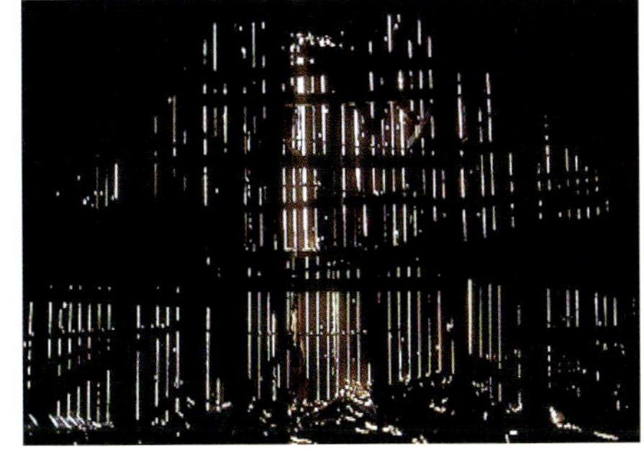

6

7

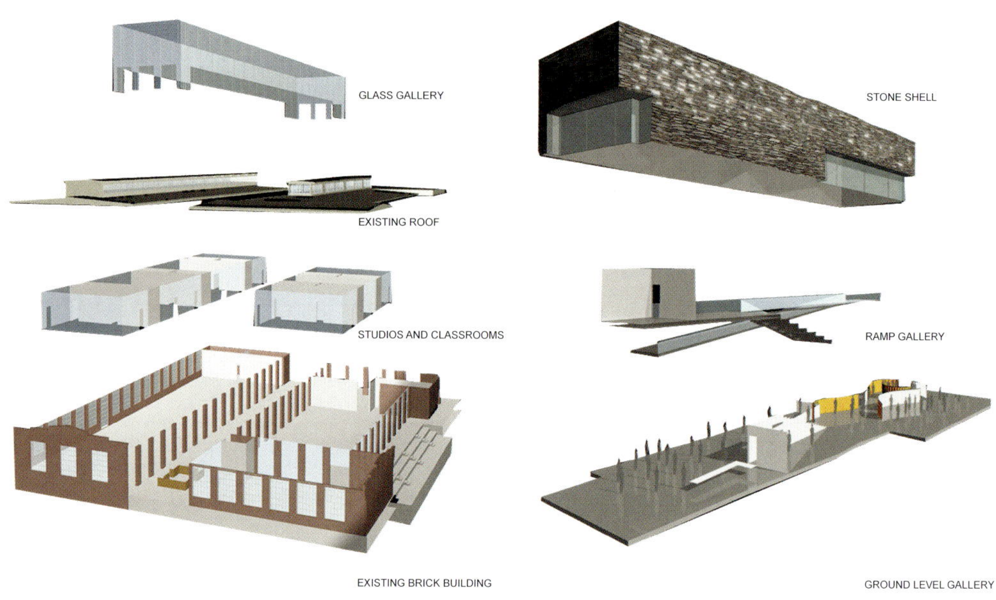

MILL GALLERY STUDIOS AND CLASSROOMS

CHILDREN'S MUSEUM

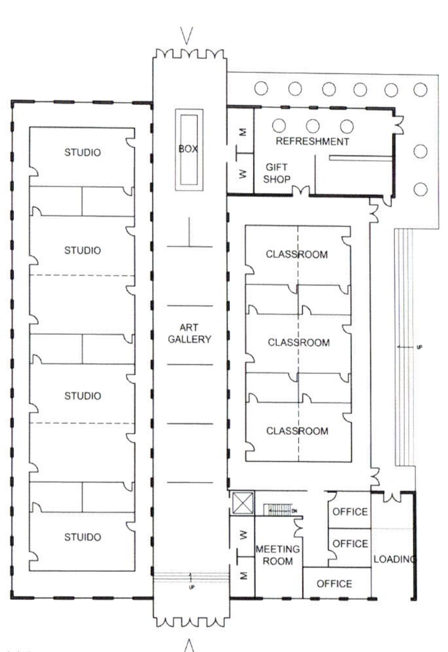

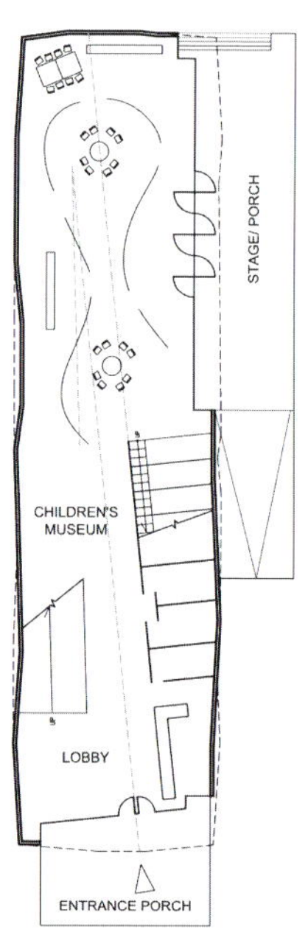

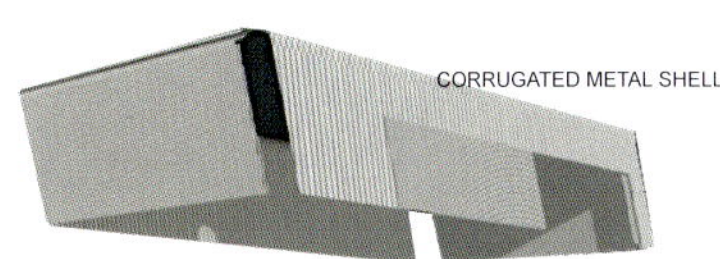

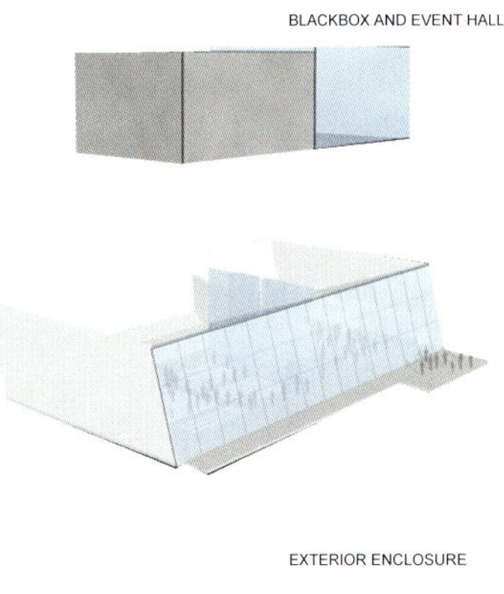

MAIN PERFORMANCE HALL

BLACKBOX THEATER AND EVENT HALL

9

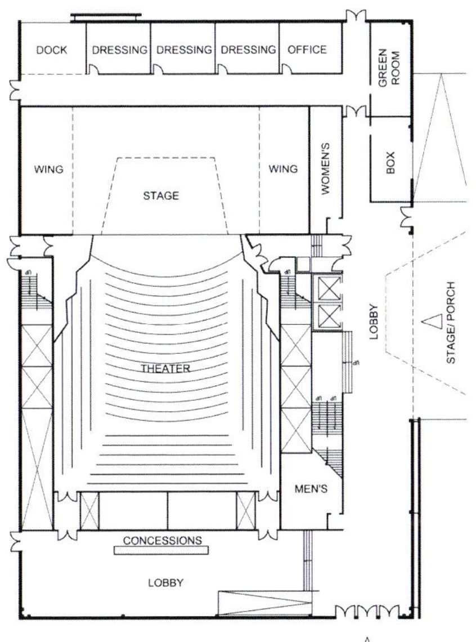

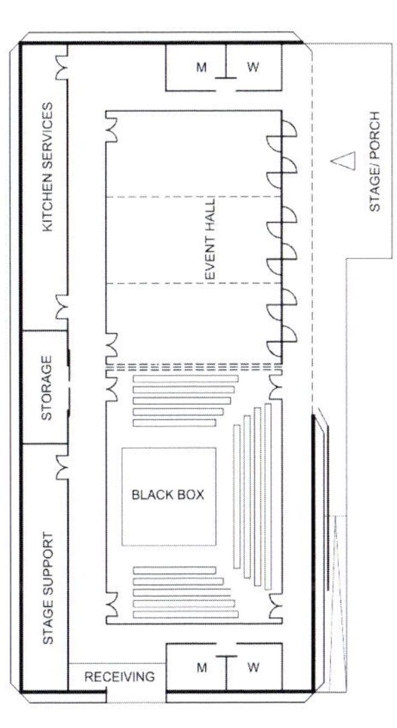

10

1 TALL GRASSES
2 DESERT SHRUBS
3 LOW TREES
4 CANOPY TREES

Kuwait Military Academy
Al Jahra, Kuwait
Designed 2006

The Kuwait Military Academy provides the Kuwait Ministry of Defense an entirely new campus facility for officer-level education and training for a total of 900 students in three classes. While the intricacies of designing for the client's educational program, military culture, and sensitive security needs presented numerous design challenges, the primary one was the environment—a harsh, windswept desert outside the bounds of Kuwait City where blinding sandstorms are a common occurrence and temperatures regularly exceed 120 degrees Fahrenheit. At every scale, the design is characterized by a consistent attempt to create comfortable, habitable spaces between and within buildings through passive techniques inspired by traditional knowledge embodied in the regional vernacular.

The campus, organized in linear programmatic bands, is oriented directly north-south to defend against the harsh hot winds that blow consistently from the northeast and invite the cool moist eastern breezes that offer a modicum of relief. A series of planted "shelter belts" offers a first level of defense against sandstorms by filtering airborne particulates through increasingly dense and tall plantings before they reach the campus itself. A continuous roof canopy linking all the buildings and pathways provides a second level of defense by keeping the hot dusty wind high above the open courtyards while offering shaded outdoor circulation routes throughout the campus. Wind tunnel testing of a physical model verified the validity of these design decisions.

Inspired by the vernacular urban morphology of desert environments throughout the Middle East, the campus is composed of numerous courtyard-type buildings spaced closely together to minimize travel distances and solar exposure at ground level. White poured-in-place concrete for the buildings, roof, and canopy creates a high level of solar reflectivity and minimizes heat gain throughout the day. Further inspired by vernacular techniques, the concrete of the internal courtyard walls and ground is tinted with cool color tones to provoke a psychological association of cooler temperatures. Shade provided by the deep canopy, fragrant eucalyptus trees, and cooling water features offer an unusual architectural experience in modern Kuwait—comfortable daytime outdoor spaces.

While the nine-meter cantilever of the continuous roof canopy provides shaded routes throughout the campus, dappled light is permitted to pass through small, circular openings reminiscent of the covered walkways of the traditional souk. Corresponding to the students' regimented and consistent daily schedule, twenty-eight uniquely-shaped openings each allow direct light to pass through at a different time and for a specified amount of time. Based on a diagram of the Kuwait sun path projected to a virtual horizontal plane (representing the canopy) these openings are nicknamed "analemmas," for the distorted figure eight shapes inherent within their geometry. Patterns of light passing through these openings gradually appear and disappear throughout the day and throughout the campus, animating different zones while tracing the movement of students.

The traditional *mashribiya* not only shades windows, but also helps control the difficult problem of glare in high-contrast interior desert environments by filtering a limited quantity of exterior light through chains of round beads that spread the light in many directions rather than focusing it. Following this vernacular tradition, the academy's window lattice design includes glass-fiber-reinforced gypsum interior panels that attempt to achieve a similar effect. Varying according to solar orientation and height, twelve panel designs take advantage of the thickness of the concrete walls to provide horizontal and vertical surfaces to shade direct light and permit a maximum quantity of reflected light to enter. As the nested panels accumulate along an interior surface, they begin to form continuous topological surfaces across which reflected light washes to relieve the contrast between interior and exterior. The SOM design team worked closely with students from the Product

Architecture Lab of the Stevens Institute of Technology to independently evaluate the performance of various design options for the window coffers. Working together, the teams developed a parametric modeling technique and genetic algorithm sequence to quickly produce and test over 100,000 randomly generated designs in a complex modeling environment. The best performers were identified and proliferated throughout the campus in residential, educational, and administrative spaces.

COURTYARD SPACES

A   OFFICER'S RESIDENCE
B   HUMAN RESOURCES
C   MILITARY STAFF DORMITORY
D   STAFF DINING HALL
E   SUPPORT SERVICES
F   CIVIL STAFF DORMITORY
G   MAIN HALL & THEATER
H   MOSQUE
I   ACADEMY HEADQUARTERS
J   ACADEMIC STUDIES
K   MILITARY STUDIES & LIBRARY
L   CADET DORMITORY: YEAR 1
M   CADET COMPANY HEADQUARTERS
N   CADET DINING HALL
O   CADET DORMITORY: YEAR 2
P   CADET DORMITORY: YEAR 3
Q   INDOOR ATHLETIC GYMNASIUM & POOL
R   FIRE STATION, WAREHOUSES, TRANSPORT & CENTRAL PLAN
S   INDOOR SHOOTING RANGE
T   MAIN GATE
U   SECONDARY GATE
V   TERTIARY GATE
W   PARADE GROUND
X   FOOTBALL STADIUM

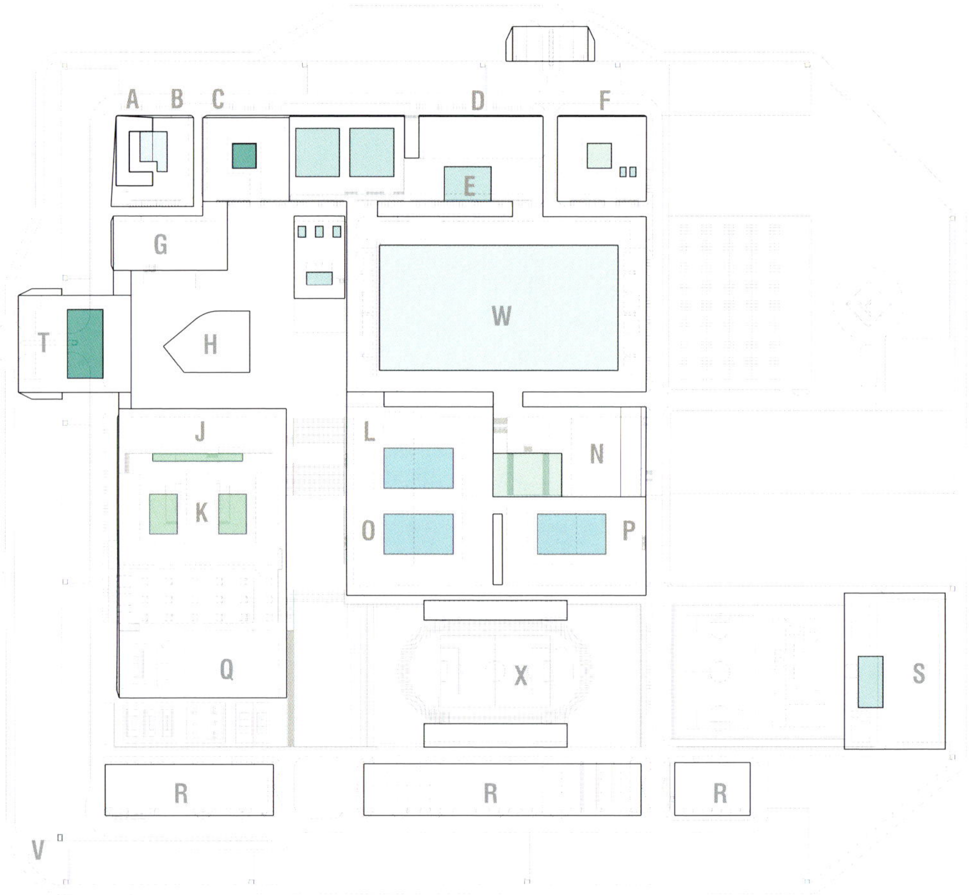

2

< 1 Site plan with protective shelter belts
2 Courtyard master plan
3 Courtyard aerial view looking toward
mosque and officer's residences
4 Library courtyard with analemma
canopy openings >

MASTER ANALEMMA LEGEND

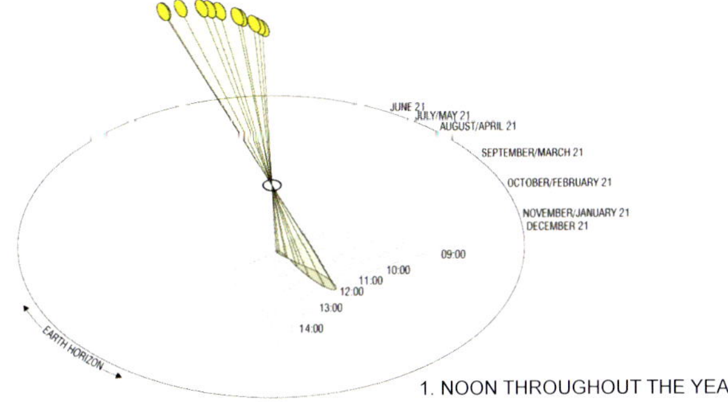

1. NOON THROUGHOUT THE YEAR

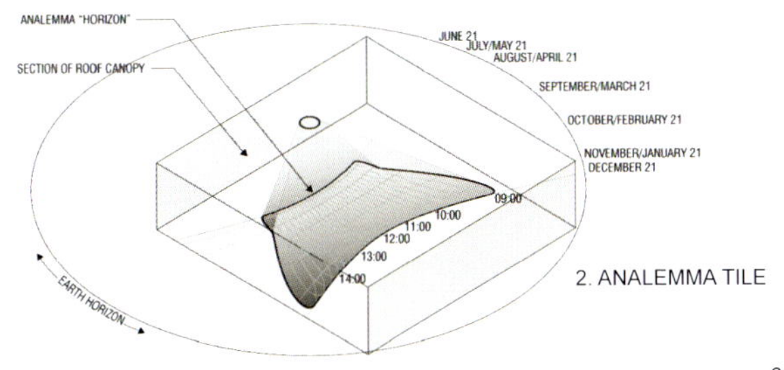

2. ANALEMMA TILE

5 Master plan with analemma zones
6 Analemma shape derivation
7 Rapid prototype analemma model of
  canopy section
8 Plans and sections of three different
  analemma types

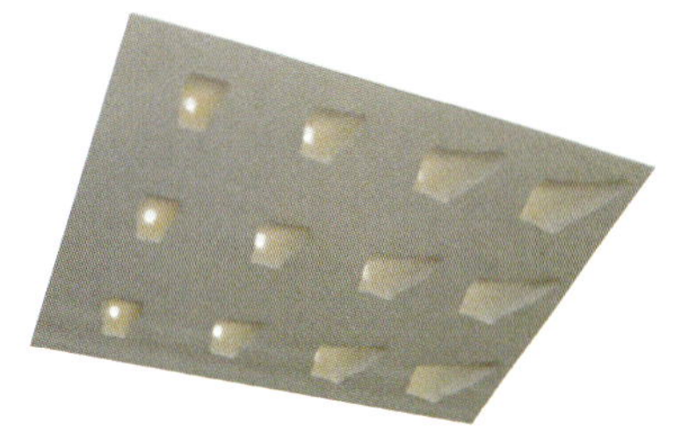

6

7

AXONOMETRIC | PLAN | SECTION | CODE

ANALEMMA: TYPE H

ANALEMMA TYPE H	
TIME FRAME	0845-1300
LOCATION	EXTERIOR
PROGRAM	WORK DAY
SKYLIGHT	NO
CANOPY DEPTH	400 MM
ZONES	

ANALEMMA: TYPE K

ANALEMMA TYPE K	
TIME FRAME	1400-1500
LOCATION	EXTERIOR
PROGRAM	REST PERIOD
SKYLIGHT	COURTYARD
CANOPY DEPTH	400 MM
ZONES	

ANALEMMA: TYPE T

ANALEMMA TYPE T	
TIME FRAME	0915-1200
LOCATION	EXTERIOR
PROGRAM	ALL MORNING
SKYLIGHT	CLEAR
CANOPY DEPTH	600 MM
ZONES	

8

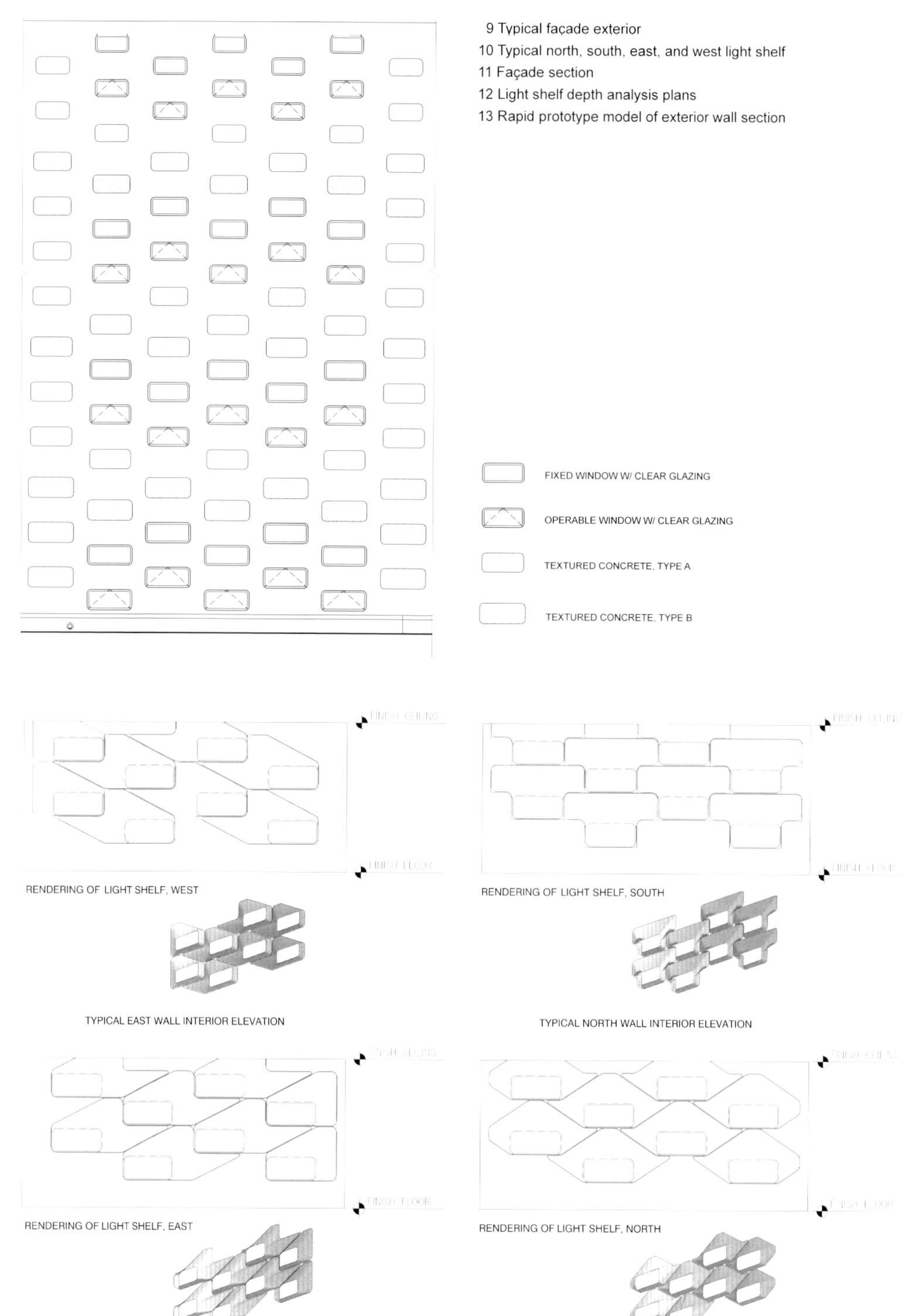

9 Typical façade exterior
10 Typical north, south, east, and west light shelf
11 Façade section
12 Light shelf depth analysis plans
13 Rapid prototype model of exterior wall section

9

10

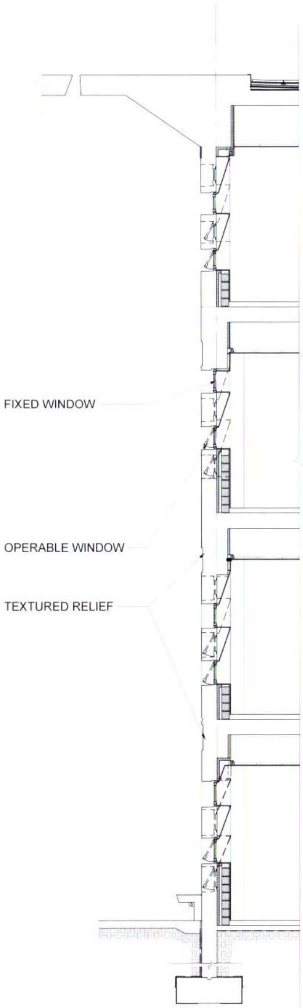

FIXED WINDOW

OPERABLE WINDOW

TEXTURED RELIEF

11

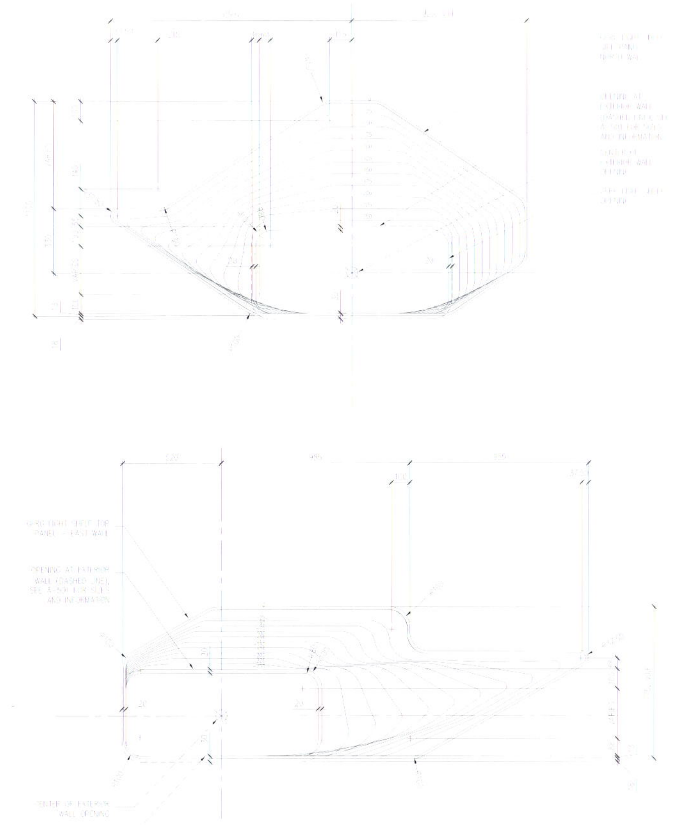

12

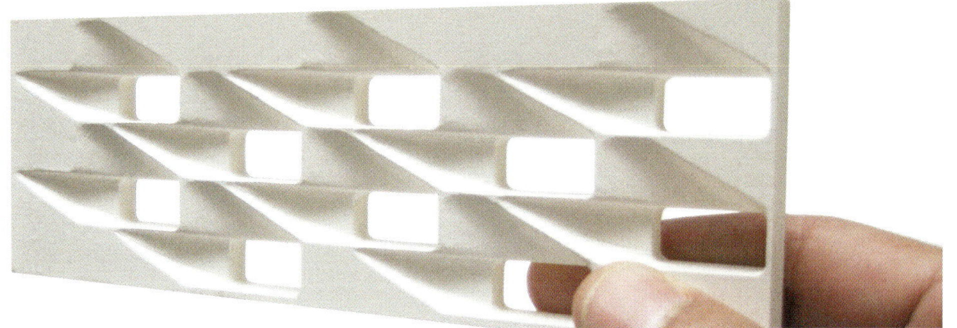

13

14

15

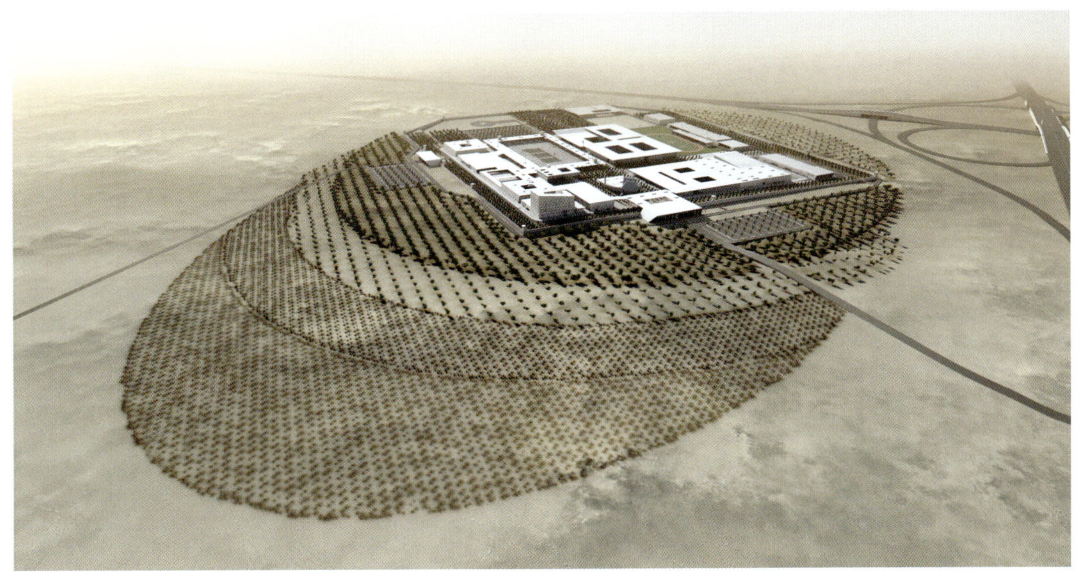

ROAD
CLOSED
AHEAD
DO NOT
ENTER
DO NOT
ENTER

Elizabeth Academic High School

Elizabeth, New Jersey
Designed 2006

This high school is planned for the civic center of Elizabeth, a city of 125,000 people, south of Newark, New Jersey. The physical context is decidedly mixed. Directly adjacent to the site are several well maintained historic buildings, including two seventeenth-century houses and the City Hall. These are interspersed with modest single and multi-family residences, a gas station, a funeral home, and a small public park.

The Elizabeth Academic High School's mission is to establish a college preparatory institution which seeks to attract and retain Elizabeth's best students, most of which historically have left the district due to its exceptionally poor reputation. The main sending high school for the district, Elizabeth High School, is, at 5000 students, New Jersey's largest and has a dropout rate of seventy percent. As a counterpoint, the new Academic High School will employ strategies which strive to create a more intimate learning environment in the spirit of a private "prep school" campus, with its array of discrete buildings disposed around green quads.

Following the high school curriculum established by faculty, the formal parti organized four separate volumes—one each for the school's academic specializations and a shared flexible resource room—on a conceptual "campus green" resting on a plinth containing shared program elements like the library, gymnasium, and administration. Termed the Law, Business, and Engineering Academies, each is conceived as an independent building within the larger building, with a student reading room along a widened connecting corridor overlooking the adjacent quad and linking it to the other academies. Over the course of the school day, students circulate from class to class in the separate academies and to activities in the two-story shared plinth. The resulting separation of program spaces strengthens the individual identities of the components and suggests a more intimate scale to the learning communities of the school. The intimate learning environment is furthered through the design of individual classrooms, where collective Harkness-style meeting tables are used in lieu of individual student desks.

The quads framed by the academies are designed as simple, garden-like areas to be used by students and faculty in nice weather. Artist Lawrence Weiner designed installations for the East and West quads which include paving arrangements and bench platforms inlayed with aphorisms in English and Spanish, as the majority of the student population speaks Spanish as a first language. Weiner's installations are intended to provoke curiosity about the relationship of "action" to "reaction" and "pursuing" versus "being pursued," themes which are pivotal for the adolescent population of Elizabeth. The roof surface of the quads also functions as the building's storm water detention system, holding rainwater and releasing it into the public system at a reduced rate to unburden the Elizabeth River watershed during large storms.

The relative modesty of the materials is borne of cost concerns (a certified construction estimate of 212 dollars per square foot was a requirement of approval) and a need for durability. The reading of the heavy masonry base contrasts with the relative lightness of the glass pavilions resting upon it, a deliberate reference to the roughness of the urban context and to the privileging of the spaces for learning above. These readings—both of the base and of the pavilions—are made more complex and inverted by the use of specially pigmented concrete masonry units which, through varying the amount of pigment in selected areas of the masonry block field, create a halo-like effect suggesting an inversion of the block and mortar arrangement to a point where the mortar overwhelms the masonry unit. Roller shades in the glass pavilions are colored to match the terra cotta tones of the masonry, suggesting a somewhat ironic monolithic reading when the shades are drawn. In these ways, the implied opposition of the threatening urban context and the protected space of the pursuit of knowledge becomes a charged dialectic.

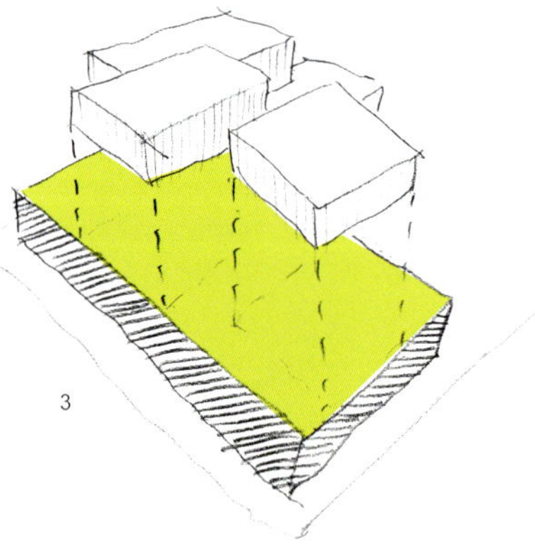

2

< 1 Context photos
  2 Overall model
  3 Parti sketch
  4 Academic program elements
  5 Exterior view of high school overlooking quads >

3

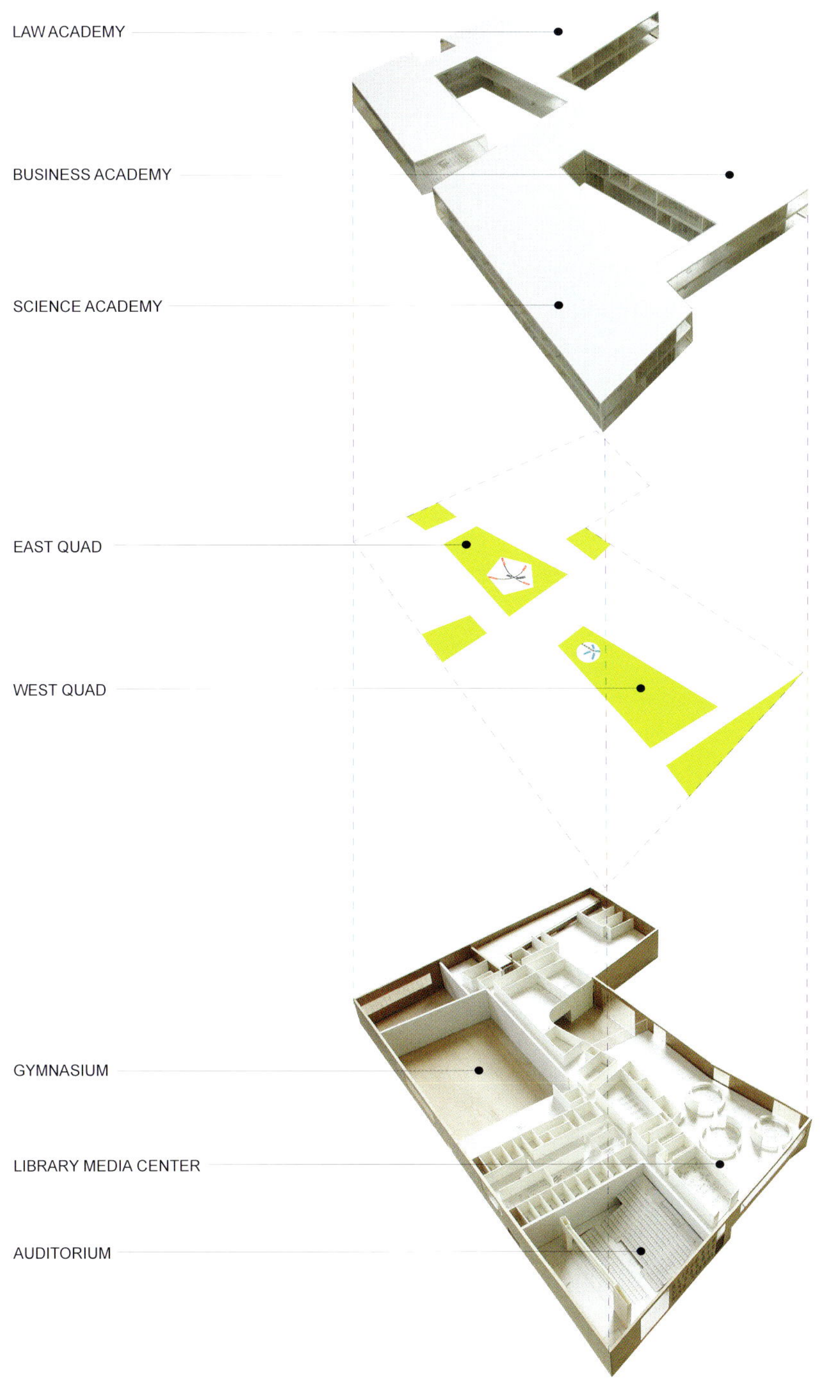

LAW ACADEMY
BUSINESS ACADEMY
SCIENCE ACADEMY
EAST QUAD
WEST QUAD
GYMNASIUM
LIBRARY MEDIA CENTER
AUDITORIUM
4

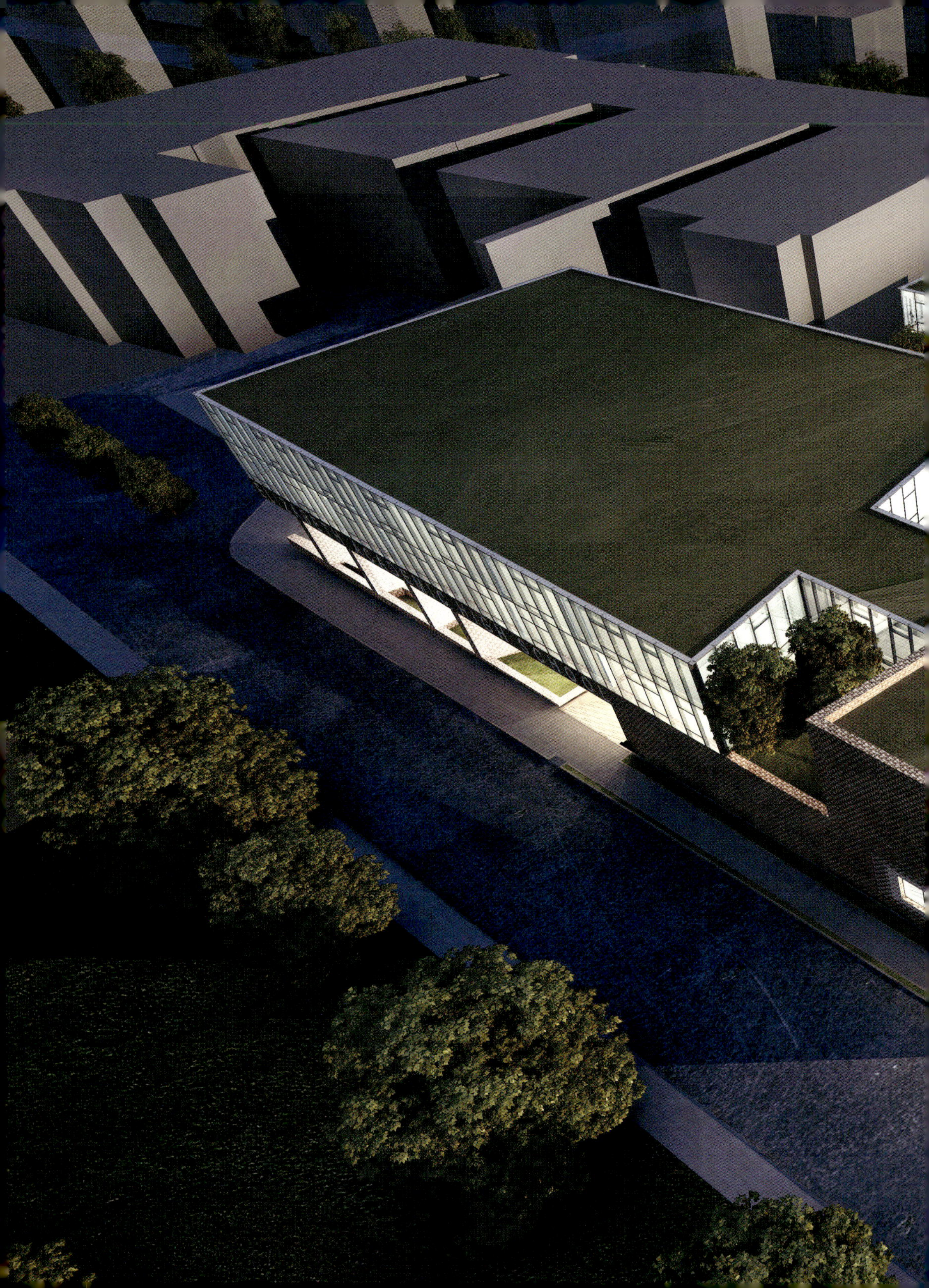

6

ELIZABETH ACADEMIC HIGH SCHOOL

7

ELIZABETH
ACADEMIC
HIGH SCHOOL

8

2 CMU
COURSES
2 CMU
COURSES
REFER TO WINDOW SCHEDULE
2 CMU
COURSES
2 CMU
COURSES
REFER TO WINDOW SCHEDULE
CMU03 (TYP)
CMU02 (TYP)
CMU01 (TYP)

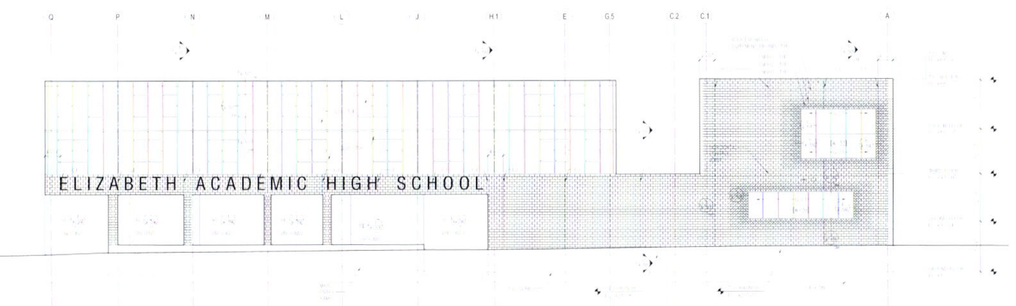

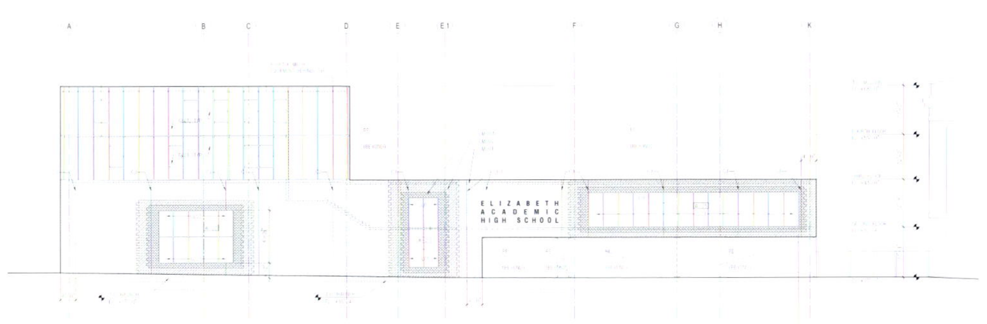

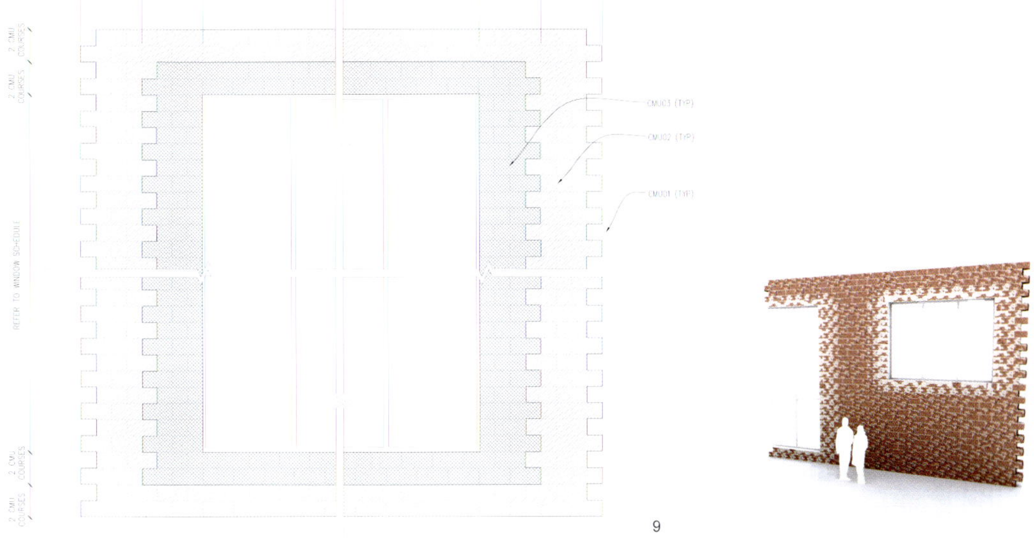

9

10

11 East north elevation overlooking front entrance to the high school

12 North elevation

13 Third floor plan with quads >

14 Lawrence Weiner's proposal for the East Quad >

15 Lawrence Weiner's proposal for the West Quad >

16 Art installation enlarged plans >

11

12

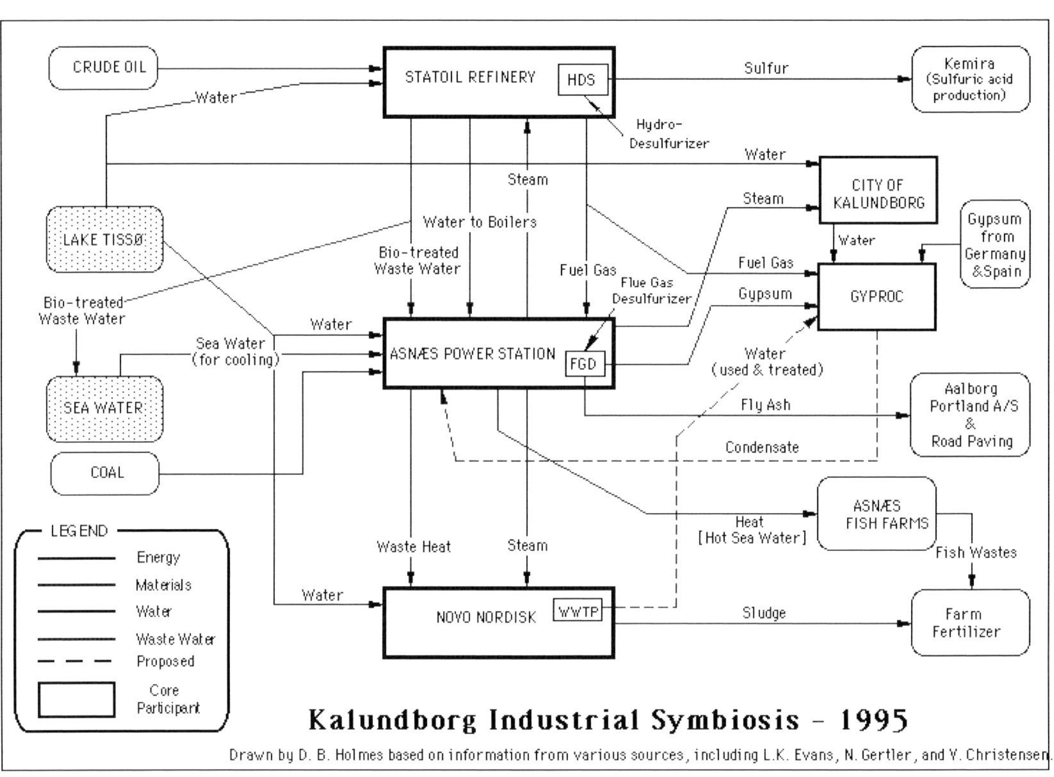

Fig. 1 Denmark's Kalundborg Industrial Institute's, explanation of "industrial ecology"

Sustaining Architecture during a Revolution

Susannah Hagan

The world will no longer be divided by the ideologies of "left" and "right," but by those who accept ecological limits and those who don't.
Wolfgang Sachs, Wuppertal Institute

Limits and revolution aren't obvious bedfellows. Surely revolution is expansive, breaking the chains of an oppressive status quo? True, but it is nature that's in revolt, not us, throwing off our chains, and as development continues at breakneck speed across the globe, throwing into question the whole of contemporary material culture: what we make, the way we make it, and the way we dispose of it—or fail to. We are being swept up by the forces of nature rather than of history, though it's difficult to distinguish between the two, given our contribution to nature's current state. Historical inevitability is this time found in unavoidable ecological limits: the exploitation of the biosphere with little or no understanding of the environmental damage done by its pursuit has become unsustainable. Social and economic turmoil follow climatic turmoil as the biosphere struggles with its gathering disequilibrium, and we are tossed around.

Doom-laden, perhaps, but the sheer volume of empirical evidence on global warming pushes in on us daily. Just as climate change will reach a "tipping point," and then accelerate dramatically, so a sizeable percentage of the world's population seems finally to be approaching a cultural tipping point, after which, perhaps, the rate of acceptance of our new situation will also increase dramatically. Whether our willingness to act on it increases in tandem remains to be seen. Certainly the built environment's role both in contributing to, and mitigating, global warming needs to be more convincingly acknowledged by architects and urban designers, given their role in the creation of it. This means pursuing "sustainability" much more consistently than most practices are presently prepared to: making root and branch assessments of the environmental impact of *all* the firm's work at *all* scales, educating clients, and, in those countries with profes-

sional bodies like the American Institute of Architects, insisting those bodies voice their members' environmental concerns to all levels of government. A tall order if you still believe things aren't that bad, and that what is really important, as it always has been, is the economy, stupid. But in these revolutionary times, the economy is no longer separable from climate change, and adjusting to that now will spare us vastly more painful adjustments later on.

A New Bottom Line

To redirect practice in this way is to call into question long-held assumptions and sacred cows. Never a comfortable exercise, and the degree of discomfort it causes one group or another can be measured by the degree of resistance to it. Businesses have always been driven by "the bottom line," architectural firms as much as any other. But "business as usual," it is now becoming clear, will soon cost more than any company can make, and those costs, environmental as well as economic, will be borne by all of us. This is part of a curious hybrid: an econo-ethical discourse in which, if you begin with economics, you end up in ethics, and if you begin with ethics, you end up in economics. Perhaps literally: *The Stern Review*, an independent study commissioned by the British government and published in 2007,[1] provides a rigorous and detailed analysis of economic consequences of climate change. Under the title "The Benefits of Strong, Early Action on Climate Change Outweigh the Costs," the report states unequivocally:

> *Tackling climate change is the pro-growth strategy for the longer term, and it can be done in a way that does not cap the aspirations for growth of rich or poor countries. The scientific evidence points to increasing risks of serious, irreversible impacts from climate change associated with business-as-usual (BAU) paths for emissions.*[2]

It would take the report's voluminous evidence to convince the sceptical of these bare-faced conclusions, but the message is easily grasped: change cultural attitudes and material practices now, or reap the whirlwind. A culture's failure to perceive the intrinsic value of nature is no longer excusable, a value rarely factored into economic calculations about the "affordability" of environmental technologies. Our attitudes to profit and nature must shift if we are not to be bankrupted by the effects of global warming.

Since the Industrial Revolution, it is the countries that industrialized first that have contributed the most greenhouse gasses globally (seventy percent up until the present [UN]). New technologies, however, have the potential to uncouple the equation of "most developed" with "biggest polluters," but only if there is the will to do so. Perhaps it takes a scientist to fully appreciate the implications of the current revolution in energy technology. German Chancellor Angela Merkel was a quantum chemistry researcher before she became a politician, and has committed the country to the most ambitious environmental targets in the world: a forty percent reduction in CO_2 emissions, and an increase in renewable energy to twenty percent of total energy generation by 2020. The Renewable Energy Sources Act means any individual or enterprise generating energy from renewable sources is guaranteed a payment of up to four times the market rate for that energy for twenty years, which has given a tremendous boost to the renewables industry and artificially reduced the pay-back time on these technologies.[3]

This top-down model of effecting technological change is vital to the eventual creation of an economically level playing field, but an equally fertile ground for change is the worldwide bottom-up activity generated by determined individuals, research groups, and businesses. The private sector is essential, not only in promoting new technologies but inventing them, and architects have an urgent role to play in transferring environmental technologies from the computer to the client, and from the developed world to the developing one. Those architectural firms committed to deep change rather than green window-dressing or the ostrich position, are the ones that will be leading us through an uncertain future.

From an environmental point of view, it's one of the two things architecture is good for, as new projects, whether individual buildings or towns, can have no appreciable material effect on the physical environment—there are too few of them. The real work, after all, is to retrofit the billions of existing buildings worldwide with insulation, double glazing, heat exchangers, solar hot water panels, bore holes, etc; so they cease to run like 1950s Cadillacs. Not the stuff of most architects' dreams. However, the other thing architecture is good for environmentally *is* the stuff of dreams: making buildings and settlements that point forward to an altered state, to a condition that barely exists, in this case, a built environment achieving the efficiencies and constructive interdependencies of natural ecosystems. This pointing forward has a cultural, more than a physical effect, but is as important, since the cultural climate must change before we can damp down the actual climate to any degree. Any architectural firm with a tradition of interdisciplinary innovation has the potential to effect that change, once its sights are set on sustainable innovation rather than innovation for its own sake. This requires change within the micro-culture of a firm, and then of the profession, something that has evolved further in European architectural practice, mainly because the European Union has been bombarding its members with environmental directives for the past twenty years, as it has learned some unknown facts of life: "50% of material resources taken from nature are building-related. Over 50% of national waste production comes from the building sector. 40% of energy consumption in Europe is building-related."[4]

This is the new, or really the renewed element of the sustainability triad, the social and the economic aspects having been part of architectural thought and practice for over a century now. It is the environmental sustainability of the built environment that demands architects acquire new knowledges and new skills. Environmental design in a contemporary context was never about a return to some pre-industrial arcadia. It is instead part of a radical reordering of material culture that will demand a constant stream of new ideas and technologies to cope with the scale of the challenge. Everything must become part of a culture that looks to nature for its operative models. Once invented they could be of great benefit in realizing a new and elegant economy of means. With our forays into bio- and nanotechnology we've only glimpsed the edge of a vast *terra incognita* where the similes we currently use to describe an improved built environment become fact: buildings won't be *like* plants, they will more likely *be* plants, at least in part, the remarkable structural and adaptive properties of plants appropriated by us through biotechnology.[5] Cities won't be *like* ecosystems in their social and economic interdependencies, they will *be* artificial ecosystems in their biomechanic metabolisms. At the moment resources and energy go in at one end, and wastes of various kinds come out at the other, most of which are dumped into the air, land, and water. In ecosystems, the waste of one process is the raw material of another—the dung beetle springs to mind—in a waste-not-want-not model of consumption that used to be ours in the West, and is still, in some developing countries. This circular consumption requires, not self-denial, but creativity to make it work in a highly complex, increasingly urbanized world. Kalundborg (fig. 1) in Denmark is one of the few working examples of a so-called "industrial ecology," where, for example, its power plant sells its fly ash to a cement manufacturer.[6] Hardly glamorous. The bowels of material culture rarely are. But operationally—and economically—sophisticated: in this model, waste is not only a source of raw materials, but of profit. Would that more contractors understood this. Transition periods are always the most difficult to negotiate, and this transition, from a carbon to a zero carbon world, requires a sustained domino effect: a change in the cultural climate that leads to a change in the political climate that leads to carbon pricing (so *we* pay for our pollution rather than future generations), which leads to the financial viability of investing in new technologies, which leads to the proliferation of "clean" technologies, which leads to a reduction in carbon emissions, which leads to the mitigation of the worst effects of climate change, which leads to greater social and economic stability. It's not happening like that, and it won't. We are proceeding by lurches forward and regressions. No matter. Out of this melee are emerging new models of being and doing, to which environmentally-informed, intellectually consistent architecture and urban design, perhaps particularly urban design, are essential. Both must be allowed to function as laboratories, to bring forward forms, techniques, and technologies that may or may not work, and, vitally, to share information on the results. The architect-as-inventor, rather than social engineer, is the model we need to retrieve from the attic of the modern movement: the inventor of new relationships between building, city, and environment, of new configurations to accommodate these relationships, of new systems to run them, of new conceptual and actual melds between nature and technology.

Two-faced Technology
Can technology cure the problems it has, at least in part, created? When we talk of environmentally sustainable design, are we talking about a different model of technology from the instrumentality with which we're so familiar, that is, exploitation to the point of ruination? It could be argued that human development has always involved the exploitation of nature. Civilizations have risen by extracting what they wanted with increasing efficiency, and sometimes fallen from over-extraction. The only reason industrialization, rather than human nature, stands accused is because technology since the nineteenth century has become so much more powerful than its earlier versions, and with an increase in power has come an increase in destructiveness. This is essentially a failure to think beyond the relationship between an intervention and its effect on us, to its effect on nature. Had we had the means earlier to transform the given as widely and swiftly as we can now, this "destructiveness" would have made itself felt earlier. In other words, the drive to control the physical environment, to use it as a means to our ends, is as old and fundamental a cultural phenomenon—at least in the West—as the necessity, so far at least, of living within its limits.

In traditional vernacular architecture, highly differentiated architectures were obliged to observe a regard for things-in-themselves—materials, climate, topography—because its makers had no technological choice other than to build with climate and context rather than against them. Instrumental technology liberated us from such traditional politesse, and given this power to order as we see fit, some ask what possible rationality there is in imposing voluntary restraints. The answer lies in the price one is prepared to pay for misperceiving restraint as retreat. Designing with technologies as sophisticated as nature's ways-of-doing demands the most from us, not a denial of it. Environmentally-designed architecture is an exemplar of a future in which technology is both constrained and limitless, operating *for* us, but *with* nature as far as possible.

Given the constraints of sustaining the economic viability of an architectural practice, how is a radically reconfigured architecture to be achieved? Internal contradictions are present in all architecture firms successfully negotiating the mainstream, and simultaneously being forced to think about changes to that mainstream. Although there is often a clear intention in many of them to improve the environmental performance of their buildings, at the same time there is a desire not to stray too far from their previous practice and a profitable status quo. What is needed is a willingness to develop a consistency of position (no more "biggest" / "tallest" simply for its own or the client's sake), and even more demanding, to choose the level of technology appropriate to the task. The first (too difficult) question is: "Does the client need a new building at all?" A refurbishment or addition to an existing building may, in environmental terms, be the rational answer—less expenditure of energy, less extraction of natural resources, less to recycle at the end of a building's life. But architecture is rarely about reason. Questions of architectural identity and client status, plus our incurable addiction to novelty, mean design is often entirely irrational. The second (slightly less difficult) question is: "What level of technology delivers the best balance between economics and environmental performance?" In other words, how much money (and energy) do you have to spend to create an environmental system that will reliably deliver, and significantly reduce environmental impact? One can be no more precise than this, as it's a moving target, but would hope that an expensive piece of architecture would do better than the CO_2 emissions allowed for a LEEDS or BREAM "excellent" rating. This may cost more, but at the high end of the market, this is what architecture can do: surpass norms, especially new, overly-tentative norms. So that for heating and cooling a private house in a moderate climate, there should be no need for anything more than a passive system. Even in a difficult urban environment with a demanding program and a big budget, the building envelope could do much more passive mediation between inside and outside before one moved on to active systems. But what kind of envelope and which active systems? Economics aside, is the expenditure of (fossil) energy to make a triple glazed envelope of high performance glass justified by its environmental performance? Is an energy-using digital building management system justified by its energy-savings? "Smart" buildings have something to teach us in terms of anticipation and flexibility, and are, perhaps, the only way of optimizing energy consumption in public buildings subject to many and contradictory user demands. Conceptually, also, digital systems are seductive, allowing the building to come much nearer the sophistication of a living organism, the new paradigm of all built culture. But the important ideas here are responsiveness and performativity, whether achieved by low or high technology.

The shift of a firm's priorities to maximizing the reduction of environmental impact in all its outputs can be considerably helped by clients who demand rather than resist this. In the United States now, as in Europe in the recent past, many of the most environmentally ambitious buildings are commissioned by clients whose business requires them to be seen as environmentally ambitious. A client can also impose a lack of environmental ambition, which is presumably why SOM's home page is neatly divided between work that explicitly declares itself sustainable (Chongming and UNC; fig. 2) and work that does not (Burj Dubai and Infinity Tower). Faced with clients keen to build "against nature" on a pharaonic scale, a firm has three choices: to reject them, to try to lead them onto a saner path, or to do what they want. Not all clients are convertible to the cause, and consistency of approach is easier for a firm that has begun its life by defining itself as "environmental" than it is for one that has in the past led the field with a pre-environmental identity.

Identity and Accountancy
It is entirely possible for firms with already-established identities to develop a more consistent environmental position, as the evolution of Richard Rogers+Partners into Rogers Stirk Harbour + Partners demonstrates. Theirs is an example of a high modernist practice that has redirected, rather than foresworn, its modernist principles. There is the same commitment to experiment, the same faith in progress, the same reliance on new technologies to fix what earlier technologies broke, but their architecture has become less universal, more responsive. There has been an embracing of a much wider palette of materials, natural as well as manufactured—

Fig. 2 Chongming Island principles

for example the bamboo strips that make up the vast un-dulating ceiling of their new Madrid airport—and, where performance demands, of a much wider range of forms, as in their new Welsh National Assembly. Why? Because they perceived a potential for innovation within a modernist interpretation of the new environmental remit: "the built environment is clumsy, damaging and inefficient, its performance always lagging behind other engineered artefacts, let's crank it up." Modernists said the same thing at the beginning of the twentieth century when faced with the machine. Now they say it faced with what the machine has done.[7]

Consistency of vision and appropriate levels of technology demand an environmental accounting that forces tough choices on architectural firms. It means the environmental cost of a project is addressed first, and its economic cost second, with the understanding that rejecting environmental costs for some will increase environmental and economic costs for all. The more expensive a volatile climate becomes, the keener government will be to make "the polluter pay." What characterizes sustainable technology, high or low, is the consideration of a building as one integrated system, not a collection of systems that may be at war with one another: "There is a breakdown of barriers between building fabric and services design. Both are part of the energy system design."[8] Given the environmental necessity of responding to a context that is as much physical as cultural, architects will be led towards a repertoire of sustainable architectures—plural. Responses can range from a contemporary take on traditional vernacular (e.g. Charles Correa's social housing in India),[9] to an existing architecture made more sustainable (most mainstream firms), to an environmental functionalism/determinism (ZED Factory,[10] some work by Future Systems[11]), to designs that are concerned not only with sustainable operation, but also with expressing a particular view of the relationship between nature and culture. The Dutch firm MVRDV (fig. 3),[12] is particularly good at witty and thought-provoking representations of the new partnership.

For many firms and clients, however, differentiating the building envelope is a highly contentious strategy if architecture-as-response contradicts their architecture-as-identity, and their identity is one of transparency, abstraction, and high culture overcoming the constraints of nature, or an indigenous culture. Though a firm could justifiably adopt all the above approaches for different commissions, most maintain their identity by specializing. If energy efficiency comes after other considerations (social, aesthetic, or particular to the client), then it will not be allowed to dominate the design process, and form won't respond to performance. If energy efficiency and reduced environmental impact are the most important considerations, and become the identity of the firm, then design will reflect that priority. In fact, there is increasingly less choice. Climate change and its social and economic consequences (environmental refugees, storm damage) are here. Changing designers' priorities from idea-driven "form giving" to performance-driven "form finding" in the interests of reduced environmental impact is now a matter of some urgency, and world class firms have a greater responsibility to lead that goes with their greater reach and reputation.

Doing Productive Design

Form finding doesn't just refer to open-ended avant-garde digital experiments. Environmental design returns

Fig. 3 MVRDV, The Garden, 2001, Hengelo, the Netherlands. Rendering courtesy of MVRDV

Fig. 4 Nicholas Grimshaw's Eden Project

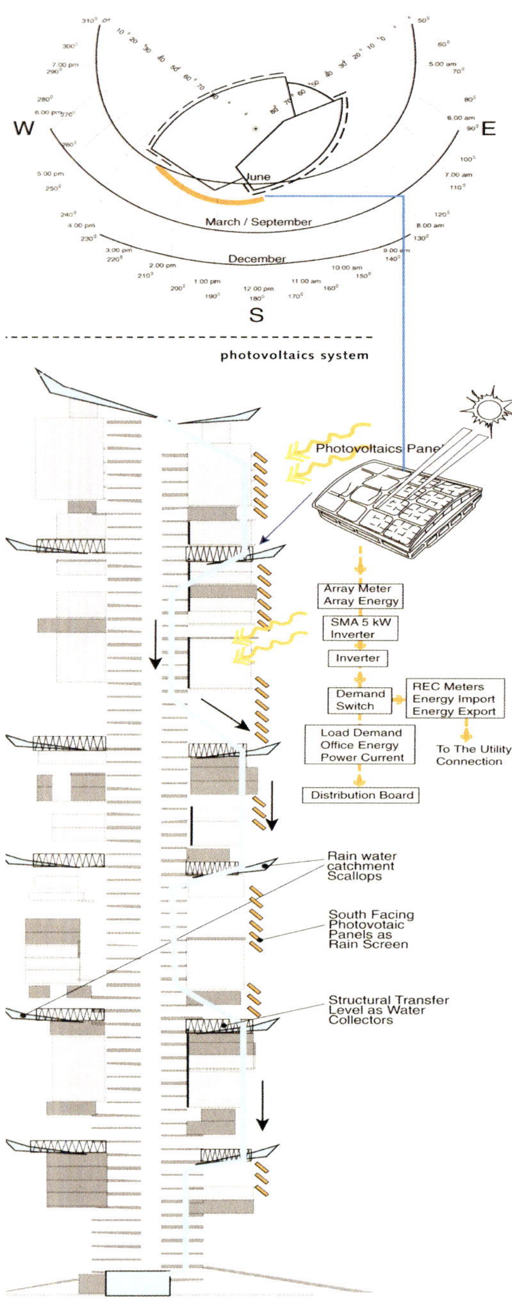

Fig. 5 Hamza and Yeang's bioclimatic skyscraper

it to its engineering origins, with the formal and the performative merging, and the building, wholly or in part, expressing a chosen environmental strategy (such as Nicholas Grimshaw's Eden Project; fig. 4, and T.R. Hamza and Yeang's bioclimatic skyscrapers; fig. 5). If kept separate, with the expression of the environmental systems suppressed in favor of a building envelope of more conventional appearance (such as Ercilla + Campo's Services Building, Catalonia Polytechnic, Spain), then performance will be less effective, but perhaps more acceptable to the client—and the culture. Environmental design at all scales is about performance, which is why it's no small wonder the Architects-Formerly-Known-as-High-Tech find it seductive: it both justifies and focuses technology transfer from various forms of engineering into architecture, which in some of their past work seemed to be more ideological than logical. Contemporary climate-responsive architecture can become power stations, producing electricity from sun and / or wind. To maximize their productivity from these sources, however, their forms must be governed by the harvesting of these renewables. At architectural scale, solar collection has for the most part produced straightforward orthogonal buildings with expanses of PVs, solar panels, and/or glazing. Sometimes these elements are designed to track the sun, altering their angle of reception as the sun moves through the day and the year, but generally solar architecture remains conventional for economy's sake. When environmental productivity of one kind or another is used to *determine* a form, the results can be startlingly similar to some of the non-linear designs of the formalist avant garde. Reservations about this design method center on one parameter—energy—dominating all others, and distorting the architectural object into a one- instead of a multi-dimensional response, but there is no reason why this has to be the case. Additional parameters can be added in subsequent iterations, and if environmentally performative architecture is to have any cultural value, this must, in fact, happen. Nevertheless, it's useful to look at an example of environmental form-finding that deliberately determines the design through the requirements of maximized energy productivity.

Optimizing wind collection is not easily done, and requires engineering the shape of the building. *Project ZED,*[13] a European Commission-funded research project

(1995–97) coordinated by the Martin Centre, University of Cambridge,[14] explicitly pursued environmental form-finding through three energy-producing designs by Future Systems (fig. 6) in three European cities: Berlin, Toulouse, and London. As Britain is rich in wind energy, Future Systems' London case study opted for wind power in a twenty-five story residential and commercial tower. Every aspect of the building's form and fabric was, to a large extent, determined by the requirements of energy productivity. Any doubts that this is so are laid to rest by the description of the evaluative process, in which both physical and digital modeling dictate changes to the building's form to optimize energy productivity. The floor plan on each side of the VAWT aperture was changed from an egg-shape to more of a boomerang shape, to reduce turbulence and increase productivity. The Mark II scheme was estimated to be capable of increasing a given wind speed by sixty percent, thereby producing four times as much energy as a building carrying turbines without this modeling.

When there is a quantified target, the reasons for ending an iterative process are much clearer than they are in formalist experiments. With an energy determined building, it is clear when one stops: when the building is judged to produce as much energy as it can under the given circumstances. Environmental determinism is itself determined by the laws of physics. The parameters for shape-generation are strictly governed by dynamic physical phenomena such as the behavior of air at different temperatures and different velocities etc. In contrast, the parameters for much form-finding in avant-garde architecture are opaque, and the cut-off point for the iterative process arbitrary. Outside the research lab, experiment is still vital to the development of a "sustainable'" architecture that is not only environmentally productive, but is architecture. Equally vital is the sharing of results. There continues to be too little post-occupancy analysis of environmentally-designed buildings because firms, for good commercial reasons, are unwilling to share their mistakes, thus flattening our learning curve. Only the most environmentally-committed practices will even privately discuss what went wrong, as well as what went right. For this reason, there is not yet a large enough body of measured precedents to help other designers

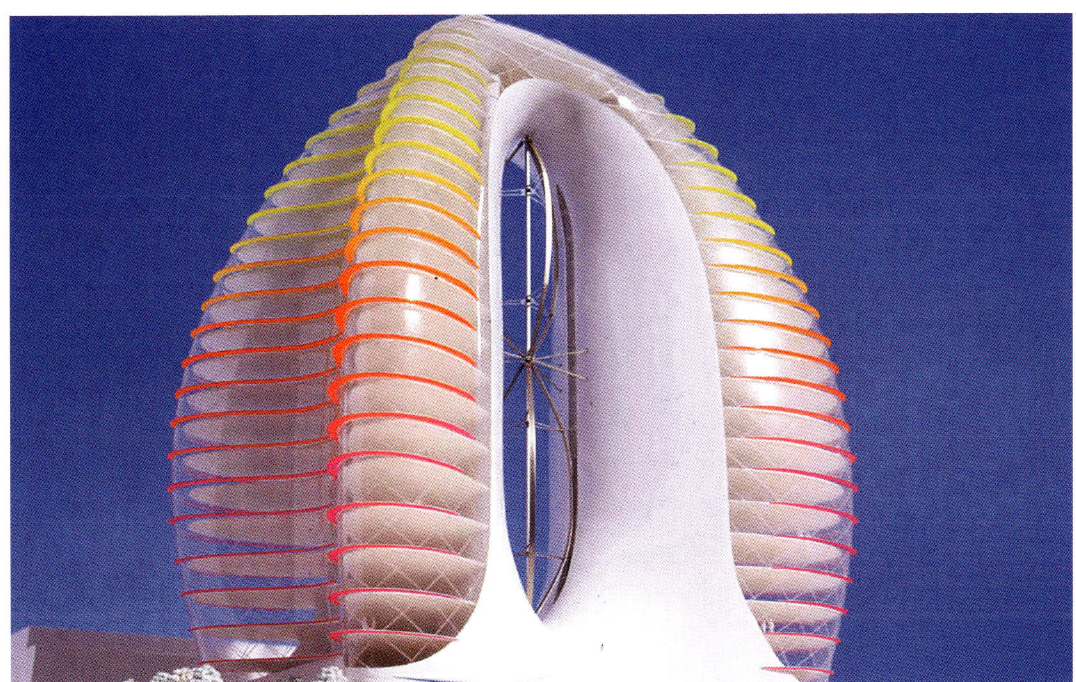

Fig. 6 Future Systems, *Project ZED: London case study*, showing vertical axis wind turbine (VAWT) to produce electricity for the building. Placing the VAWT within the body of the building creates a Venturi effect, and increases energy productivity by increasing wind speed across the turbine.

and engineers. Experiment needs to be seen as part of the role of architecture, and failure as part of the process of learning how to mitigate climate-change. If this is important at building scale, it is crucial at urban scale, where the most damage is being done.

Making Artificial Ecologies
Environmental design revolves around a particular idea of imitating nature in operation—its productivity, production of energy, of clean(ed) water, of filtered air, of acoustic protection, of food, of (public) health. This is true at architectural and urban scales, but it is at the urban scale that it may find its most radical expression, requiring design methods that bring about a reconfigured nature within intensely urban contexts, and / or environmentally productive landscapes, in which buildings are part of the same productivity. This challenges conventional conceptions of the city as the site of built culture, of non-nature. The emerging practice of landscape urbanism has taken much of its meat from the ecological sciences, and is contributing to the linguistic and actual blurring of city and place-specific nature now so important for the city's

survival, in particular to cities already in environmental meltdown. Environmentally productive "urbscapes" require the quantification of nature, something resisted by practices that are design- rather than engineering-led. The muddy-boots-practicalities of engineering, however, are the *sine qua non* of a new artificial nature that may one day appear on urban sites as a matter of course. At present, such models are experimental and the technologies emergent.

Arup's design for the zero carbon new town of Dongtan (fig. 7) is a case in point, as is SOM's Chongming, an even more ambitious experiment with eight new high-density towns proposed to house a million people, and yet compact enough to preserve eighty-five percent of the island for organic agriculture and water management, and protect it from the continuing sprawl of neighboring Shanghai. If the client pursues the project past the construction of the new neighborhood now being added to Chongming City, we will have two large-scale urban experiments in sustainable design to learn from *in operation*. In Dongtan, a city intended for half a million people, Arup is using the concept of the ecological foot-

Fig. 7 Dongtan by Arup Associates

print to drive its spatial planning. Ideally, in any environ mental design, whether building or city, nature's supply and human demand are in equilibrium. This requires the analysis of a complex set of quantified relationships, and Arup used a modeling tool called REAP (Resources and Energy Analysis Program), developed by the Stockholm Environment Institute (SEI) and the Center for Urban and Regional Ecology, University of Manchester. This helps calculate the quantity of natural resources on site to sustain life (energy, food, water), and the quantity of waste and pollution that can be absorbed there.

The comparative dispersal into the landscape of the first phase of Dongtan is one model of an eco-city, based on a careful assessment of the carrying capacity of the site, an ideal scenario, but an unlikely template for a country with 1.3 billion people, and a planet that currently falls short of recovering from the rate at which we exploit it by over twenty percent. Dongtan's average density will be about 190 people per hectare, or roughly 75 dwellings per hectare, extraordinarily modest by Chinese standards. Other firms are pursuing another, more fashionable model of compaction and densification, which is based, for the most part, on a very different parameter: transportation. There is another reason for compaction, however, which has emerged from the studios of two other international practices, Office for Metropolitan Architecture (OMA) and Foster and Partners, and that is climate. Both OMA, in Ras al Khaimah, with the design for a new city, called RAK Gateway (fig. 8), and Foster's in Abu Dhabi, with the eco-city Masdar (fig. 9), have used the traditional desert vernacular morphology of narrow self-shading streets and compacted city footprint to reduce the amount of surface exposed to intense solar radiation, and the consequent overheating and evaporation of what moisture is available. The results are two surprisingly similar masterplans: perfect squares sitting in their respective deserts, RAK Gateway with a density of 400 people per hectare, or roughly 100 dwellings per hectare, almost twice as dense as Dongtan.

What is interesting in the new "eco-cities" of the Middle East and China is a new responsiveness to physical, as well as cultural, context. The new cities near Shanghai are in an area blessed with fertile soil and rain, and both Arup and SOM have responded accordingly. SOM's

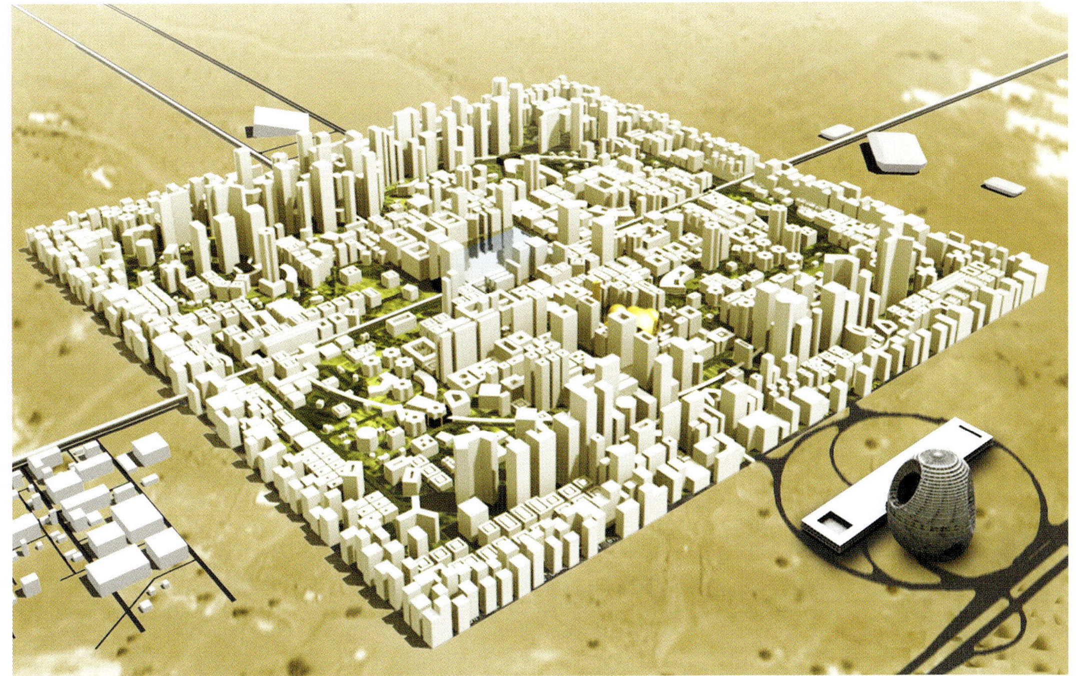

Fig. 8 RAK Gateway by Office for Metropolitan Architecture, OMA

Fig. 9 Masdar City; carbon-neutral, waste-free, car-free eco-city by Norman Foster and Partners

Chongming is an interesting hybrid: eight dense and compact cities, but compacted, not for climate, but in order to preserve surrounding land doing valuable agricultural and ecological work. The cities will rely on this land to close the loop of their metabolic processes. If it is completed, and does what it says, Chongming's new altered urban state will be incomparably more powerful an influence than a settlement that looks different and does the same old thing. Arup's Dongtan will be the first to become what its design leader, Alejandro Gutierrez, calls an "ecological demonstrator," with it's first phase due for completion in 2010. Again, there is follow-through, an intellectual consistency to technological innovation that has sent them in every appropriate direction to avoid fossil fuels at urban scale: biomass, biogas, solar power, wind. Because the practice has the requisite new knowledge, it is able to understand and use what physical resources are available. Dongtan and, if it's built, Chongming, are laboratories and symbols of what might be to come. Their real value lies in the new thinking of their clients and designers, and in the transfer of that thinking to existing cities worldwide.

Conclusion

A design needn't be environmentally-determined to be environmentally sustainable, but will inevitably be environmentally influenced if one is thinking in a "whole life'" or "cradle to cradle" way about the building or the city. Innovation in environmental performance is too often discounted in the design world if it doesn't assume an innovative form. Future Systems is one of a few exceptions to what is at present a surprisingly conventional-looking output, considering environmental design's potentially revolutionary effect on building form. The canyon that habitually divides the good from the cool is a curious thing, and one that may finally be bridged by young architects trained in goodness (environmental design) and coolness (formal innovation)—both / and. The modern movement pioneers never had any difficulty deriving new forms from new technologies, though the case is interestingly different. Modernist forms anticipated building technologies it took another fifty years to develop into reliability. Today, it is more the case that our new technologies are ahead of the forms appropriate to them, and they are ahead because of the architecture profession's unwillingness to embrace the fact of nature's revolt. Finding those forms may entail looking back (as in Masdar and RAK Gateway), as well as ahead, but some of the upcoming generation of architects have a similar ecumenism that allows them to slide from formal experiment to practical effect and back again, untroubled by distinctions between beauty and utility. They have, and will continue to have, just as much difficulty as the rest of us in precisely defining "sustainability," but perhaps less difficulty in achieving it.

1 Nicholas Stern, *The Economics of Climate Change* (HM Treasury, 2007), *Tho Storn Roviow* (Cambridgc, 2007).

2 Ibid., p. 1, 3.

3 Angela Merkel, interviewed in *The Guardian Weekend* (London, January 5, 2008), p. 19.

4 David Anink et al., *Handbook of Sustainable Building* (London, 1996), p. 8.

5 Michael Hensel, *Emergence: Morphogenetic Design Strategies* (New York, 2004), p. 74.

6 Sym Van der Ryn and Stewart Cowan, *Ecological Design* (Washington, DC, 1996), p. 114.

7 Catherine Slessor, *Eco-Tech* (London, 1998)

8 Berrie Evans, "Windows as Climate Modifiers," *The Architects' Journal* (August 1993), p. 39.

9 Kenneth Frampton, *Charles Correa* (London, 1999).

10 Bill Dunster, *The ZED Book* (Oxford, 2008).

11 Jan Kaplicky, *Future Systems* (London, 2008).

12 A+U Special Issue, *MVRDV Files* (November 2002).

13 *Zero Energy Design*, also known as "zero carbon" or "net zero." Total renewable energy autonomy on site for electricity as well as heating / cooling is very difficult to achieve, and for complex programs in cities, even more so.

14 *Project ZED: Towards Zero Emission Urban Development*, a research collaboration between The Martin Centre, University of Cambridge; Future Systems; GRECO, Ecole d'Architecture de Toulouse; RP + K Sozietat, Germany, and TUV Rheinland, Germany. The English version of the report is held in The Martin Centre library, University of Cambridge.

Ceiling view of Antoni Gaudí's Sagrada Família

Exterior view of Mies van der Rohe's Seagram Building

Structure Between

Less Is More and More Is More:
The Philosophy and Structures of Mutsuro Sasaki

Those looking to understand why contemporary Japanese architectural culture enjoys such indisputable success can find useful answers in Mutsuro Sasaki's book, *Flux Structure* (Tokyo, 2005). Sasaki, a structural designer primarily known in more sophisticated engineering circles, bases the findings in his book in part on research of physical model experiments of the seminal undulating forms by Antoni Gaudí. Though primarily rooted in creating organic forms, Sasaki is no stranger to modernist principles and seeks to combine the two in his work. Evident in perhaps his most important project, the Sendai Mediatheque (in collaboration with Toyo Ito), he joins the Gaudíesque curving shell form with the modernistic column and concrete slab floor structure. This is what sets Sasaki apart from most structural designers; the simple design philosophy that fuses the ubiquitous Miesian truism: "Less is more" with the counter aphorism: "More is more." To Sasaki, these two approaches are not incompatible. On the contrary. It is the dialogue that falls between the "Less": Mies van der Rohe's Seagram Building and the "more": Gaudí's Sagrada Família that has formed the basis for his inspiration in structural research. It is noteworthy that a structural designer has found a way to connect the two ideologies rather than simply follow the rapid diaspora from modernism to the trendy freeform architectural movement.

Only after understanding the root of Sasaki's design position can the science be properly appreciated. In consideration of Gaudí's effort expended creating trial and error models, Sasaki wondered, "… if a computer could be used for the application of mathematically based mechanical theory to generate structural shapes for the shape analysis of a real structural design." His dedication to answering this has lead to the creation of two successfully proven methodologies; Sensitivity Analysis method and the Extended Evolutionary Structure Optimization.

What follows is a series of projects designed using these methods, along with Sasaki's explanations on the inspiration and execution of his collaborations with some of the best Japanese architects practicing today.

Francesco Dal Co

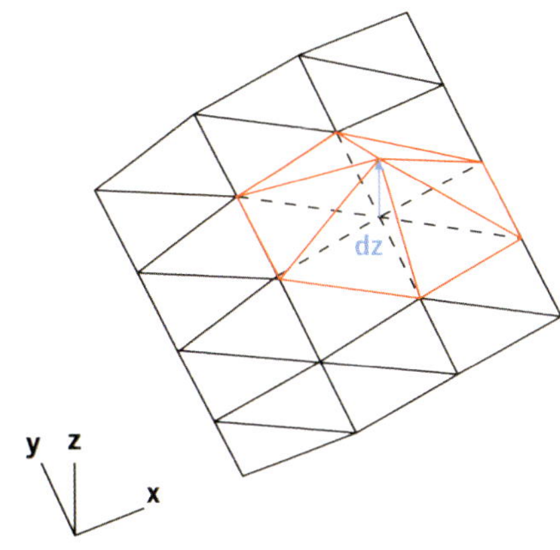

Sensitivity Coefficient

$$\alpha_i = \frac{dC}{dz_i} = -\frac{1}{2}\{u\}\ \frac{d(\sum_e [K_e^{(i)}])}{dz_i}\{u\}$$

$\sum_e [K_e^{(i)}]$: Sam of Element Stiffness Matrix relating to node No. i

$\{u\}$: Nodal Displacement Vector

Morphogenesis by Sensitivity Analysis: methods of shape determination

"As an ultimate model for a futuristic layered architecture, this was a proposal for a minimal, pure *Dom-Ino* structure composed of seven plates supported by thirteen tubes."
Sasaki on Sendai Mediatheque by Toyo Ito

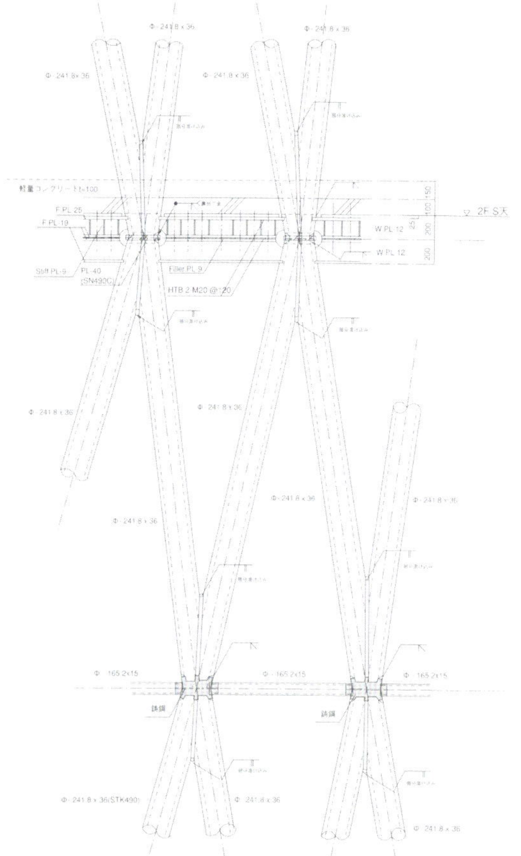

Sendai Mediatheque, enlarged detail of column structural steel

Sendai Mediatheque, inside view of column shaft

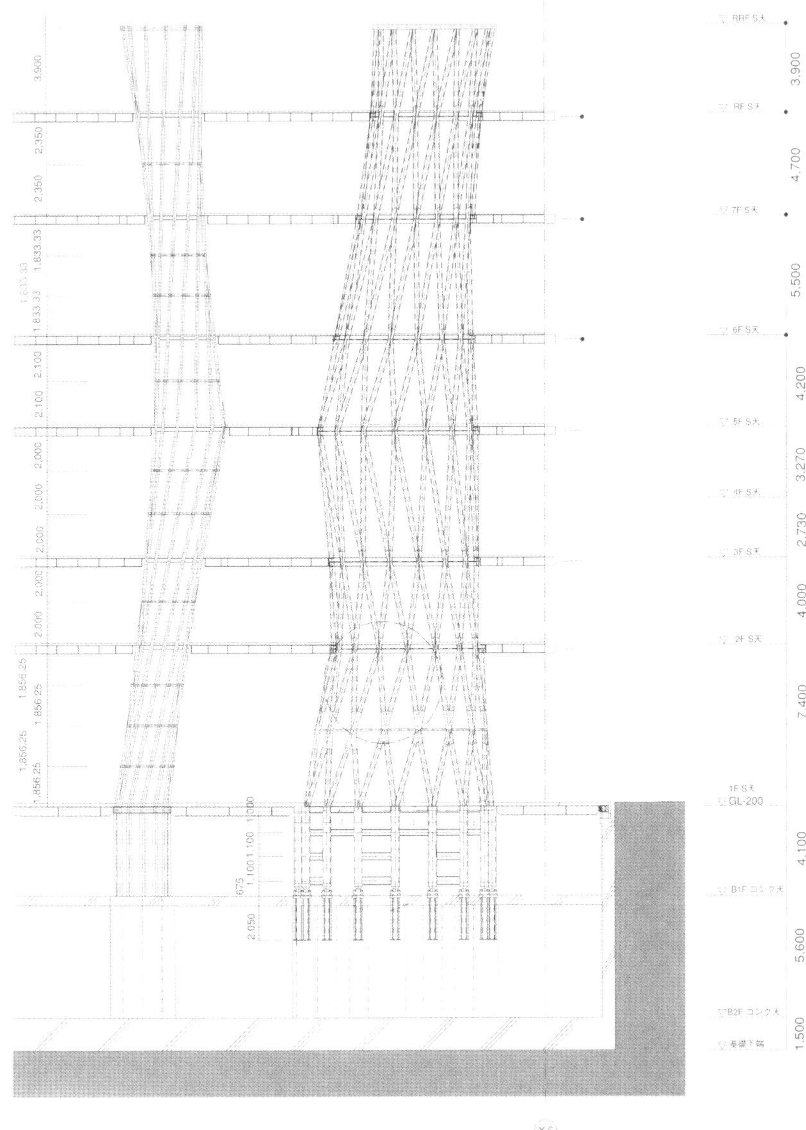

Sendai Mediatheque, section

"An abstract transparent architecture implemented by means of a *thin roof* and *thin wall* composed of small elements, and *slender columns*."
Sasaki on 21st Century Museum of Contemporary Art by Kazuyo Sejima + Ryue Nishizawa, SANAA

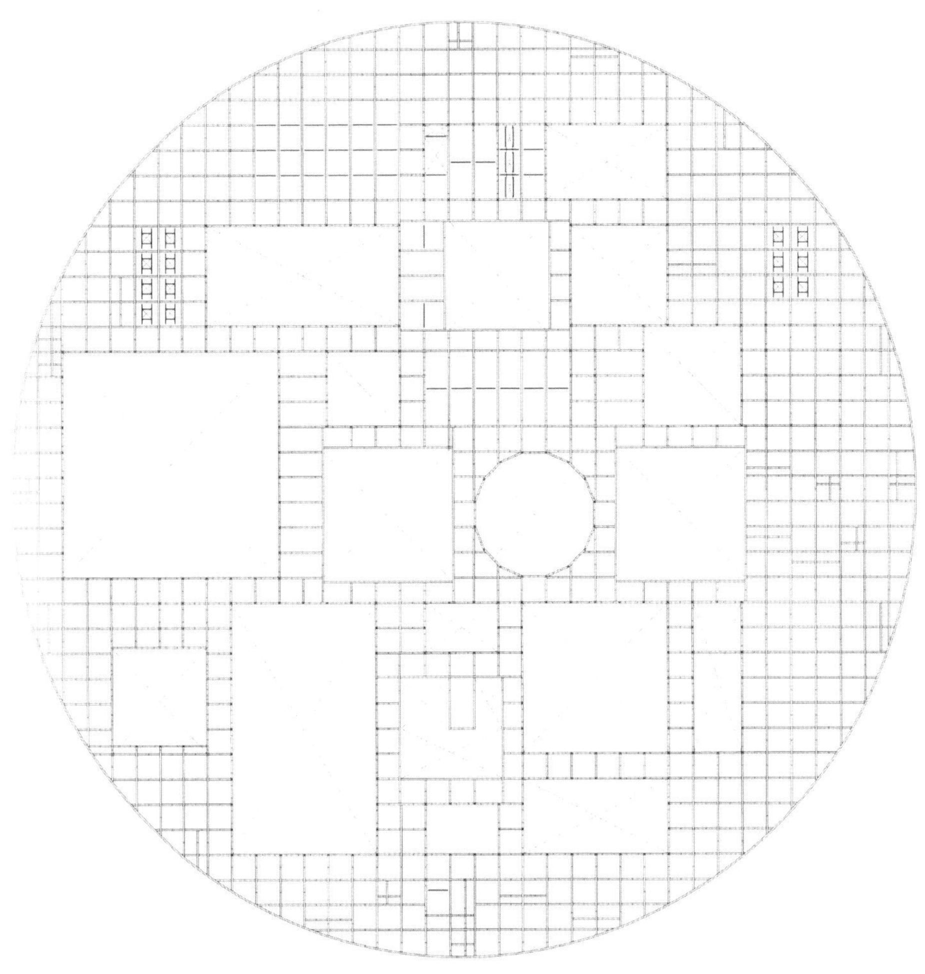

21st Century Museum of Contemporary Art, structural framing plan

21st Century Museum of Contemporary Art, exterior overall view

21st Century Museum of Contemporary Art, exterior view

"Shape design (Sensitivity Analysis method) was used to modify the initial shape imagined by Toyo Ito for the main roof structure. This generated the optimum structural shape with the least possible bending stresses, and a minimum of strain energy and deformation."
Sasaki on I Project by Toyo Ito

I Project, shape design by Sensitivity Analysis showing deformation at the roof by lowering a uniformly distributed vertical load (1.5t / m²)

I Project, shell formwork

I Project, arrangement of steel rods

"Having established Arata Isozaki's image and the initial conditions requested by the architecture, the main roof structure was sought through shape design (Sensitivity Analysis method), producing an amorphous shape as well as a structure that follows mechanical principles."
Sasaki on Kitagata Community Center by Arata Isozaki

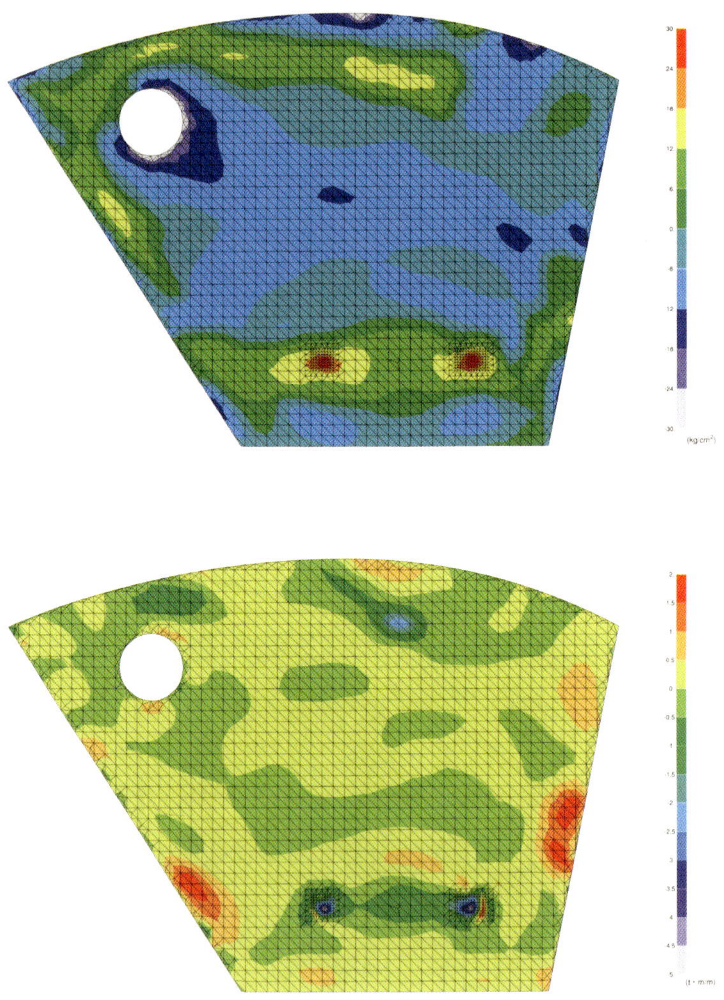

Kitagata Community Center, distribution of main vertical stress (vertical load) and flex distribution (vertical load)

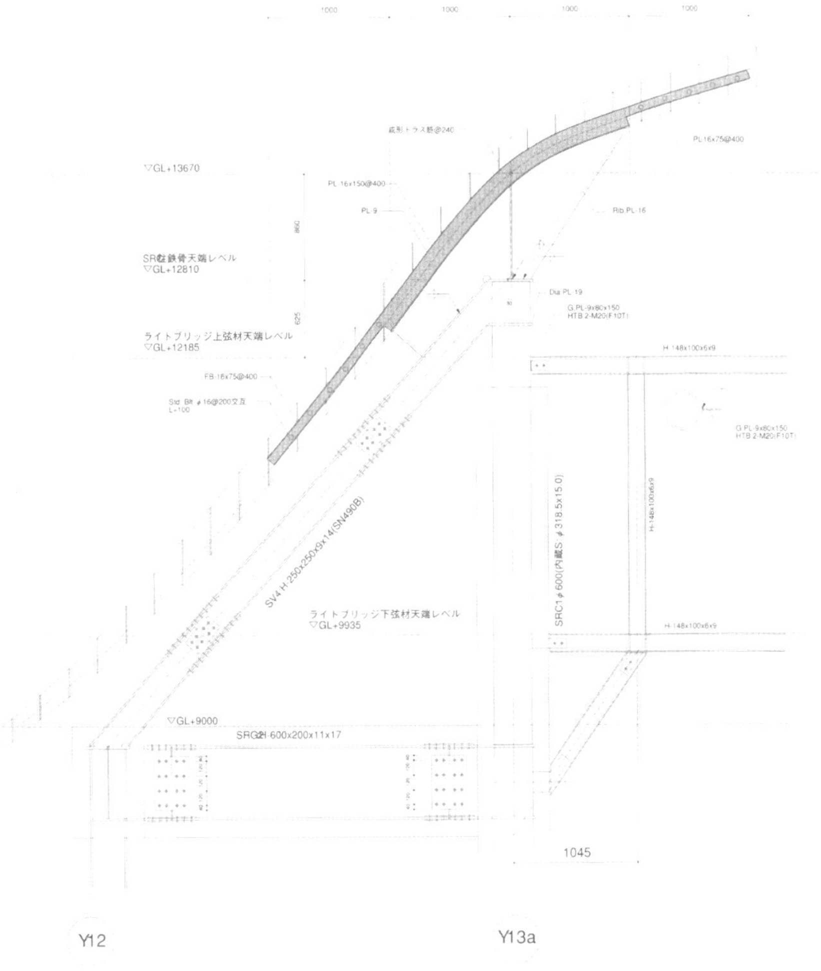

Kitagata Community Center, roof section

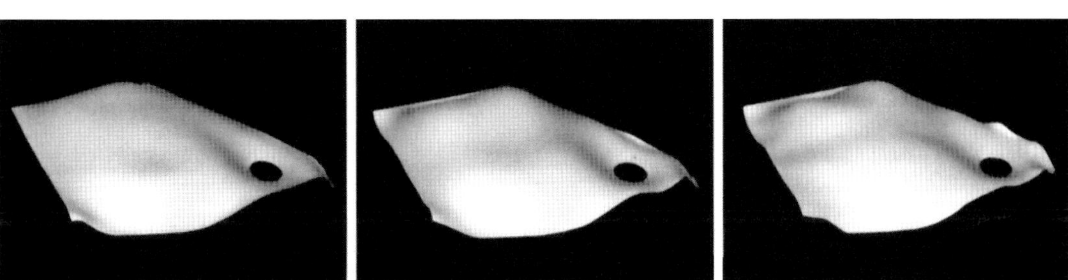

Kitagata Community Center, working models of the roof

"Using shape design (Extended Evolutionary Structure Optimization method, Extended ESO method), an enormous flux structure was created, 400 meters long by fourty meters wide by twenty meters high. The structural elements were optimally formed within a three-dimensional space while satisfying the given design conditions, and the structural shape thus obtained maximum mechanical efficacy with a minimum use of materials."
Sasaki on Florence New Station by Arata Isozaki

Florence New Station, exterior view

Full model

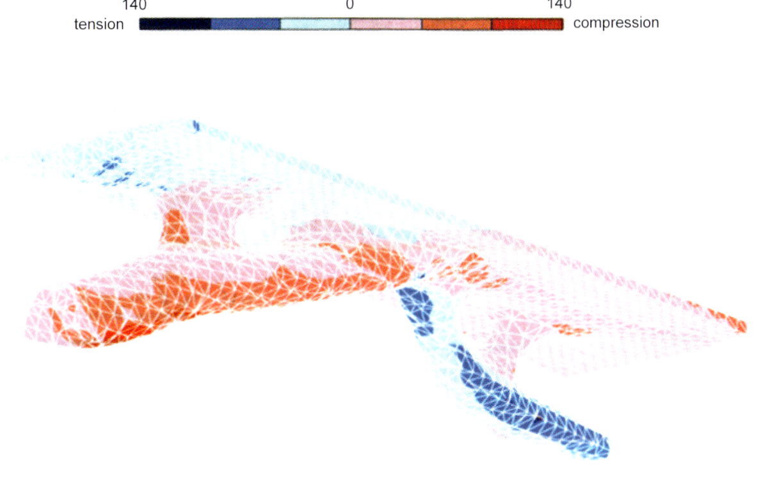

Distribution of principal stress

Florence New Station, Extended Evolutionary Structure Optimization (ESO) analysis of structure

"The gently curving structural shape imagined by SANAA, something like rolling up the surface of the ground, was given mechanical rationality by shape design (Sensitivity Analysis method). The steel-framed roof is supported by the floor structure below, which is a reinforced concrete free-curved shell."
Sasaki on EPFL Learning Center by Kazuyo Sejima + Ryue Nishizawa, SANAA

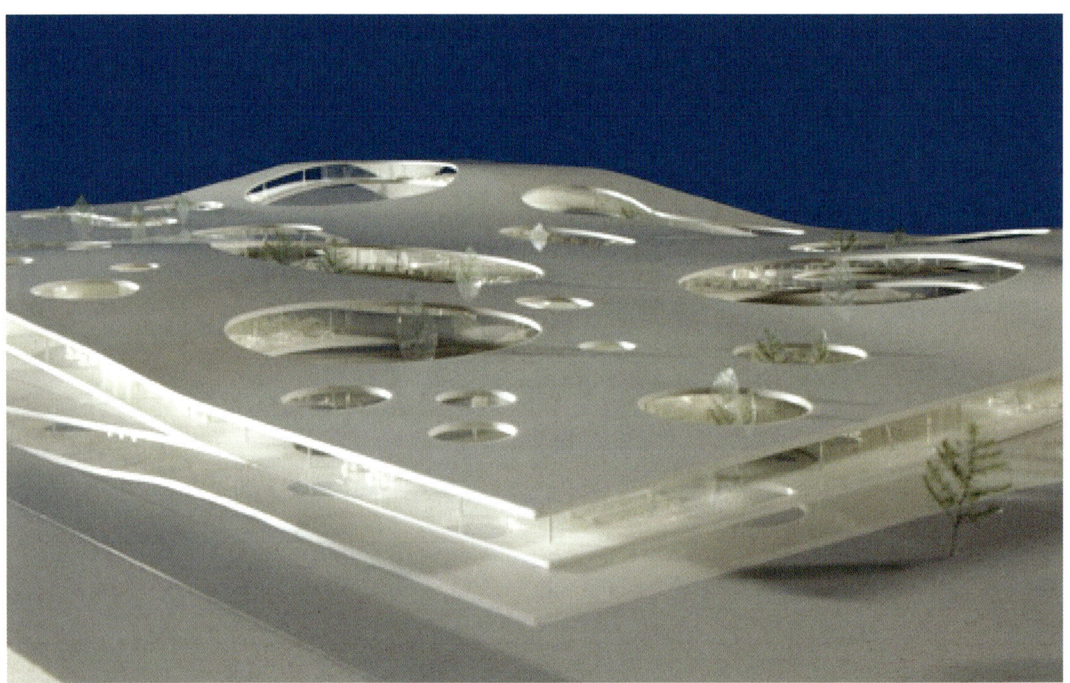

EPFL Learning Center, exterior view

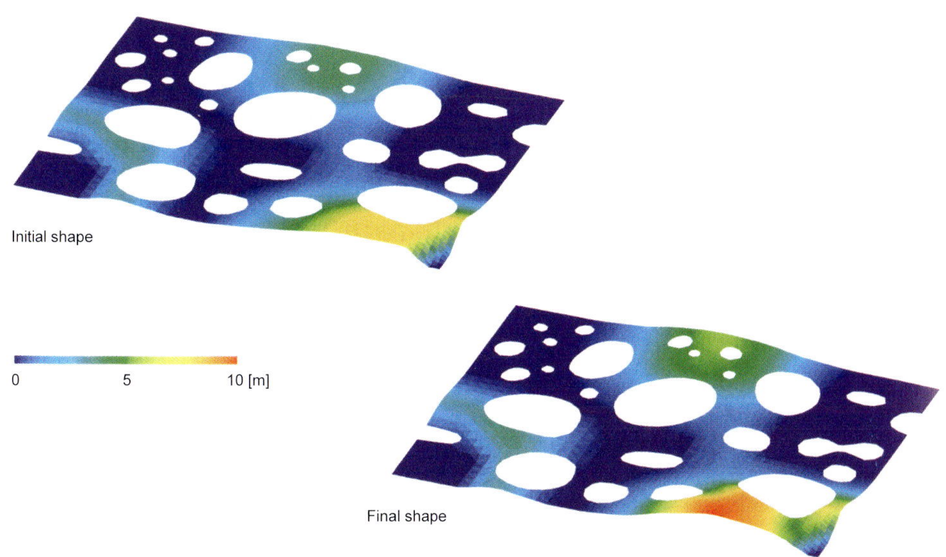

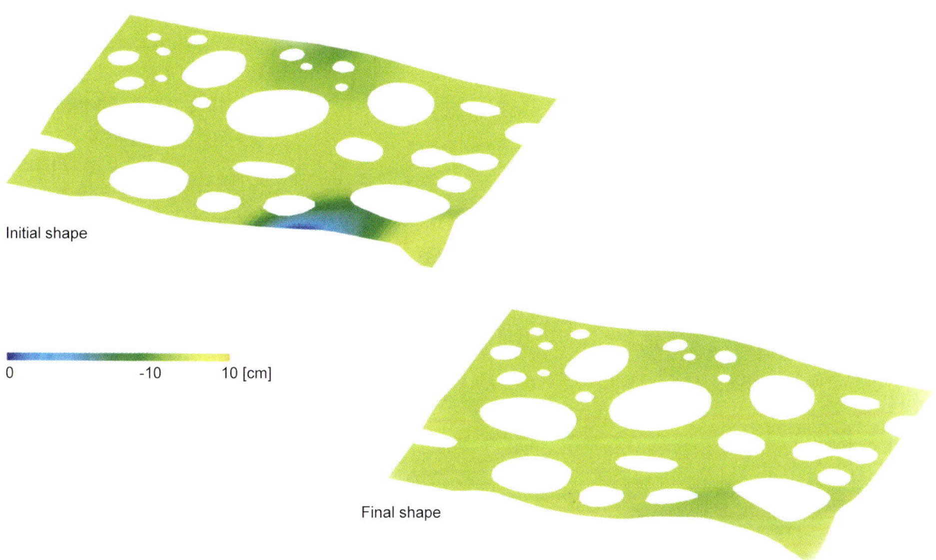

EPFL Learning Center, final shape configurations

"The building's roof is composed by complex free curved surface with various curvatures and can be described as if fluttering in the air. It is realized by twenty centimeters thick free edge shell with smooth surface by means of economically rational way. By full use of 3D digital data, a special formwork is newly devised for this project, which includes sleeper, joist, sheeting and supporting column by improving an ordinary plywood formwork."
Sasaki on The Crematorium in Kakamigahara by Toyo Ito

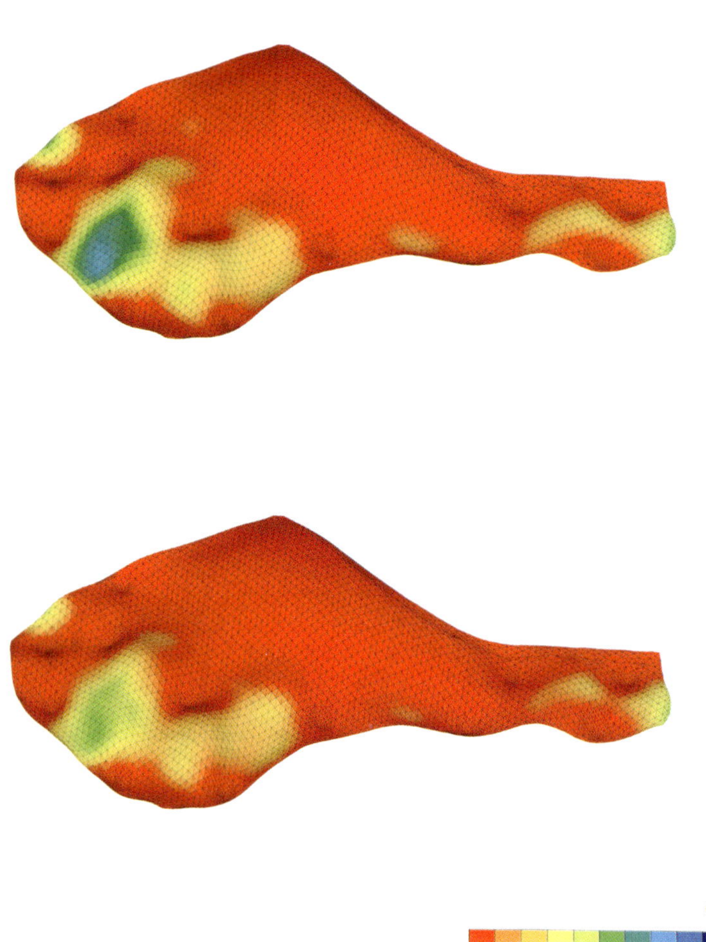

The Crematorium in Kakamigahara, shape design by Sensitivity Analysis

The Crematorium in Kakamigahara, exterior view

The Crematorium in Kakamigahara, arrangement of steel rods for the shell concrete pouring

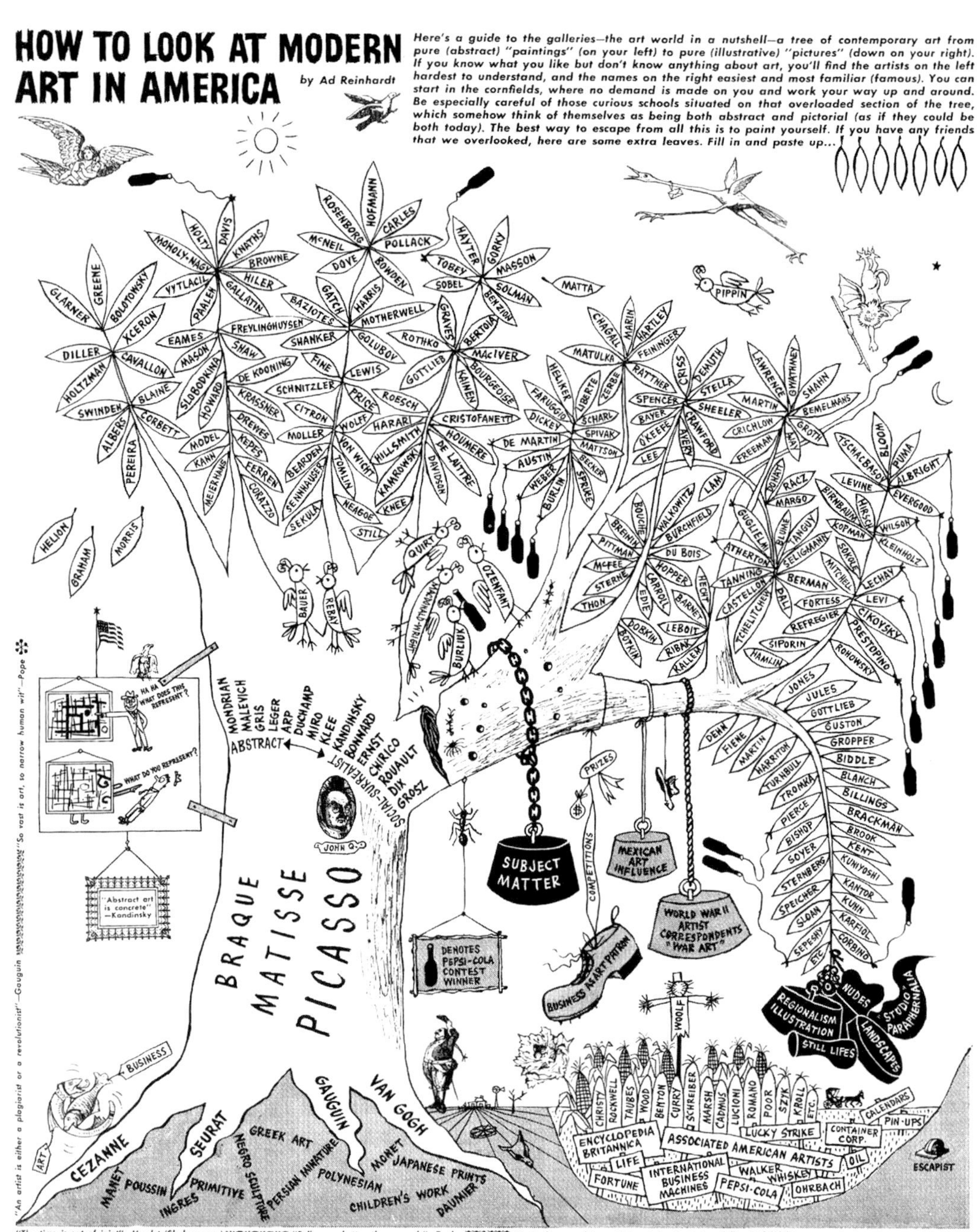

Fig. 1 Ad Reinhardt, "How to Look at Modern Art in America," published in *PM* magazine, June 2, 1946

Art, Soul of the Corporation:
Patronage, Public Relations, and the Interrelations of Architecture and Art after World War II

Joan Ockman

The corporation has, in fact, become one of the most powerful and conscientious art patrons of our day, and has established itself not only as a purveyor of tasteful objects but as an arbiter of taste as well…. Capitalism is not the same free-for-all it was in the last century, and the men who head our modern corporations are not the same princes of industry and finance who lived in marble palaces surrounded by artistic plunder and were a law unto themselves. The modern corporation has a conscience, or if it hasn't, the laws of the land and the new folklore see to it that it behaves as though it had.

Russell Lynes[1]

In the societies of control, on the other hand, what is important is no longer either a signature or a number, but … codes that mark access to information, or reject it…. [N]ineteenth-century capitalism is a capitalism of concentration, for production and for property. It therefore erects a factory as a space of enclosure, the capitalist being the owner of the means of production…. But in the present situation, capitalism is no longer involved in production, which it often relegates to the Third World…. This is no longer a capitalism for production but for the product, which is to say, for being sold or marketed…. Even art has left the spaces of enclosure in order to enter into the open circuits of the [data] bank…. Marketing has become the center or the "soul" of the corporation. We are taught that corporations have a soul, which is the most terrifying news in the world.

Gilles Deleuze[2]

Today the role of the corporation as arts patron and underwriter is so integral to the economy of American culture that it is nearly impossible to draw the line between not-for-profit cultural institution and for-profit business. One can hardly imagine a contemporary museum putting on a large exhibition without major funding by business, just as it is *de rigueur* for corporations to hire consultants and in-house curators for purposes of building up prestigious art collections, establishing their own cultural foundations and sponsorships, and displaying artwork in their headquarters and exhibition spaces. These corporate-art practices began to become well-established in the United States by the 1960s, but they took shape during the period immediately following World War II, when the hand of managerial capitalism became increasingly visible and munificent. Within this development the contribution of the firm of Skidmore, Owings & Merrill was exemplary, starting with its design of the Terrace Plaza Hotel in Cincinnati in 1946–48.

While powerful American financiers and industrial magnates with names like Frick, Morgan, Hearst, and Mellon amassed ambitious art collections in the early decades of the twentieth century, usually based on the European masters, and constructed grandiose buildings to house them, such ostentatious dispositions of private wealth largely came to a halt by the Depression. Under the New Deal, the federal government took on a new mantle as patron of the arts, especially through the programs of the Works Progress Administration, which created jobs for thousands of unemployed painters, sculptors, architects, and artisans at a moment when "social consciousness" strongly permeated American culture. This massive public arts support in the United States—resulting in edifying murals in the lobbies of state capitols and monumental friezes on the pedimented façades of post offices—was derailed by the nation's entry into World War II. But the social agenda and patriotic solidarity of those years set the tone for private patronage both during the war, when corporations recognized the benefits of keeping a high profile and cultivating public trust, and especially the period afterward, as the domestic economy rapidly expanded.

Negative perceptions of the monopolistic control and impersonality of American business had, in fact, been widespread since the late nineteenth century. As Roland Marchand elaborates in his book *Creating the Soul of the Corporation* (1998), the desire to counteract the public's mounting accusations of venality and aloofness encouraged a quest on the part of those in the top echelons of management for greater social and moral legitimacy.[3] Nor did such humanizing efforts abate with the stock market's crash, especially as big business was largely blamed for the debacle and corrupt corporate practices in the 1930s further soured public opinion. Strategies for dispelling the image of soullessness ranged from well-publicized benefits programs for employees, to patriotic and community-friendly service initiatives, to cultural undertakings focused on art and design. Already in 1935 a congressional ruling had created an incentive for corporate largesse, allowing businesses to deduct up to five percent of before-tax income for charitable gifts; during the war years, such deductions would enable them to circumvent high excess-profits taxes. In the name of good public relations, men like Thomas Watson at IBM and Walter Paepcke at Container Corporation of America took the lead in establishing generous corporate art programs, and the heads of companies like Standard Oil of New Jersey, Miller, Pepsi-Cola; pharmaceutical manufacturers like Abbott Laboratories and Upjohn soon followed suit. These programs were variously geared to the purchasing of work from leading artists, incorporating fine art in company advertisements, and setting up sponsorships and competitions.[4]

The term *public relations* was coined as early as 1908 by the president of the American Telephone and Telegraph Company, Theodor Vail, to supersede the older term publicity. The latter was primarily associated with "press agentry" and sales promotion. Public relations, in contrast, connoted a civic duty on the part of business to inform the community about its responsibilities, actions, and contributions. In the 1920s the concept was transformed by a master technician of mass persuasion, Edward Bernays. A Viennese emigré and the nephew of Sigmund Freud, Bernays made "PR" a modern, professional field, grounding it in psychology, market research, and the social sciences.[5]

Among the forward-looking businessmen who subscribed to the value of good public relations was the Harvard- and Oxford-educated John Josiah [Jack] Emery (1898–1976), scion of a Cincinnati fortune in candle-making and real estate, who took over his family's business in the mid-1920s and turned it into a successful chemical company. Known as a man of excellent taste, he was married to the daughter of the artist Charles Dana Gibson, creator of the Gibson Girl. In 1931 Emery had put up the 48-story Carew Tower complex in downtown Cincinnati, which included the Art Deco-style Netherlands Plaza Hotel. The Carew was touted at the time as the tallest building west of the Alleghenies and the city's Rockefeller Center. Thirteen years later, with the end of World War II in sight, Emery co-founded the Citizen's Planning Association in Cincinnati together with a group of other business leaders, and this association (in 1948 renamed the Citizens' Development Committee) produced a comprehensive master plan for the revitalization of the downtown core. Emery also began developing the Terrace Plaza on a half-block site at the edge of the central business district.

Cincinnati's first large public building to be constructed after the war, Terrace Plaza opened in July 1948 in what was touted as "a blaze of public relations" in an article published in *Harper's* magazine the previous month.[6] The ultramodern brick-faced building consisted of an eleven-story hotel set back from the lot lines to meet zoning requirements, placed atop a mostly windowless built-out seven-story base housing two department stores, Bond and J. C. Penney, as well as street-level shops (fig. 2).

SOM was fresh from completing its first phase of work on the "atomic town" of Oak Ridge, Tennessee. Emery chose the young firm because he felt that precisely its architects' lack of experience in hotel design would make them more likely not only to come up with something unhackneyed but to work cooperatively with him. The project was indeed remarkable in its collaborative and systematic approach to programming, finance, and design.

Both the New York and Chicago offices of SOM were involved in the project, with William Brown in New York as partner in charge and William Hartmann in Chicago

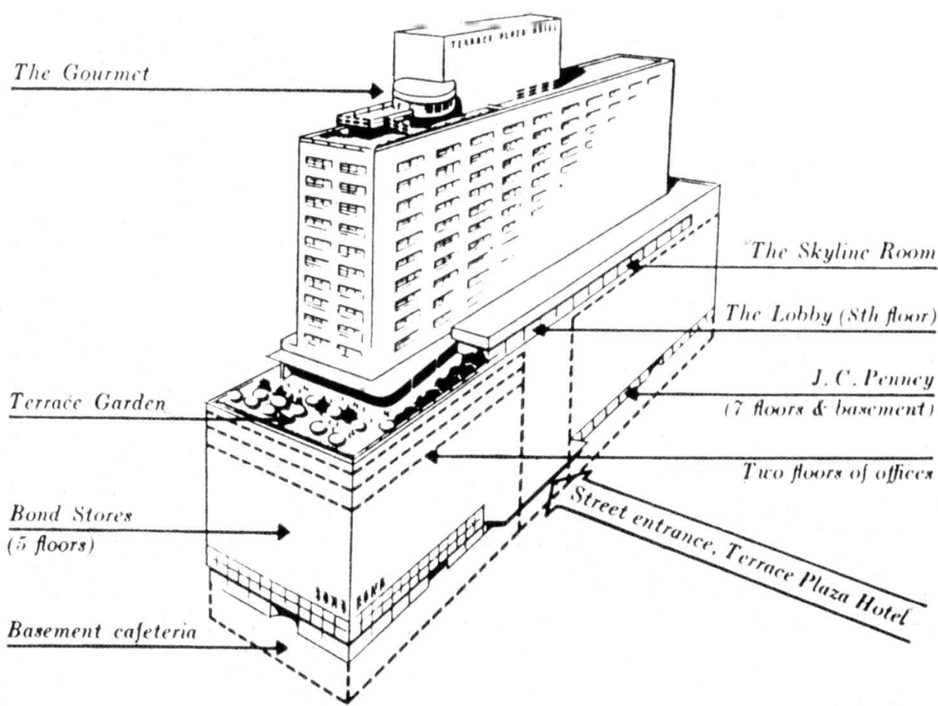

Fig. 2 Terrace Plaza Hotel, Cincinnati, 1946–48

responsible for overall design.[7] The coup of lifting the hotel 130 feet above street level allowed for the provision of attractive amenities like a rooftop terrace garden adjoining the lobby and an outdoor dining space that could be converted into a skating rink in winter. The base-and-slab *parti,* anticipated in an ideal scheme designed and enthusiastically promoted by Nathaniel Owings in 1947 as an "office building of tomorrow," also looks forward, of course, to the seminal Lever House, shortly to be on the firm's drawing boards. The use of materials developed during World War II like Formica and other plastic laminates; the custom-designed textiles and the variegated color schemes in the individual hotel rooms correlated with different sun exposures; the built-in air conditioning and lighting fixtures; the motor-controlled couch-beds and the retractable metal wall partitions that could alter the size of suites; and the fully automated elevators and advanced mechanical systems regulated on a large central console, all contributed to the sense that Terrace Plaza was the last word in modernity and planning, and

that its owner had spared no expense on behalf of the public's comfort and enjoyment.[8]

Equally noteworthy and integral to the overall conception at Terrace Plaza was the inclusion of important works of painting and sculpture. These were by four contemporary artists. The main dining space on the lobby floor, the Skyline Room, boasted an 89-foot-long by 16-foot-high mural by Saul Steinberg, depicting Cincinnati landmarks interspersed with other real and imagined urban scenes (figs. 3, 4). According to William Brown, the designers were searching for a "quiet" treatment for the long interior wall facing the windowed east elevation of the restaurant and had rejected paneling and fabric when the idea of a flat, continuous mural emerged. Ben Baldwin, of the interiors team, had been in the Navy with Steinberg, and proposed him for the commission.[9] The thirty-three-year-old Romanian-born artist had emigrated from the Dominican Republic, where he had waited a year for a US visa, having been forced to flee fascism a year after completing a degree in architecture in Milan. ("The study of architec-

Fig. 3 Terrace Plaza Hotel, Skyline Room restaurant, with mural by Saul Steinberg. Photo: Ezra Stoller

Fig. 4 Terrace Plaza Hotel, Skyline Room restaurant, with mural by Saul Steinberg. Photo: Ezra Stoller

174

ture is marvelous training for anything but architecture," Steinberg once commented. "The frightening thought that what you draw may become a building makes for reasoned lines.") His witty and droll drawings—which did not hesitate to poke fun at an overly rationalist and abstract modern architecture, as in the grid-paper-façade buildings he would publish for a special issue of *Architectural Review* titled "Man Made America," published in 1950—were already widely known and had appeared in *The New Yorker* since 1941. Steinberg was especially interested at this period in exploring a wall-size scale for his work, and had recently realized a mural at the Bonwit Teller department store in New York. The execution of the Bonwit's job had been botched by assistants who were hired to transfer the mural to the wall, though, so he elected to carry out the Cincinnati mural by himself. After a preliminary trip to look at the unfinished restaurant space and make sketches, he rented a large studio in New York, where he projected slides onto stretched canvas and laboriously began working on the mural in ten sections. He also extrapolated from postcard views of the city and other picture material. When he finished the sections of the mural, he rolled them up and shipped them to Cincinnati, and then followed to install them, assisted by an artist friend, Costantino Nivola. Admitting that he would have preferred to have worked directly on the wall with "no blueprint" and under less rushed conditions, Steinberg nonetheless pronounced himself pleased with the result.[10]

Twelve floors above, in the more intimately scaled and expensively appointed Gourmet Room, located in a drum of thin-shelled concrete with a sloping glass window-wall cantilevered over the penthouse terrace, was a second mural, by Joan Miró. It occupied a curving 32-foot-long by 7-foot-high expanse behind the diners' banquettes, and featured the Catalan artist's signature abstract forms (fig. 5). Ever since his first major retrospective at the Museum of Modern Art in 1941, as well as through his representation at the prestigious gallery run by Pierre Matisse on New York's 57th Street, Miró's reputation in the United States had been growing. Matisse was acquainted with Emery through his wife Alexina, a native of Cincinnati, and was instrumental in securing the commission for Miró. Philip R. Adams, the recently appointed

Fig. 5 Terrace Plaza Hotel, Gourmet Room restaurant, with mural by Joan Miró. Photo: Ezra Stoller

curator at the Cincinnati Art Museum, seconded the recommendation (while also suggesting Braque and Dufy for the job).[11] By his own admission Emery was not sure how to tell "a good Miró from a bad one," but he willingly allowed himself to be persuaded: "The whole thing is so screwy and modern."[12] In October 1946, Pierre Matisse wrote to Miró in Spain about the potential project, telling him that Emery was "in the process of constructing an immense building in Cincinnati, part of which is reserved for shops and the upper part for a very nice hotel," and noting that "on the terrace will be a very exclusive restaurant, where I suggested to him that a big painting might be installed."[13] Miró, desirous at this date both "to engage in collaborative projects and to integrate his art with the most advanced form of modern civilization"[14] reciprocated Emery and Matisse's enthusiasm about the project. "The mural painting excites me, too bad one can't do a fresco!" he wrote back to his art dealer, adding, "Every mural must be done in view of the surroundings and in close collaboration with the architect."[15] Two months later an agreement was reached, with Matisse telegramming Miró to confirm the fee of $12,000. In February 1947, the artist flew with his family to New York, where he moved in for several months with his emigré compatriot and friend José Luis Sert in the latter's apartment on 59th Street, and set up painting operations in the Harlem studio of the artist Carl Holty. Miró found his first encounter with New York overwhelmingly stimulating, like "a blow to the solar plexus."[16] He was in turn warmly welcomed by the American public, who found his Parisian charm, in Clement Greenberg's words, "the very spirit and embodiment of the Left Bank."[17]

Before commencing work on the mural, Miró traveled to Cincinnati to view the hotel building under construction and make sketches. He was especially struck by a construction photograph taken of the restaurant's circular framing telescoped through the building's skeletal steel grid, and he tacked this image on the wall of his studio alongside an artist's rendering of the hotel for inspiration (fig. 6). Painted without assistants, the mural was completed in time for a temporary exhibition at the Museum of Modern Art in October—arranged through Sert and underwritten by Emery, who was happy to publicize his hotel in New York—before being shipped to Cincinnati. Its playful red, yellow, green, orange, and black

arabesques on a cobalt-blue ground were reminiscent of the figuration in Miró's 1940–41 *Constellation* series, although more simplified. The mural "brilliantly" fulfilled its festive purpose, according to the art critic James Thrall Soby, who visited the studio while the painter was working on it, even if, in Soby's view, it "lack[ed] the profundity of Miró's finest easel pictures" and, as installed in the restaurant, was "arrested at impertinent intervals by supporting columns in front of the wall."[18] From the architects' point of view, it admirably served its role as décor. As William Brown commented retrospectively:

> *We had no other thought than to incorporate some abstract pattern in the room. Although this was to be his first mural [sic], we chose Joan Miró because his work is very colorful and amusing, the right mood for a drinking and dining room…. [Miró] went pretty much along with what we suggested, that the mural should harmonize with the rest of the room…. There is something childlike about his drawings—very good…. Although people make fun of the mural, most of them like it.*[19]

Two other site-specific works were executed for Terrace Plaza. "Twenty Leaves and an Apple," a twelve-foot mobile made of piano wire and sheet-metal cut-outs (fig. 7), was solicited from Alexander Calder in 1946. Although less well documented than the Miró mural, the Calder commission also came through Emery's connection with Pierre Matisse and his association with the Cincinnati Art Museum, which had shown Calder's sculptures in exhibitions in 1942 and 1946. The selection of Calder actually preceded that of Miró, as Emery was more familiar with his work and initially favored using only American artists.[20] In any case, Calder's close personal friendship with Miró, which went back to the late 1920s, and the aesthetic affinities of their work made the juxtaposition of the two artists in the hotel particularly appealing to those involved in the decision. In a project sketch submitted for approval in May 1947, Calder specified that his metal shapes were to be red, yellow, blue, and white (fig. 8). Ultimately, they were all painted black with the exception of one red "apple." The spot-lit mobile was suspended from the ceiling in the reception area of the hotel's lobby. Spirited by the powerful air-conditioning system—one of the building's technical bragging points—it cast con-

Fig. 6 Joan Miró in Carl Holty's studio, New York, with mural for Terrace Plaza Hotel at right. Behind him are preliminary sketch for the mural, a photograph of the hotel under construction, and an artist's rendering. Photo: Arnold Newman

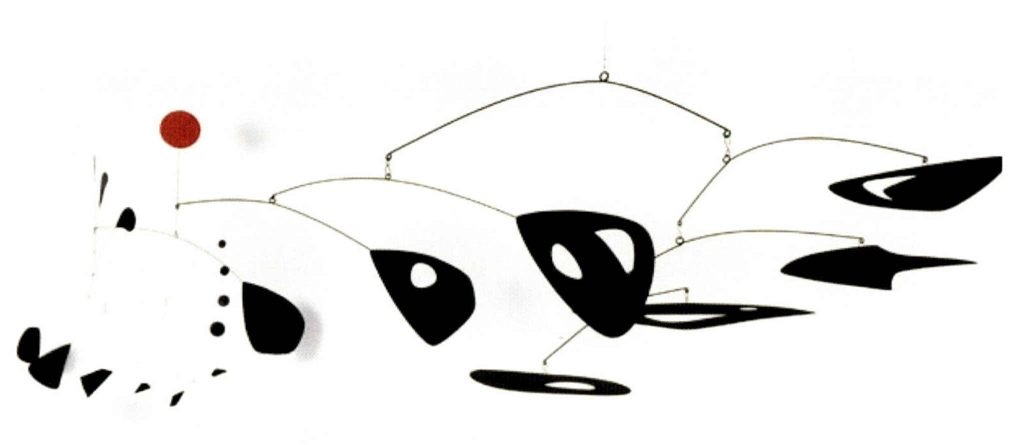

Fig. 7 Terrace Plaza Hotel, with *Twenty Leaves and an Apple* mobile by Alexander Calder hanging in lobby area. Photo: Ezra Stoller

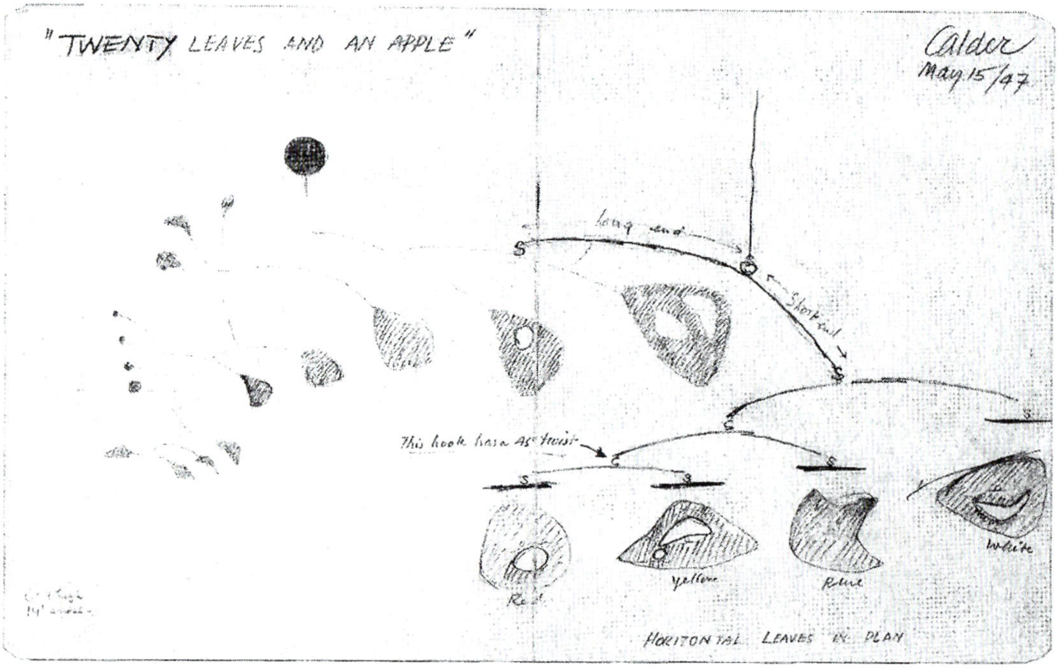

Fig. 8 Alexander Calder, preliminary sketch for *Twenty Leaves and an Apple*, dated May 15, 1947. Cincinnati Art Museum

stantly moving shadows on a white wall across from the elevator bank. Finally, reinforcing the theme of kinetics was a group of plastic light sculptures by the artist James Davis, which floated off the wall behind the bar in the cocktail lounge (fig. 9). Based on experiments with new industrial materials and artificial light, Davis's work bore kinship with that of László Moholy-Nagy at this date. Later Davis would become better known for his kaleidoscopic "flow of energy" films. Classically trained, he was also acquainted with Charles Dana Gibson, Emery's father-in-law, and this may have been the source of the commission.[21]

By all accounts, the citizens of Cincinnati appreciated Emery's gifts of art. If the charming Steinberg mural paid tongue-in-cheek homage to an older form of civic representation, humorously evoking a Better Business Bureau ethos of Fourth of July parades on Main Street and playing to local interest, the other contributions were equally well calibrated. At once contemporary and crowd-pleasing, innovative and free in expression, they helped forge a bond between American business and modern art that would contribute to making modernist aesthetics domi-

nant in the United States in the period ahead, shifting the center of the art world—and the art market—from Europe to America. At the same time, with the emergence of Abstract Expressionism in the late 1940s, the disparities between "hot" and "cold" abstraction, and between high art and mass culture, would become increasingly contentious, especially in the context of the cultural politics of the Cold War, as the heroic and vitalist "new American avant garde" confronted the rigorist geometric abstraction imported from Europe and subsequently the desecrating imagery of Pop.[22] In the immediate postwar moment, however, the work of artists like Miró and Calder proved broadly appealing to a wide spectrum of taste cultures. The painter Ad Reinhardt, who satirized art-world politics from the 1930s to the early 1960s in a series of occasional cartoons for publications like *PM* and *Art News,* included in one of them a lineup of contemporary painters ranging from the most abstract (Piet Mondrian) to the most "social-surrealist" (George Grosz). Miró appeared in the middle, above a cameo of John Q. Public. Published in 1946, this same cartoon by Reinhardt, titled *How to Look at Modern Art in America*

Fig. 9 Terrace Plaza Hotel, Terrace Garden lounge, with light sculptures by James Davis. Photo: Ezra Stoller

Fig. 10 Le Corbusier, *Painting Toward Architecture*, catalogue of The Miller Collection of Abstract Art, 1946, frontispiece spread

(fig. 1), also included a little vignette of two fish labeled "Art" and "Business" swimming in a circle and biting each other's tail.[23]

The artwork at Terrace Plaza also garnered a favorable reception from contemporary architecture critics. An especially enthusiastic admirer was Henry-Russell Hitchcock. He singled out Miró's mural in his introduction to the 1948 catalogue of a traveling exhibition of the art collection of the Miller Company, a lighting equipment corporation based in Meriden, Connecticut, headed by Burton Tremaine, Jr. Tremaine and his future wife, Emily, had launched their collection in 1944 with the prescient acquisition of Mondrian's *Victory Boogie-Woogie*. The Miller catalogue and exhibition, entitled *Painting Toward Architecture,* were intended, according to a statement by Tremaine accompanying the catalogue's frontispiece (a 1925 still-life by Le Corbusier), both to illustrate the influence of abstract twentieth-century art on the development of modern architecture and to showcase abstract painting and sculpture "of potential value to contemporary architects" (fig. 10). "If architects are to utilize the work of painters and sculptors in their buildings," Hitchcock elaborated in his introductory essay, "painting or sculpture that is partially representational, or at least very free in form and color, seems to complement most effectively the geometrical and spacial [*sic*] character of the architecture itself."[24]

Hitchcock would return at greater length to Terrace Plaza and the subject of modern art in architecture in his introduction to the monograph on the work of SOM published in 1963, documenting the previous dozen years of the firm's work:

Especially notable in [SOM's] more luxurious interiors has been the incorporation of works of painting and sculpture, both commissioned items designed for particular situations in lobbies, banking rooms, and restaurants and items bought in quantity to hang on the walls of reception rooms and individual offices. It is not irrelevant that several partners are themselves active and knowledgeable collectors of contemporary art; but so are several other rival architects who have had on the whole considerably less success in converting clients to their own tastes or in persuading them, regardless of personal taste, to spend corporation money on such often controversial extras. But it has been a fortunate circumstance that several of SOM's most important clients, from John Emery of the Terrace Plaza Hotel to Leigh Block of Inland Steel, Jack Heinz of Heinz Research Center, and David Rockefeller of Chase Manhattan, have been themselves avid collectors and hence very ready to collaborate on such programmes. These prominent men have thus enthusiastically set the pace for other clients who might not otherwise have been so readily persuaded in this direction.[25]

In the same passage, Hitchcock went on to compare SOM's success in integrating art with that of other architects:

Where two of the greatest individual architects of the 20th century, Frank Lloyd Wright and Le Corbusier, have characteristically insisted on providing themselves both the landscape settings and the associated art works for their buildings, the SOM partners could hardly do the same, and this has on the whole worked to their advantage. One may properly feel, not merely that Miró is a better painter than Le Corbusier, but that the Miró mural in the circular penthouse restaurant of the Terrace Plaza Hotel in Cincinnati, the first notable instance of SOM's use of commissioned works of art, is a happier instance of collaboration between architect and artist than Le Corbusier's own mural in the Swiss Hostel of 1930–32 in Paris or his painted windows and enameled door in the Ronchamp church of 1950–55. For that matter, the incorporation of Miró's mural in Cincinnati was far more successfully handled than were his contributions to the Harvard Graduate Center in Cambridge by Gropius and TAC or to the Unesco Building in Paris by Breuer, Zehrfuss and Nervi. By commissioning such things as mobiles by Calder, screens by Bertoia and constructions by Lippold to provide focal interest in monumental interiors they have certainly shown in practice a more effective devotion to the ideal of making important use of collaborating painters and sculptors than many architects who have been more vocal on this subject.[26]

In praising SOM, Hitchcock attributes the firm's aptitude in incorporating artwork into its buildings to the sophistication and sensibility of many of its partners and associates. Foremost among those at SOM in this regard was undoubtedly Gordon Bunshaft. Bunshaft would not only put together a distinguished personal collection of art with his wife, Nina, starting in 1954 (with an oil by Miró among their early acquisitions), and subsequently serve on MoMA's board of trustees, as well as the federal Fine Arts Commission, but he even dabbled in painting himself early in his career, producing imitative canvases to which he self-deprecatingly referred as his "Mondrians."[27] The only other American architect whose passion for modern art and art collecting in the postwar period matched Bunshaft's was Philip Johnson; and in suggesting in 1963 that SOM had had a more successful record than other architects in working between artists and clients, it is possible that Hitchcock had in mind the fiasco that occurred a couple years earlier in the case of another restaurant mural. Johnson had engaged Mark Rothko to paint a cycle of murals at the Four Seasons restaurant in the Seagram Building in New York, on which he was collaborating with Mies van der Rohe, and Rothko had notoriously pulled out of the commission, refusing to allow his high-serious work to be used for the frivolous purpose of embellishing an elite eating establishment.[28] Again, the implicit contradictions between "art-as-art" and "lobby art"—between high modernism and corporate public relations—would not come to a head until the 1950s, and Bunshaft, who established close personal and working relationships with artists like Noguchi, Henry Moore, Dubuffet, and others over the course of his career, would prove especially adept in mediating this divide.

Already in his first design for SOM, however—the Venezuela Pavilion at the New York World's Fair of 1939 (fig. 11)—the young Bunshaft had displayed an affinity for art in modern architecture, boldly incorporating a 170-foot-long mural by a Venezuelan artist, Luis Alfredo López Méndez (assisted by Miguel Arroyo). The representational painting was executed on the underside of the building's slab-like canopy, which projected at an angle above the rectangular glass box of the pavilion. With this gesture coupling modern architecture and mural art, Venezuela sought to project a dynamic image of both its modernizing culture and its *bellas artes*, transcending

Fig. 11 Venezuela Pavilion, New York World's Fair, Queens, New York, 1939, with mural by Luis Alfredo López Méndez on underside of canopy

the country's more familiar identification with the national oil industry. While clearly rooted in the social representation of the 1930s and the nationalist politics of world's fairs, this early project by Bunshaft looks forward to the elegant integration of architecture and art in his postwar work.

As far as the more discursive culture of architecture was concerned, what emerged from the war years in both the United States and Europe was an important debate on a theme that came to be known as the New Monumentality. In their "Nine Points on Monumentality," a position statement of 1943 written by three prominent Europeans sitting out the war years in New York, the architectural historian Sigfried Giedion, the architect-planner José Luis Sert, and the painter Fernand Léger called for a grand-scale "synthesis of the arts." Their statement puts forth an idealistic vision of monumental collaborative civic projects to be undertaken in postwar cities by modern architects, painters, and sculptors. Elaborating on the theme a year later in a symposium contribution entitled "The Need for a New Monumentality," Giedion emphasized modern art's potential to infuse the function-

alist-utilitarian language of interwar modern architecture with greater emotional resonance and lyricism. Among the key images Giedion presented in support of his argument for the "new magnitudes" demanded of postwar symbolic representation was a grotesque head painted by Picasso in 1930 as a sketch for a colossal sculpture (fig. 12). Its intended size is indicated by a tiny scale figure in the painting's bottom lefthand corner. In his caption, Giedion notes that the head's yawning mouth and nightmarish features register the horror of war with all the *"terribilità"* of Michelangelo's late sculptures.[29]

The image anticipates Picasso's famous *Guernica,* painted by the artist seven years later for display in Sert and Luis Lacasa's Spanish Pavilion at the 1937 World's Fair in Paris, together with other artworks condemning the Spanish Civil War, among them Miró's mural *El Segador* (The Reaper), depicting an anguished but defiant farmer, and a fountain by Calder protesting Franco's siege of the mercury mines at Almadén. If this charged political and emotional content seems, very literally, a far cry from the Picasso sculpture that would grace the plaza in front of SOM's Chicago Civic Center (now Richard J. Daley Cen-

Fig. 12 Pablo Picasso, *Monument en Bois*, 1930, as published by Sigfried Giedion with his essay "The Need for a New Monumentality" in 1944. Giedion's caption reads in part, "Sketch for a modern sculpture of enormous scale (the human figure at the lower left corner may indicate the approximate dimension).... Its forms have the *terribilità* that—for his contemporaries—emanated from Michelangelo's sculptures. A threatening which Picasso translates in present day language."

Fig. 13 Chicago Civic Center (now Richard J. Daley Center), Chicago, 1967, with sculpture by Picasso in front

tor) in 1967 (fig. 13), it nonetheless has a genealogical relationship with that later exemplar of large-scale public art. Likewise, Giedion, Sert, and Léger's civic ideal of the new monumentality would be radically translated after the war by SOM and its capitalist clients into the skyscrapers and corporate headquarters of the postwar urban landscape.

Arthur C. Keating Hall from the west under the elevated train line. Photo: ESTO

Arthur C. Keating Hall, interior. Photo: ESTO

Myron Goldsmith: Keating Hall at IIT

Nicholas Adams

*Myron Goldsmith (1918–96) was one of the most origi-
nal architects at Skidmore, Owings & Merrill (SOM).
Closely associated with Mies van der Rohe, a recent
study has suggested that he was the source for many
of the theoretical concepts around highrise construction
as practiced at SOM. Certainly, he pursued an original
line. As an architect he was methodical, careful, and
considerate and he produced striking buildings and
projects: the United Airlines Hangar and Wash Hangar,
San Francisco (1956–58), the McMath Solar Telescope
at Kitt Peak (1959–62), the Republic Newspaper Plant,
Columbus, Indiana (1969–71), Ruck-a-Chucky Bridge
project (1978), and many others. The following article
has two goals: to summarize Goldsmith's philosophy of
architecture and show how this philosophy expressed
itself in one of his most intriguing, albeit lesser-known
buildings, Arthur C. Keating Hall, the gymnasium at the
Illinois Institute of Technology. Seemingly a simple glass
box on the outside, the building reveals how Goldsmith
combined the philosophy of a structural architect with a
light, even a delicate touch.*

Myron Goldsmith

Arthur C. Keating Hall from the east, main entrance. Photo: ESTO

Though he designed buildings that depend thoroughly on modern engineering techniques, Myron Goldsmith was in many respects a very traditional architect.[1] As he wrote in 1987, he was not wed to a particular building system or constructional technique, but "part of the long historical tradition of structural architecture…a complex realm of the art of building in which architecture, engineering, and aesthetics interact to make structure the central expressive element of design." Among Marcus Vitruvius's descriptive triumvirate *firmitas*, *utilitas*, and *venustas*, Goldsmith gave priority to *firmitas* because he believed that "structure, once determined, contains within itself the promise of commodity and delight."[2] Servant to a greater idea, linked by a historical chain of previous solutions to the problem of structural architecture, knowing that "he must inevitably be judged by the standards of the past," he produced work with a rigor matched by few architects in the twentieth century. In Goldsmith's work there is no switch in direction, no shift from one position to another; only one big idea, structural architecture, refined and purified, redefined and reconsidered in the light of each new architectural challenge.[3]

Born and raised in Chicago, Goldsmith received degrees from the Illinois Institute of Technology (IIT) in Chicago (BS, 1939; MS, 1953). He served in the United States Corps of Engineers (1944–46) and then worked in the office of Mies van der Rohe (1946–53). In 1953 he received a Fulbright grant that enabled him to spend two years in Italy (1953–55) studying with Pier Luigi Nervi. On his return he joined Skidmore, Owings & Merrill, first in San Francisco (1955–58), where he lamented the risks of "being a structural engineer in a high seismic risk zone," and then in his native Chicago (1958–83) where he became a design partner in 1967. Appointed to the graduate teaching faculty at IIT in 1961 he also directed a series of important graduate theses that further explored the nature of structural architecture.

Goldsmith's name is often linked to Mies van der Rohe. He was an undergraduate when Mies arrived at IIT in 1938. He later worked in Mies' office, most notably on the Farnsworth House (1946–53). At SOM he used many devices, formal and structural that recall the buildings of Mies. His two Indiana newspaper plants, *Franklin Journal* (Franklin, Indiana, 1963–65) and *The Republic* (Columbus, Indiana, 1969–71), with their simple steel supports recall Mies's spare industrial American buildings. The exposed steel support beams on the Inland Steel Research Laboratories (East Chicago, Indiana, 1966–68) are equally Miesian. When called on to design additional buildings for the Mies-designed IIT campus, Goldsmith built structures that are all but indistinguishable from those of his teacher (Engineering 1 Building, 1966–68; Life Sciences Building, 1966–68; Stuart Building, 1969–71).[4] Yet the formal character of Mies' architecture neither frames his importance to Goldsmith nor adequately explains Goldsmith's own work. Mies inducted Goldsmith into the fellowship of structural architecture; Mies was among the twentieth century's most prominent practitioners of structural architecture; and both he and Goldsmith were followers of the principles of structural architecture. Thus, when Goldsmith explained the McMath Solar Observatory at Kitt Peak (1959–62), a work looking quite unlike anything designed by Mies, he called it "very Miesian, trying to make architecture out of the fact, the plan, the planning limitations, the limitations of normal structures. . . . "[5] In Goldsmith's narrative account of the history of structural architecture, Mies was one link in a chain that began with the Gothic and traditional Japanese architecture, included nineteenth-century iron and steel architecture and engineering, and ultimately, the work of Robert Maillart and Pier Luigi Nervi.[6] In fact, Goldsmith came to conclusions about the interaction of structure and form—"that complex realm of the art of building," as he called it—which demonstrated an experimental approach to structure that differed from Mies. Mies remained focused on the idealized wide-flange steel structural beam, commonly called the I-beam, as a representative symbol of modern structure and as the dominant structural form of the age. By contrast, Goldsmith sought to express structure, sometimes using Mies's I-beam, but sometimes not. Kitt Peak seeks "to make architecture out of the fact," but does not isolate or idealize "the fact"; its symbolic achievement of Kitt Peak is as a whole structure and its spatial environment rather than at the level of the individual structural element. In that respect, Goldsmith was as much a follower of Nervi as Mies: like Nervi, the individual structural component registers less.

Goldsmith lived along the boundary of engineering and architecture. Although he took the licensing exam to be-

Republic Newspaper Plant (Columbus, Indiana, 1969–71). Photo: ESTO

United Airlines Hangar (San Francisco, 1956–58). Photo: ESTO

McMath Solar Telescope at Kitt Peak (1959–62)

come a professional engineer in 1943, his degree from IIT was in architecture and he considered himself an architect. Travels with Goldsmith always included site-seeing great works of engineering. His master's thesis, "The Tall Building: The Effects of Scale" (1953) focused on a tall concrete skyscraper with an exoskeleton, yet the broader significance of the study lay in its theoretical analysis. Using sources from Galileo to Sir D'Arcy Wentworth Thompson, Goldsmith provided a model for thinking about change in structural engineering, specifying (against practices of the day rooted in the Chicago skeleton) that as the scale of structure increased the structural system must change. The thesis was optimistic and open-ended, typical of postwar thinking about architecture: there may be natural limits to structure, natural points of culmination, but they will of necessity be rethought or reconceptualized when the time comes. Mies had identified steel and concrete as the structural materials of the epoch: simple steel plates, channels, and L-shapes, and the I-beam formed the Miesian grammar; Goldsmith claimed only that structure would have to change to meet new requirements; it is an operative theory, pragmatic stance.[7]

The Fulbright grant in 1953 allowed Goldsmith to leave the office of Mies van der Rohe, live in Italy and work with Pier Luigi Nervi. When he returned to the United States he did not return to Mies' office as he might have done (and as Mies probably expected), but rather, on the invitation of William Dunlap, to take a position as a structural engineer with SOM in San Francisco. There he designed the monumental United Airlines Hangars at the San Francisco Airport (1956–58). Later he joked about the problem of being a structural engineer in a seismic zone, but it seems possible he thought that, like Nervi, he could practice architecture as an engineer. What prevented the realization of that plan is not known. Did he recoil from the responsibility, as the joke suggests? Was the professional division in America such that he could not maintain design control without the status of designer?[8]

In any case, when he moved to Chicago in 1958, he moved to the architectural design department at SOM and never practiced exclusively as an engineer. Chicago's own structural tradition and the environment of SOM provided sufficient opportunity in which to prac-tice structural architecture as an architect. Chicago also provided the environment for experimentation.

In 1961 Goldsmith returned to IIT as a thesis adviser in the Graduate School of Architecture. IIT was more than just a convenient outlet for an architect consumed with day-to-day problems but a place for Goldsmith to explore his ideas about structural architecture. Regular class meetings with graduate students were held on Saturday mornings (still the practice at IIT as it is the day that working professionals can be present) and other faculty, SOM engineers, and special friends would come to these sessions. The debate was lively, amicable, and often concluded with more discussion over a long lunch at a local restaurant. Each master's thesis, developed over two years or more, culminated in a single building project elaborating the connection between architecture, engineering, and aesthetics. Thesis topics generally involved the development of building type on an unspecified site: an open-plan school, a tall office building in a seismic zone,[9] a sports center. In some instances these theses became the basis for a building at SOM; at other times they remained exercises in building technology. Importantly they elaborated the critical possibilities of a structural architecture, as their inclusion in Goldsmith's edition of his major works makes clear.[10]

Although Goldsmith worked on many different types of building at SOM (from tall towers to train stations) over time he developed specializations. There are, for example, the two newspaper plants, four telescopes (the 60 inches Solar Telescope and the 150 feet Stellar Telescope, Kitt Peak, 1962 and 1972; the Lindheimer Astronomical Research Center at Northwestern, 1967; Cerro Tololo north of Santiago, Chile, 1971). Sports facilities formed another specialization. While with SOM in San Francisco, Goldsmith prepared a thin-shelled, clear-span skating facility for the Winter Olympics in Squaw Valley (planning, 1956; design work 1957). Post-dating thin-shelled concrete structures such as Minoru Yamasaki's Lambert Field Airport, St. Louis (1951–56) and predating Eero Saarinen's TWA Terminal (1956–62), had it been built, it would have represented a significant penetration of Nervi's influence in the United States.[11] Thereafter Goldsmith built two major sports facilities on the west coast, the Portland Coliseum (1959–61) and the Oakland Coliseum (1964–68), the latter a pair of gigantic circular concrete bowls, one for basketball and hockey with a striking suspended ribbed roof structure, the other open to the sky for baseball.[12] In roughly the same years Goldsmith directed two masters' theses dealing with sports facilities: Emmanuel Glyniadakis, "A Sports Center" (1964); Peter Doyle, "A Sports Arena" (1965). Overseen by Goldsmith, Fazlur Khan, and David Sharpe, Doyle's design, though original in form, has some of the characteristics of the Oakland Coliseum, notably its use of cables shielded by concrete to support the roof. Glyniadakis's thesis was for a monumental universal space public sports facility. Over 810 square feet in plan, the building would have included an arena (13,000 spectators), a track and field area (2000 spectators), a swimming pool (2000 spectators), and a fourth flexible arena for other sports. Surmounted by a two-way grid roof structure of 17-foot deep steel girder spaced 45 feet apart, it is a dauntingly monumental work, but despite the difference in scale it calls to mind another SOM athletic facility from the same period, Arthur Keating Hall at the Illinois Institute of Technology.[13]

Arthur Keating Hall (1965–68) was built in that slightly awkward period after SOM had replaced Mies van der Rohe as the campus architect at IIT. Walter Netsch had already built the Paul V. Galvin Library (1962) and the Grover M. Hermann Hall (1962), buildings that aroused a great deal of ire for responding so independently to the original campus. Arthur Keating Hall came at a critical time, both for the campus and for Goldsmith. Though the typology was novel, Goldsmith sought to erase the impression of indifference to Mies's plans left by Netsch.[14]

In siting Keating Hall, alternative plans show that the original idea was to empty the entire block bounded by 30th and 29th Streets, South Wabash Avenue, and South State Street, and build a gymnasium, apartment-style dormitories, and playing fields. Plans for the sports fields advanced to point of a perspective proposal for an entry pavilion, grandstands, and custom-designed chain link fencing. Community opposition, notably from the Mount Carmel Baptist Church at the north side of the lot considerably reduced the land available and IIT narrowed the scope of the program to the gymnasium as the final perspective plan shows. Sports fields occupied the remainder of the available lot.

The program for the gymnasium required facilities for basketball, tennis, a swimming pool, squash courts, and a training room. Moveable grandstands allowed both tennis and basketball to be spectator sports; public viewing stands for swimming were also available. Over the fall and winter of 1964–65 design work proceeded with the development of different functional options: stacked within an expressive box or stacked under a single universal space. By March 1965, Michael Pado, Goldsmith's senior designer noted "all design efforts will be directed toward the "compact scheme" for the gym" as issues of exterior articulation dominated the design team.[15] The alternatives, sketched by Pado and discussed with Goldsmith show that the team was assiduously working to eliminate breaks in the surface plane and vertical projections as they developed alternative systems to accommodate the program. At the same time, they worked to

Emmanuel Glyniadakis, "A Sports Center" (1964), photograph of the model Both are from Myron Goldsmith, *Buildings and Concepts*, pp. 156, 153.

Peter Doyle, "A Sports Arena," Masters Thesis, 1965, model photo

Keating Hall, alternative site plan proposals, November 1964 (Skidmore, Owings & Merrill, LLP, Chicago, IL. Drawings, Tube 1966A)

perfect the internal support system. Although the athletic department expressed concern about placing a gymnasium over the pool, the organizational *parti* held firm with basketball and tennis above; swimming, training room, and squash courts below.[16] Service functions migrated to the sub-basement. As this "compact scheme" came together Goldsmith and Pado established the size of the building at 72,800 square feet (ultimately reduced to 68,300) divided into three levels: seating capacity for basketball (2000), tennis (270), swimming (300), and squash and handball (100).[17] The basic grid was 6 feet square with windows six feet long and three feet eight inches high. The roof consisted of exposed steel plate girders 110 feet long, spaced at thirty-foot intervals, with roughly thirty feet from floor to ceiling (floor to beam = thirty-six feet and three inches; floor to the top of the window = thirty-three feet). Piers supporting the beams on the east and west side also serve to carry heating and water pipes, exposed at the ceiling line as they wiggle up past the beams.

The greatest controversy concerned the proposal to use floor-to-ceiling glass for the walls. "There was," wrote

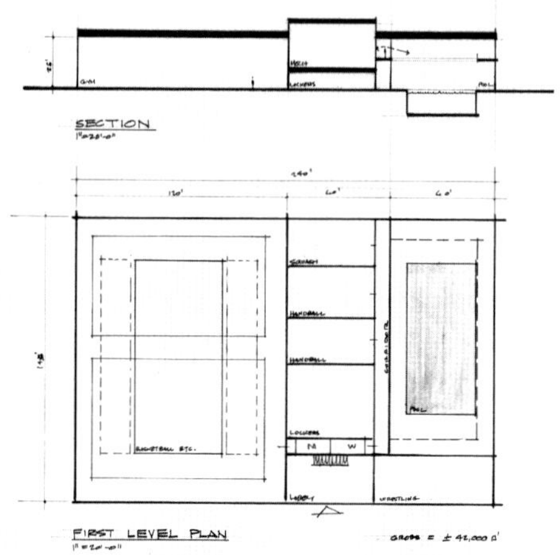

Keating Hall, stacked solution, winter 1964 (Skidmore, Owings & Merrill, LLP, Chicago, IL. Drawings, Tube 1966B)

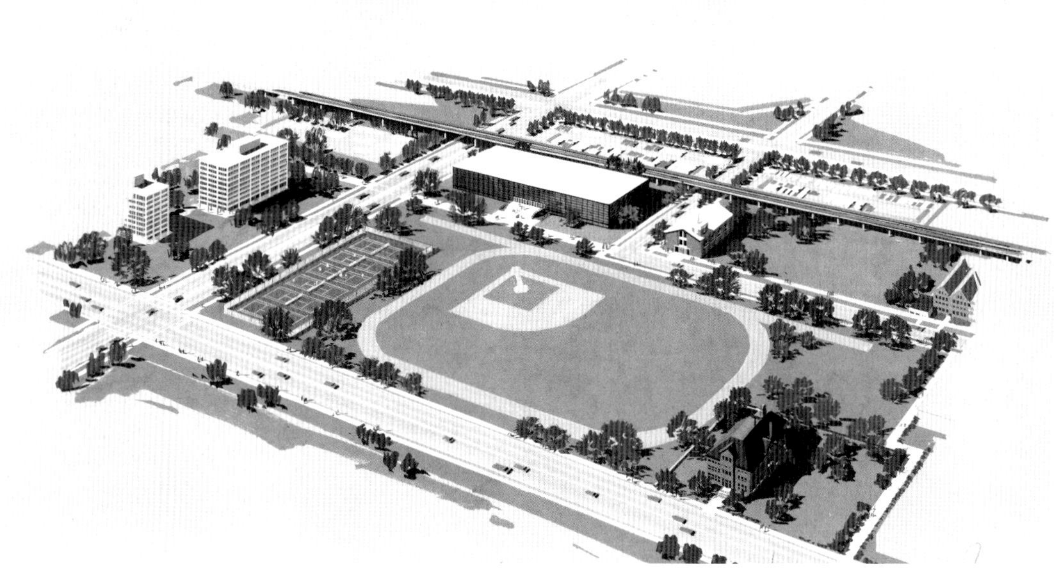

Keating Hall, aerial view (Skidmore, Owings & Merrill, LLP, Chicago, IL. Drawings, Tube 1966A)

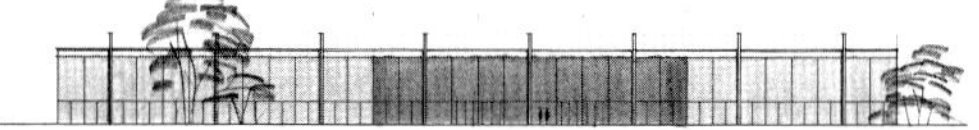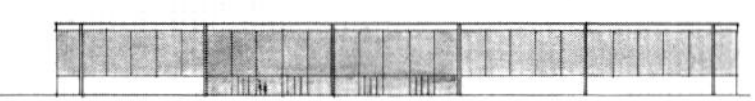

Keating Hall, studies of the exterior, spring 1965 (Michael Pado, Chicago, IL, designer, Skidmore, Owings & Merrill, LLP, Chicago, IL. Drawings, Tube 1966B)

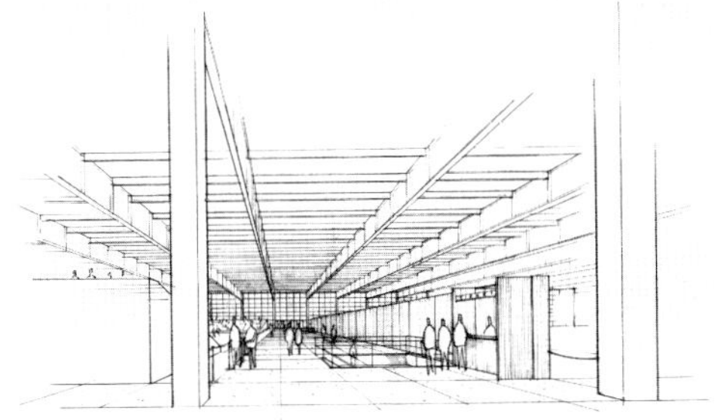

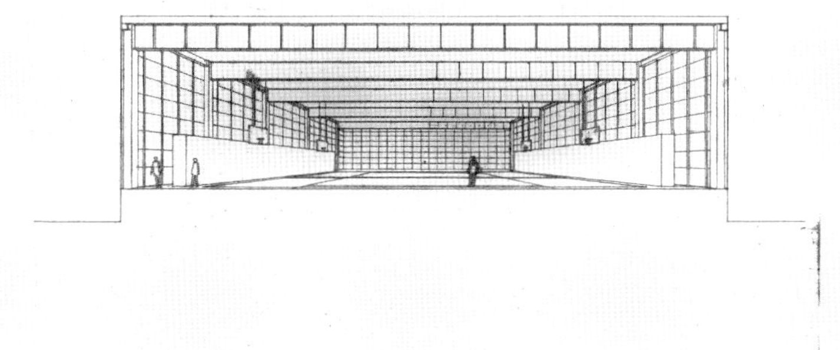

Keating Hall, studies of the interior, spring 1965 Skidmore, Owings & Merrill, LLP, Chicago, IL. Drawings, Tube 1966E)

Keating Hall, view of the Ekco Pool (basement level) and gymnasium floor. Photo: ESTO

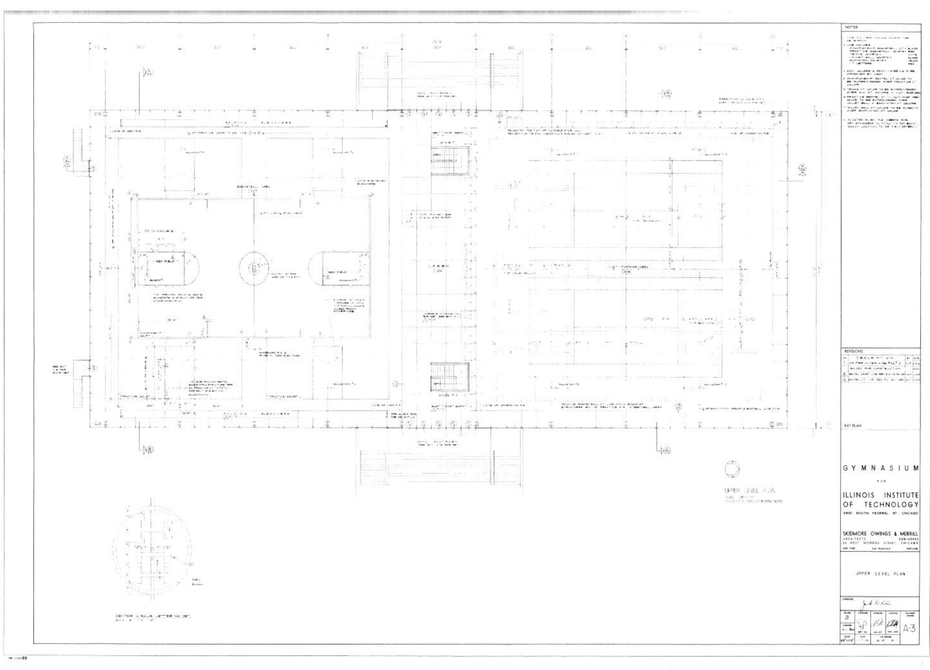

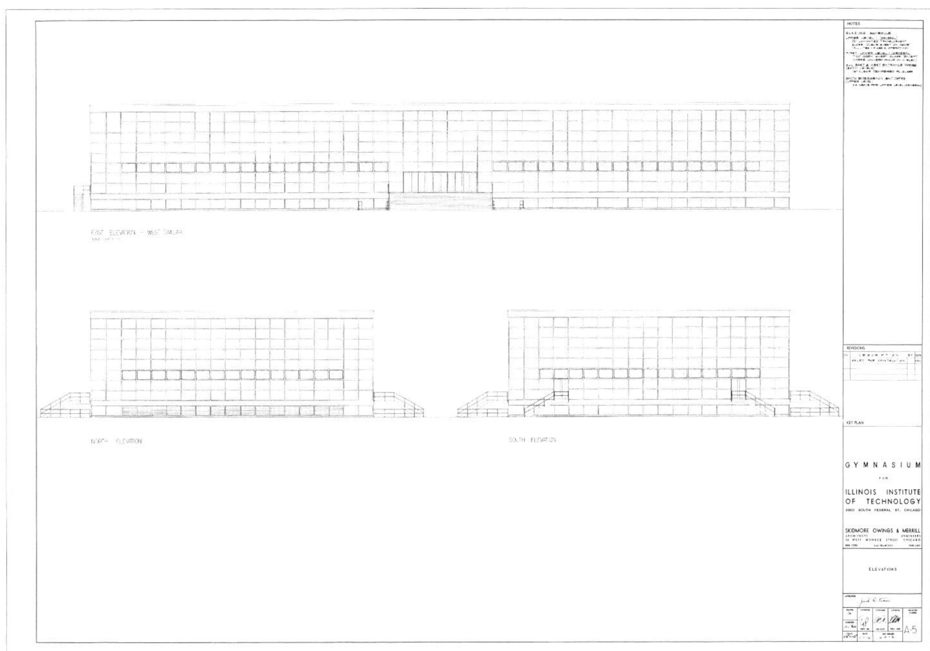

Keating Hall, main level floor plan; exterior elevations Skidmore, Owings & Merrill, LLP, Chicago, IL. Drawings

R. J. Spaeth, IIT's vice president and treasurer to SOM, "no agreement on the part of the institute that the walls of this building should be of glass. Whether they are of glass or nor will depend entirely upon providing a satisfactory solution to the program discussed at the meeting.… In my own thinking at this point, glass is not a satisfactory wall, and until we have a solution to the problem glass presents we can make no decision as to these exterior walls."[18] A sketch from May 1965, possibly developed for presentation to the client, explains the nature of the wall. To answer the client's concerns, SOM worked with Pittsburgh Plate Glass to create a glass sandwich consisting of $^{1}/_{32}$ of an inch thick Pennvernon Graylite "56" glass and $^{1}/_{32}$ of an inch heavy sheet of "A" quality Pittsburgh plate glass. Between the two sheets the fabricators inserted a fifteen-gauge polyvinyl butryal interlayer with sixty-four percent light transmission.[19] To test the glass the architect set up a mock-up panel in Crown Hall and the architects threw baseballs and basketballs at it.[20] Over the summer of 1965 Goldsmith and the clients made the final decisions about the articulation and SOM completed the model and presentation drawing and offered them to the donor for study. By August definitive design drawings had been prepared.[21] At a press conference in October 1965 the president of IIT, J. T. Rettaliata introduced the donor, Arthur Keating, president of Ekco Products Co. and the "king of the U.S. kitchenware business."[22] His bust, on a plinth designed by SOM, was initially located in the upstairs entry lobby. On Keating's request the pool was to be named for Ekco, the company's name composed from his father's initials: Edward Katzinger.

Keating Hall has something in common with Crown Hall. Set over a half-floor basement, the building is a simple glass and steel box. The articulation of the framing piers and the floor level articulation at Crown have been eliminated: the comparatively humble business of a gymnasium requires only a low-relief gridded box relieved by the nine-portal entrance and monumental staircase. Whereas at Crown Hall only the lower level of the main floor is translucent, at Keating Hall gray translucent glass runs consistently from floor to ceiling.[23] Warm gray translucent glass thus became the defining characteristic, muting the exterior light, creating a calm, ordered interior in which the open space of the gymnasium is contained by the gray walls—providing public open

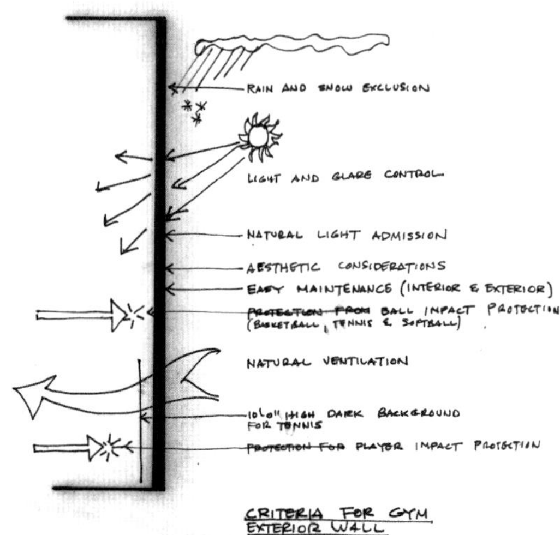

Crown Hall Exterior Wall Section

space for the athletes and shielding them from the campus. At the north and south ends of the gymnasium, without the support piers that rest under the beam ends on east and west, the walls recall the delicate effects of a *shoji* screen, the wall like a light scrim. Fixed elements, for example, the right-angled water fountain, stand out against the glass; the athletes seem like ballet dancers on the polished floor, floating against a *sfumato* wall. The building sustains an astonishing ambivalence: a rigidly modernist box with a slightly blurred sense of luminescent space recalling the effects of Giorgio Morandi, one of Goldsmith's favorite painters.

Although Keating Hall draws on Mies van der Rohe's formal arsenal—the stair railings leading down to the lower level basement are identical to those in Crown Hall (and elsewhere on the IIT campus)—trussed ceiling universal spaces had already been developed by SOM. At the Great Lakes Naval Station, Bruce Graham and William Priestley had designed and built a completely glazed trussed roof box to house the Gunner's Mate School (1954). Comparatively simple in form with strengthened beams to articulate the curtain walls, the glass is clear, making the interior effect more like an airplane hanger or a factory.[24] Gymnasia with glazed walls could also have been a model. Sanza Architects built a trussed beam ceiled gymnasium in Osaka (1957) that

Keating Hall, glass panel as set up in Crown Hall for testing, 1965. Photo: Michael Pado

Keating Hall, Exterior night time view. Photo: ESTO

Keating Hall, Interior view. Photo: Michael Pado

Keating Hall, interior detail of the drinking foundation. Photo: Michael Pado

Keating Hall, stairs to the basement level. Photo: ESTO

has much in common with Keating Hall: both deriving from the long-beam spaces of Mies.[25] But the relation with Mies and the comparison with the Osaka gymnasium also underline Goldsmith's ability to modulate the stricter virtues of a structural architecture. In the United Hangars in San Francisco, the beams are lithe, expanding at the moment points to express the role that weight plays; in the Oakland Coliseum, the ceiling ribs form an iconic pattern creating a great concrete tent over the heads of the spectators recalling Nervi's Palazzetto dello Sport (1958–60); at *The Republic* newspaper plant the pavilion is detailed with authoritative clarity but scaled (and colored) to be a humane and surprisingly warm presence on the street. And Goldsmith had seen the implications of a clear glass large-scale *palaestra* in the thesis of Glyniadakis. Thus the changes—the floor-to-ceiling gray glass, the logical variation from side to end in the handling of the beams, the sleek exterior skin, even the elevation over a half basement—all represent refinements to ideas that had been developed in other circumstances to different solutions. Crown Hall, though the program was entirely different, also offered guidance. Here, indeed, was the strength of the structural architect for whom no problem is unique, for whom each new solution truly belongs to a linked series of former solutions.[26] Here, too, are Goldsmith's strengths. Having determined the appropriate form of structure he had a delicate touch when it came to color, materials, and texture. Keating may have its problems as a gymnasium, as some of the recent renovations reveal, but the building confirms the principles of structural architecture in the right hands. And Keating found enthusiasts. "I expressed my feeling about the new gym," John Hejduk, a comrade from the early days in Italy wrote to Goldsmith, in October 1969: "It is nice to see a friend produce what I consider a master work. I think it extremely important that our students here at Cooper [Union] see a complete set of working drawings on that particular building. You had indicated that you would send us a set. Would you send us a set as soon possible?"[27]

Arthur Keating Hall provides an imaginative structural and aesthetic solution for a gymnasium in an educational institution turning the transparent modernist box into a translucent container. It provides a liberating space without exposing or revealing the visitor. Warm in tone and highly rational it also responds sympathetically to Mies van der Rohe's campus plan and structural patterns. Anticipating the character of works such as Herzog & de Meuron's Sammlung Goetz, Munich (1992), Steven Holl's Nelson-Atkins Museum addition in Kansas City (2007), or the experimental glass screens of James Carpenter (Rochofsky Screen, 1994–96; Light Tunnel, German Foreign Ministry, Berlin, 1998–2003). Goldsmith demonstrated some forty years ago modernism could occupy a range of emotional territories. In *Aesthetics and Technology of Building*, Pier Luigi Nervi uses words that might have been spoken of Keating Hall: "One can say that despite an abundance of impersonal technical solutions, correct building entails that warmth of human intuition and sensibility which characterized the structural architecture of the past."[28]

1 I am grateful for conversations and correspondence about Myron Goldsmith with William Baker (December 7, 2007) and John Zils (December 20, 2007), Skidmore, Owings & Merrill. Michael J. Pado generously shared his archive of materials related to Keating Hall with me (December 21, 2007). His photographs grace this article. Edward Windhorst provided an attentive and critical reading and I have tried to respond to his sharp observations. Barbara Muller provided careful editorial suggestions for which I am extremely grateful. Robin and Chandra Goldsmith met my awkward queries with generous recollections and helpful insight. Thanks also to Karen Widi for help in examining the files related to Keating Hall at Skidmore, Owings & Merrill in Chicago. Sarah Goldstein at Vassar College provided technical help in the processing of images. Francesco Dal Co proposed Keating Hall as the subject of study; I am very grateful to him.

2 Myron Goldsmith, "Structural Architecture," Werner Blaser, ed., *Myron Goldsmith: Buildings and Concepts* (New York, 1987), p. 24. Of this statement he commented: "To fulfill that promise, in structures of our own time, has been my chief purpose as an architect."

3 Thus, for example, in a lecture at the RIBA in 1966 Goldsmith noted: "If I have a vision of architecture, it is that the majority of buildings should be a structural solution." "RIBA Annual Discourse," *Royal Institute of British Architects Journal* (June 1966), pp. 252–57. (In underlining Goldsmith's connection to structural architecture I do not mean to imply that he did not consider other factors in design to be important.)

4 Franz Schulze notes Mies subdivides the windows in works such as Pearlstein Hall; by contrast Goldsmith leaves the windows undivided. See Franz Schulze, *Illinois Institute of Technology: The Campus Guide, An Architectural Tour* (New York, 2005), p. 64

5 *Oral History of Myron Goldsmith*, interview by Betty J. Blum, Chicago Architects Oral History Project (Chicago, 2001), p. 87

6 Colleagues and friends remember that Goldsmith rarely, if ever, spontaneously cited Mies van der Rohe as an authority. This reticence to speak of his teacher is in contrast to the *Oral History*. Similarly the collection of material donated by Goldsmith to the Canadian Centre for Architecture, Montréal privileges his connections with Mies van der Rohe at the expense of his work for SOM. See *Myron Goldsmith: Poet of Structure* (Montréal, 1991).

7 The thesis was a text—like structural architecture itself—that he continued to revise on and off for the next thirty-five years. See Goldsmith, "The Effects of Scale," in Blaser 1987, pp. 8–22. Colleagues recall that his lectures consisted of the same slides played over and over; that when one was lost he simply dropped it from the schedule.

8 Goldsmith's own thoughts as recorded in his oral history ties the departure of William Dunlap to SOM Chicago and the arrival of Charles Bassett in San Francisco. "Chicago was the direction I wanted to go. I also wanted to leave structural engineering…." And a little later: "I decided the thing I wanted to work with most was on the aesthetic problems of structure, engineering, architecture and aesthetics. I didn't want the narrow responsibility of the technical responsibility for something." *Oral History of Myron Goldsmith*, p. 95.

9 Among the theses directed by Goldsmith are: an open-plan school with walls of precast panels (Ali Afshar, 1973); a tall office building (Mikio Sasaki, 1962); an office building (Jin H. Kim, 1963); a sports center (Emmanuel Glyniadakis, 1964); a sports arena (Peter Doyle, 1965); a harbor study for Lake Calumet (Paul A. Zorr, 1967); an ultra high-rise concrete office building (Robin Hodgkison, 1968); a railway station for Chicago (Lawrence Kenny, 1968); an office building using a long span tube structure (Wayne Petrie, 1981); a cable-stayed bridge (Bankimkumar Mehta, 1982); A technical high school for Algiers (Mohammed Yala, 1984); a 142-story steel K-braced multi-use building (Kay Elizabeth Vierk, 1986). All theses had multiple advisers including Ray Clark, Mahjoub Elnimeiri, Fazlur Khan, T.Y. Lin, David Sharpe.

10 Blaser, 1987, pp. 147-83. I can think of no other architect who so prominently included "student work" in his or her own self-presentation.

11 Nathaniel A. Owings, *The Spaces in Between: An Architect's Journey* (Boston, 1973), quotations from pp. 265–66.

12 Allan Temko, "Portland's Great Hall of Glass." *Architectural Forum* 114 (April 1961), pp. 108–11, 181; "An elegant sports and recreation center," *Architectural Record*, 143 (June 1968), pp. 121–28

13 Goldsmith is listed as design partner; Kenneth Mullin was the project manager; Senior Designer was Michael J. Pado. Design assistants included David Wild and Paul B. Marxen (1912–2007). The structural engineer was Y. E. Yamamoto. Construction: A. J. Maggio and Company.

14 In discussing how his buildings related to Mies, Goldsmith's comment in his oral history is telling: "The question was whether to do it in the same constructive way but change it somewhat. You might use the black steel and the same brick, but you might find a different solution. I thought about it for a while and even probably made some sketches on what could be done. I decided to stay with the old appearance of things, the old system, for a couple of reasons: I seemed not to have been able to come up with anything better or as good; and the other thing was that we had no guarantee that after doing a building we would be invited back to do another, that they wouldn't go to another architect. It was a building-by-building agreement, one at a time. I felt that once you broke down the discipline of the campus, the look of it, and opened it up to something different, then some future architect, not us, would feel absolutely free to do anything." *Oral History of Myron Goldsmith*, p. 119. Goldsmith's sense of horror, however, was reserved for the possibility that "you would get some concrete buildings in the academic part" of the campus. (p. 120)

15 Memorandum from Michael Pado to Jack Train, Myron Goldsmith and others, March 11, 1965. Skidmore, Owings & Merrill, LLP, Chicago, IL. Correspondence Files, microfilm roll 37. Hereafter SOM, Correspondence Files, 37.

16 Letter from R. J. Spaeth, vice president and treasurer to John Schruben, Skidmore, Owings Merrill, March 22, 1965. (Schruben worked in management and was responsible for helping develop computer programs at SOM.) SOM, Correspondence Files, 37.

17 IIT Gymnasium Preliminary Study, March 19, 1965. SOM, Correspondence Files, 37.

18 Letter from R.J. Spaeth to Kenneth R. Mullin, project manager, Skidmore, Owings & Merrill, May 21, 1965. SOM, Correspondence Files, 37.

19 Skidmore, Owings & Merrill, Chicago, Keating Hall, Tube 249.

20 According to Michael Pado the first mock-up failed and the thickness of glass had to be increased by 1/8th inch.

21 Letter of Arthur Keating to J. T. Rettaliata, president of IIT, June 15, 1965; letter of R. J. Spaeth, vice president and treasurer to Kenneth R. Mullin, Skidmore, Owings & Merrill, August 17, 1965. SOM, Correspondence Files, 37.

22 Arthur Keating (1894–1967) was the son of a tinsmith, Edward Katzinger, an Austrian immigrant to the United States. Katzinger moved to Chicago and opened a factory to make tin pans for bakeries and confectionaries, Edward Katzinger Inc. Arthur (Katzinger) Keating attended Armour Institute of Technology and graduated with a degree in mechanical engineering in 1916. A twelve-letter athlete and captain of the football, basketball, and track teams, he took over the family business and, with the help of his father and through shrewd world-wide acquisitions converted it to the world's largest manufacturer of non-electric houseware products: pots, pans, vegetable peelers, cutlery. On the death of his father in 1939 Arthur Katzinger changed his name to Keating and took the company public as Ekco Products Company. (The name of the company formed from the initials for Edward Katzinger.) The donation to IIT for the Arthur Keating Hall coincides with the sale of Ekco to American Home Products Inc. in 1965 for $145

million in stock. Keating died two years later. Keating seems not to have had a strong interest in design. Ekco products, generally, speaking have a reputation for sturdy functionality: few are the Americans who have not held an Ekco vegetable peeler in their hand! Ekco employed Raymond Loewy for some design work, but I have not found testimony of his special engagement in art or architecture. (Sources of information: *New York Times*, Obituary, December 13, 1967; www.fundinguniverse.com; Raymond Loewy Archives at the Hagley Museum and Library, Wilmington, Delaware.) See, Proposed Agenda and Participants for Announcement of the Arthur Keating Gift," press release from the Illinois Institute of Technology. See also "Arthur Keating Hall is Newest Project at IIT," *IIT Reports* 5:2 (October 1965), p. 1

23 Ironically restoration problems at Crown Hall in 1975 required the replacement of the original fragile 1/4th inch sandblasted glass used at Crown Hall. In 1981 the sandblasted glass was replaced at 860–880 Lake Shore Drive. At both locations Michael Pado used the same laminated glass type from Keating Hall. The result is that today there is greater visual similarity between the three buildings than originally. (Information from Michael J. Pado who also pointed out that laminated glass also provides excellent soundproofing. This feature enabled IIT to use Keating Hall for rock concerts without bothering the neighborhood.)

24 The Gunner's Mate Building is currently under threat of demolition, see Blair Kamin, "Why the Navy Should Act to Save This 'Box': Building 521 Priceless Relic of Naval, Chicago History," *Chicago Tribune*, February 3, 2008.

25 "A Gymnasium; flat roof truss supported by four columns," *Kenchiku bunka* 12/7 (1957), pp. 5–8.

26 In that respect the structural architect is a prime example of ideas elaborated by George Kubler whose book, *The Shape of Time: Remarks on the History of Things* (New Haven, 1962) was published at this time.

27 John Hejduk to Myron Goldsmith, October 10, 1969, SOM, Correspondence Files, 37.

28 Pier Luigi Nervi, *Aesthetics and Technology in Building* (Cambridge, MA, 1966), p. 8. (The translation probably uses the false phrase "reassumes," as a translation of the common Italian verb "reassumere." A better translation is "summarizes" or, as given here, "entails.")

Approach view from the gate and driveway. Photo: Heikki Havas (Alvar Aalto Museum)

North facade with the main entrance and the hallway behind. Photo: Heikki Havas (Alvar Aalto Museum, AAA 101817)

Maison Louis Carré

To guarantee the independence of the Jury of the *SOM Journal,* the Editorial Board, consisting of persons not related with SOM, appoints the Jury and selects an architecturally significant setting outside of the United States as the meeting place of the Jury. After having considered several alternatives, the Editorial Board of *Journal 5* selected the residence of the famous French art dealer and collector Louis Carré (1897–1977), outside of Paris, designed by Alvar Aalto (1898–1976) in 1956–59, as the venue.

The Maison Louis Carré is one of Alvar Aalto's most important and refined residential designs, along with the Aalto House in Helsinki (1935–36) and the Villa Mairea in Noormarkku (1938–39). It is also one of Aalto's complete works of art for which he designed a number of special pieces of furniture light fixtures, and fittings.

In 1955, Louis Carré purchased a four hectare farmland plot in Bazoches-sur-Guyonne, some forty kilometers, southwest of Paris, opposite the estate of his friend Jean Monet, the founder of the European Union. He first planned to commission Le Corbusier with whom he was well acquainted, but he became critical of Le Corbusier's preference for concrete. After visiting the Villa Mairea and other buildings in Finland by Alvar Aalto, in 1956, Louis Carré chose the Finnish architect, whom he had met first at the Venice Biennale earlier that year.

The site, located on the border of the Rambouillet forest between Versailles and Chartres, slopes gently towards south and west. Mr. Carré did not want a house with a flat roof, and Aalto agreed on a sloped roof that would blend with the features of the landscape and terrain. The single roof of blue slate from Normandy integrates the composition of volumes, surfaces, and materials. Typical for Aalto, the house, garage, swimming pool, and pool house, and the asymmetrically stepped terrain and tiny amphitheatre motif, create a complete architectural microcosm. The atmosphere of an enclosed world is reinforced today by the fact that full-grown trees cut off the original distant views of the French countryside.

To satisfy Mr. Carré's desire for elegant materials that would age well, Aalto chose limestone from Chartres, limewashed bricks for the walls, teak and ash wood to articulate the façade openings, and copper for the gutters, edges of walls, lamps, and exterior columns.

The house is approached through a gate up a winding road that reveals the house only at the top of the rise. The main entrance is situated on the north side of the house, living areas and bedrooms on the west and south, kitchen and service areas on the east, and servants' bedrooms on the first floor. The ground floor is dominated by the high undulating ceiling of the entrance hall that steps down to merge with the lower living room level.

The materials of the interiors were also carefully chosen; Finnish red pine for the ceilings of the hall and the living room, oak for parquets and library shelves, ash and teak for doors, columns, and fittings, bronze and leather for the door handles. A remarkable aspect of the ensemble is the fusion of the Finnish character of Aalto's architecture and a distinct French atmosphere; this mixed cultural ambience reveals Aalto's exceptional contextual sensitivity.

The house was designed as a combination art gallery and private residence. Paintings by Fernand Léger, Pierre Bonnard, Pablo Picasso, Raoul Dufy, Jacques Villon, André Lanskoy, and Paul Klee, and sculptures by Henri Laurens, Alexander Calder, and Alberto Giacometti, along with African art were displayed in the house. Louis Carré lived in the house until his death in 1977. His widow Olga continued to live there, surrounded by paintings and sculptures, until she passed away in 2002. As the Carré couple did not have children, Olga's family inherited both the house and the artworks; the artworks were sold in an auction in 2002. The house, listed *monument historique* in France, in 1996, was purchased by Association Alvar Aalto in France, in 2006. The building has recently been renovated and is open to the public on weekends. The Association has received financial support from the Finnish Cultural Foundation, the Finnish

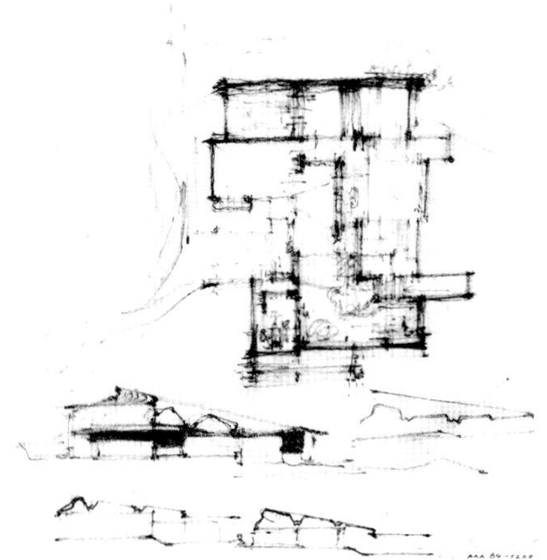

Alvar Aalto's early sketch of the floor plan and section (Alvar
Aalto Museum, 84-1267)

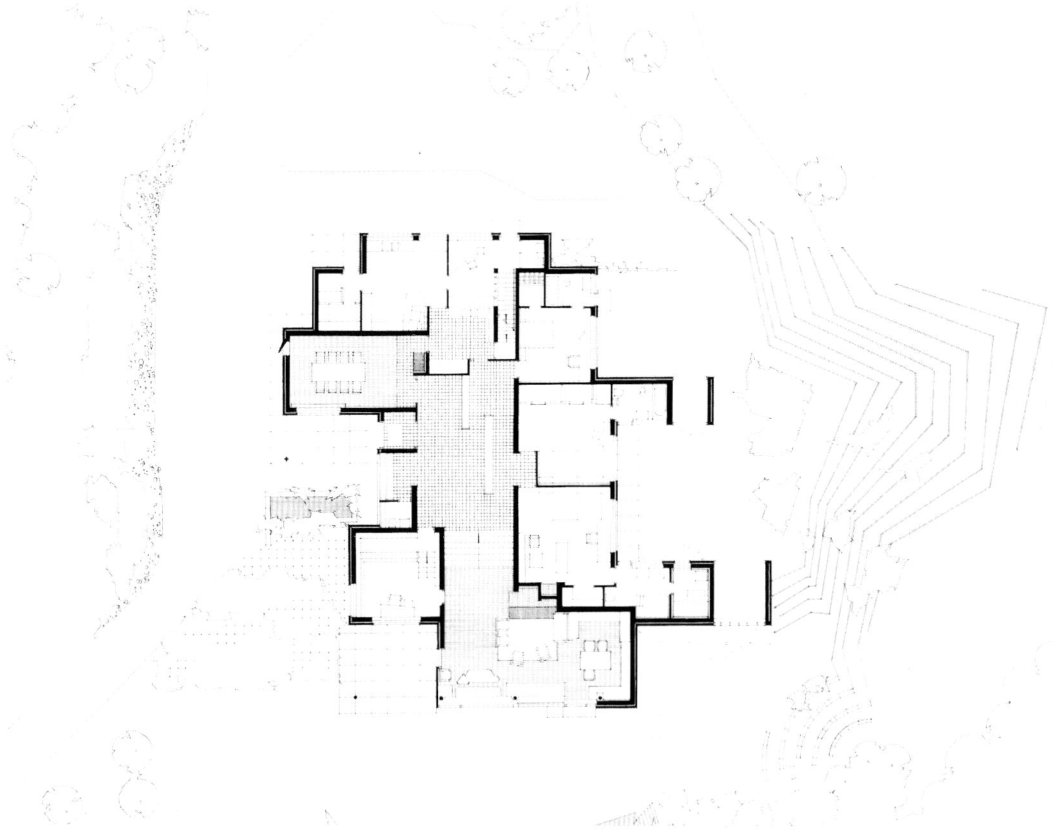

Ground floor plan (Alvar Aalto Museum, 84-1374)

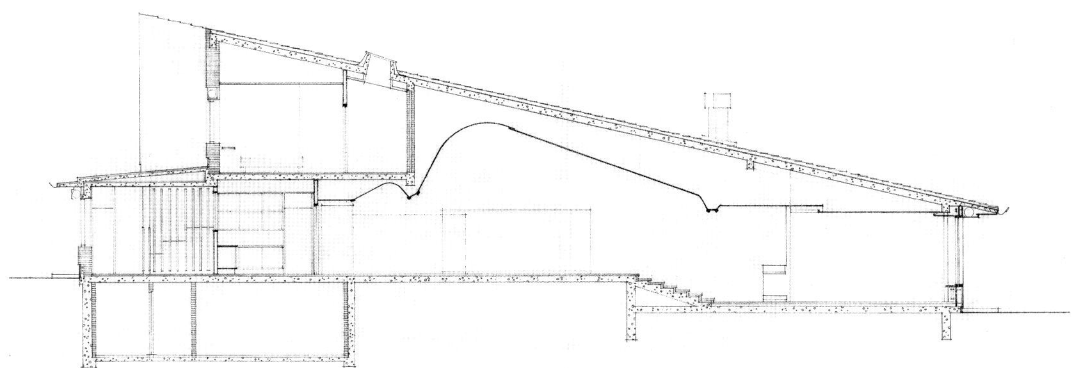

Section through the hallway (Alvar Aalto Museum, 84-1382)

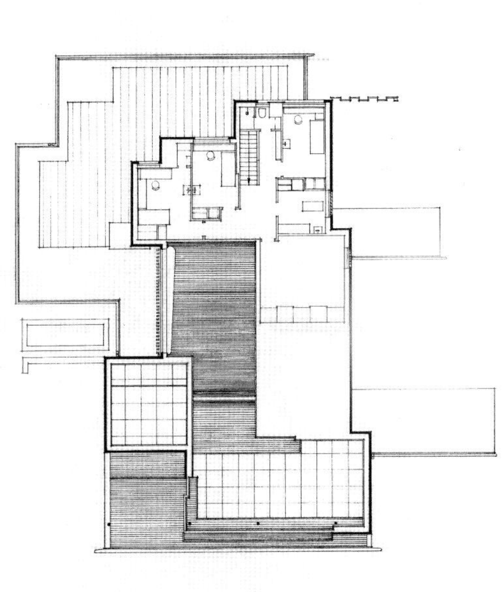

Second floor plan (Alvar Aalto Museum, 84-1374)

The hallway with an undulating ceiling made of red pine. The light fixtures are similar to the fixtures in Aalto's church of the Three Crosses at Vuoksenniska (Alvar Aalto Museum, AAA 102060)

The living room that includes furniture pieces and light fittings specially designed by Aalto for the Maison Carré (Alvar Aalto Museum, AAA 102086)

Detail of the hallway (Alvar Aalto Museum, AAA 107668)

North façade and the open landscape immediately after the house was finalized. Photo: Heikki Havas (Alvar Aalto Museum, AAA 101821)

The landscape context seen from the entrance area. Photo: Heikki Havas, 1959 (Alvar Aalto Museum, AAA 101824)

Ministry of Education and Culture, and the French Ministry of Culture.

The *SOM Journal 5* Jury met in the Maison Louis Carré on October 12 and 13, 2007, under special arrangement by the Association.

Juhani Pallasmaa

Editorial Board Biographies

Francesco Dal Co

Francesco Dal Co is the chair professor of History of Architecture at the Istituto Universitario di Architettura di Venezia. He has taught History of Architecture at the School of Architecture, Yale University, and the Accademia di Architettura della Università della Svizzera Italiana. He has served as a Senior Fellow of the Center for Advanced Studies of the National Gallery, Washington D.C., and of the Getty Research Center, Los Angeles, as well as Director of the Biennale di Venezia. He is also a member of the Accademia Nazionale di San Luca. Currently he is the director of the Italian architecture magazine *Casabella*, and of architectural publications at Electa, in Milan.

Among his recent books are: *Il tempo e l'architetto. Frank Lloyd Wright e il Guggenheim Museum* (2004); *Piranesi* (2006); *Carlo Scarpa e la Fondazione Querini Stampalia* (2006); Carlo Scarpa. *Villa Ottolenghi* (2007).

Kenneth Frampton

Kenneth Frampton was born in the United Kingdom in 1930 and trained as an architect at the Architectural Association School of Architecture, London. He has worked as an architect and an architectural historian and critic, and is currently the Ware Professor of Architecture at the Graduate School of Architecture, Preservation and Planning, Columbia University, New York.

He has taught at a number of leading institutions in the field including the Royal College of Art, the ETH in Zurich, the EPFL in Lausanne, the Accademia di Architettura in Mendrisio, and the Berlage Institute in The Netherlands.

He is the author of numerous essays on modern and contemporary architecture, and has served on many international juries for architectural awards and building commissions. His most recent writings include *Modern Architecture: A Critical History* (2007), *Studies in Tectonic Culture* (1995), *Le Corbusier* (2001), and a collection of essays entitled *Labour, Work & Architecture* (2005).

Juhani Pallasmaa

Juhani Pallasmaa established his Helsinki office, Juhani Pallasmaa Architects, in 1983 after twenty years of collaboration with a number of architects. In addition to architectural design, he has been active in urban, product, and graphic design.
He has taught and lectured widely in Europe, North and South America, Africa, and Asia, and has held positions as Professor and Dean at the Helsinki University of Technology, State Artist Professor, Director of the Museum of Finnish Architecture, and Rector of the Institute of Industrial Arts, Helsinki. He has held visiting professorships at Washington University in St. Louis, the University of Virginia, and Yale University.
Pallasmaa has published books and numerous essays on the philosophy and criticism of architecture and the arts in thirty languages. His recent books include *Encounters: Architectural Essays 1976–2000* (2004), *Sensuous Minimalism* (2002), *The Architecture of Image: Existential Space in Cinema* (2001), *Alvar Aalto: Villa Mairea* (1998), *The Eyes of the Skin* (1996 and 2005).

Project Credits

The North Mosque

Manama, Kingdom of Bahrain

Designed 2006

Client

Bahrain Bay Development
B.S.C.

Design Partner

Roger Duffy

Managing Partner

Peter Magill

Senior Designer

Michael Kirchmann

Team

Jose Munoz-Villers, Kwong
Yu, Katherine Wong, Reinaldo
Leandro, John Fawcett, Ellie
Khadr

Project Manager

Thomas Behr

Technical Coordinator

Brian Kleiver

Structural Engineering

Werner Sobek

Mechanical Consultant

MMM Group

Cost Estimating Consultant

Davis Langdon

Bridging the Rift

Border of Israel (Central Arava) & Jordan (Wadi Araba)

Designed 2005

Client

Bridging the Rift Foundation

Design Partner

Mustafa Abadan

Managing Partner

TJ Gottesdiener

Senior Designer

Chris Cooper

Team

David Maestres, Kat Park

Technical Consultant

Buro Happold

Structural Consultant

Buro Happold

Environmental Consultant

Buro Happold

BioPods

Chapel Hill, North Carolina

Designed 2007

Client

University of North Carolina

Design Partner

Jaime Velez

Architectural Design Partner

Peter Ruggiero

Managing Partner

Richard Tomlinson

Senior Designer

Jennifer Kolstad

Collaborating Artist

Jennifer Kolstad

Project Manager

Mike Lingertat

Technical Coordinator

Don Stark

Kinetic Curtainwall Prototype

New York, New York

Designed 2007—ongoing

Design Partner

Gary Haney

Managing Partner

TJ Gottesdiener

Senior Designer

Jason Klimoski

Team

Daniel Silva, Wilhelm Neusser,
Michael Dziubek, Hormuz Batliboi

Project Manager

Ken Lewis

Environmental Consultant

Buro Happold

Project Credits

Balance Bridge

Bergen, Norway

Designed 2005

Client

City of Bergen

Design Partner

Ross Wimer

Structural Design Partner

Bill Baker

Senior Designer

Aaron Jensen

Team

Tracy Ting, Roimon Hepburn, Evran Alper, Yousef Nawas

Model Team

Matthew Fiely, Mark Nagis, Robert Guyser, John Schmidt

Project Manager

David Horos

Structural Consultant

Dmitri Jajich

The Mill Center for the Arts

Hendersonville, North Carolina

Designed 2005

Client

The Mill Center for the Arts

Design Partners

Ross Wimer

Leigh Breslau

Senior Designer

Aaron Jensen

Team

Tracy Ting, Tim Kleinert, Manuel Martin Rivas, Samuel Zeller

Kuwait Military Academy

Al Jahra, Kuwait

Designed 2006

Client

Special Projects Division, Military Engineering Projects, Kuwait Ministry of Defense, State of Kuwait

Design Partner

Roger Duffy

Managing Partner

Peter Magill

Senior Designer

Scott Duncan

Team

Monica Adair, Douglass Alligood, Jason Bouthillette, Richard Choi, Peter Dougherty, Mandy Edge, Robert Finger, Daniel Fletcher, Lauren Friedman, Axel Haeusler, Peter Halkias, Themistocles Haralabides, Jason Horton, Colin Koop, Stephen Kopp, Robert Kretschmer, Claire Masick, Olin McKenzie, Fred Mosher, Alfredo Munoz, Angelynn Nakaguchi, Carrie Nesvig, Yuji Nishioka, Nicholas Cotton, Cynthia Mirbach, Adam Semel, Karen Seong, Robert Simmons, Kwong Yu

Project Manager

Donald Williams

Technical Coordinator

Mark Igou

Structural Consultant

Gulf Consult

Mechanical Consultant

Gulf Consult

Landscape Consultant

Gulf Consult

Geotechnical Consultant

Gulf Consult

Environmental Consultant

Battle McCarthy

Elizabeth Academic High School

Elizabeth, New Jersey

Designed 2006

Client

New Jersey Schools Construction Corporation

Collaborating Artist

Lawrence Weiner

Design Partner

Roger Duffy

Managing Partner

Anthony Vacchione

Senior Designer

Scott Duncan

Team

Monica Adair, Nicholas Desbiens, Peter Dougherty, Axel Haeusler, Eric L. Ho, Joseph Walter

Project Manager

Christopher McCready

Technical Coordinators

Walter Smith / Peter Cho

Structural Consultant

Consulting Engineers Collaborative, Inc.

Mechanical Consultant

Concord Engineering Group, Inc.

Landscape Consultant

MKW & Associates

Information Technology Consultant

Thomas Communications & Technology

Food Service Consultant

Hopkins Food Service Specialists, Inc.

Cost Estimating Consultant

Bovis Lend Lease

Image Credits

SOM Journal 5 Jury Report

© Roland Halbe Fotografie: p. 15

Juror Essays

© Sean Godsell Architects: p. 22

© Marc Mimram: p. 26

© Mary Miss: p. 30

North Mosque Bahrain Bay

© Futurebrand: ill. 1

© PMB Design: ill. 14

Bridging the Rift

© Archimation: ills. 6, 8, 9, 10, 12

Kuwait Military Academy

© MIR Visuals: ills. 3, 4, 14, 15, 16, 17

Elizabeth Academic High School

© Crystal CG Middle East FZE: ills. 5, 11, 12

© 2008 for the reproduced works by
Lawrence Weiner: VG Bild-Kunst, Bonn

Essays
Sustaining Architecture During a Revolution

© MVRDV: ill. 3

© Sealand Aerial Photography: ill. 4

© Hamza and Yeang: ill. 5

© Future Systems: ill. 6

© Arup Associates: ill. 7

© Office for Metropolitan Architecture, OMA: ill. 8

© Foster and Partners: ill. 9

Structure Between

© Mutsuro Sasaki

Art, Soul of the Corporation

© 2008 for the reproduced works by Alexander Calder
and Ad Reinhardt: VG Bild-Kunst, Bonn;

for Le Corbusier: FLC / VG Bild-Kunst, Bonn;

for Joan Miró: Succesió Miró / VG Bild-Kunst, Bonn;

for Pablo Picasso: Succession Picasso / VG Bild-Kunst,
Bonn;

for Saul Steinberg: The Saul Steinberg Foundation / VG
Bild-Kunst, Bonn.

Myron Goldsmith: Keating Hall at IIT

© Michael Pado: p. 201, 204 (top two images)

Maison Louis Carré

© Alvar Aalto Foundation, Helsinki

All images courtesy of SOM unless otherwise noted.

We have made every effort to find all copyright holders.
However, should we have neglected to contact copyright
holders in any individual instances, we would be most
grateful if these copyright holders would inform us forth-
with.

Acknowledgment

The Partners of SOM extend their thanks to the
Editorial Board, Juhani Pallasmaa, the Jurors,
the Alvar Aalto Foundation, Asdis Olafsdottir,
and to all those who have contributed to the
represented work. We would also like to thank
Amy Gill, Scott Duncan, Mersiha Veledar, Nancy
Cheung, Aaron Jensen, Yuji Nishioka, and SOM
librarian Susan Lane for assistance in assem-
bling, writing, and coordinating the materials for
Journal 5.

Edited by
Juhani Pallasmaa

Editorial Board
Francesco Dal Co
Kenneth Frampton
Juhani Pallasmaa

Associate editors
Amy Gill
Mersiha Veledar

Editorial coordination
Tas Skorupa

Copyediting
Eugenia Bell

Typeface
Arial MT

Paper
Nopacoat matt

Binding
Kunst- und Verlagsbuchbinderei GmbH, Leipzig

Reproductions
Weyhing digital, Ostfildern

Printing
Dr. Cantz'sche Druckerei, Ostfildern

© 2008 Hatje Cantz Verlag, Ostfildern; Skidmore,
Owings & Merrill, LLP; and authors

Published by
Hatje Cantz Verlag
Zeppelinstrasse 32
73760 Ostfildern
Germany
Tel. +49 711 4405-200
Fax +49 711 4405-220
www.hatjecantz.com

Hatje Cantz books are available internationally at
selected bookstores. For more information about
our distribution partners, please visit our home-
page at www.hatjecantz.com.

ISBN 978-3-7757-2279-7

Printed in Germany